MACKENZIE'S GRAVE

MACKENZIE

Frontispiece

MACKENZIE'S GRAVE

by

OWEN CHADWICK

WIPF & STOCK · Eugene, Oregon

Wipf and Stock Publishers
199 W 8th Ave, Suite 3
Eugene, OR 97401

Mackenzie's Grave
By Chadwick, Owen

ISBN 13: 978-1-60608-954-5
Publication date 8/5/2009
Previously published by Hodder & Stoughton, 1959

ACKNOWLEDGEMENTS

I OWE thanks to the custodians of the Bishopscourt Archives at Cape Town and particularly to the Reverend Cecil Wood for his knowledge of the Gray papers and his kindness in communicating information; to Dr Desmond Clark, the Director of the Rhodes-Livingstone Museum at Livingstone, Northern Rhodesia and to V. W. Hiller, Esq., Chief Archivist of the National Archives of Rhodesia and Nyasaland, for their help and for permission to quote from documents under their care, and, in Mr Hiller's case, from the documents so splendidly printed in the Oppenheimer Series; to Lieutenant-Colonel J. W. C. Kirk, for his help with Kirk's Journal and for allowing me to make extracts from it; to the assistants at the Public Record Office and the Bodleian Library; to the librarian at Rhodes House, Oxford, for his help with the Waller Papers and the Thornton Papers; to the archivists of the Society for the Propagation of the Gospel and of the London Missionary Society; to Canon G. W. Broomfield and John Pearson, Esq., at the headquarters of the Universities Mission to Central Africa, for their generosity in making access to their manuscripts as easy as possible, and for answering my questions; and to Miss Angela Wale.

Normally I have given to geographical places names which will be recognizable to moderns. But in some cases it has seemed better to preserve the original spelling of the early days and to write (e.g.) of Ajawa rather than Yao. This inconsistent policy will sometimes be found to produce incongruity; especially that Nyasa is Nyasa when it is a lake but Nyassa when it is a ship.

CONTENTS

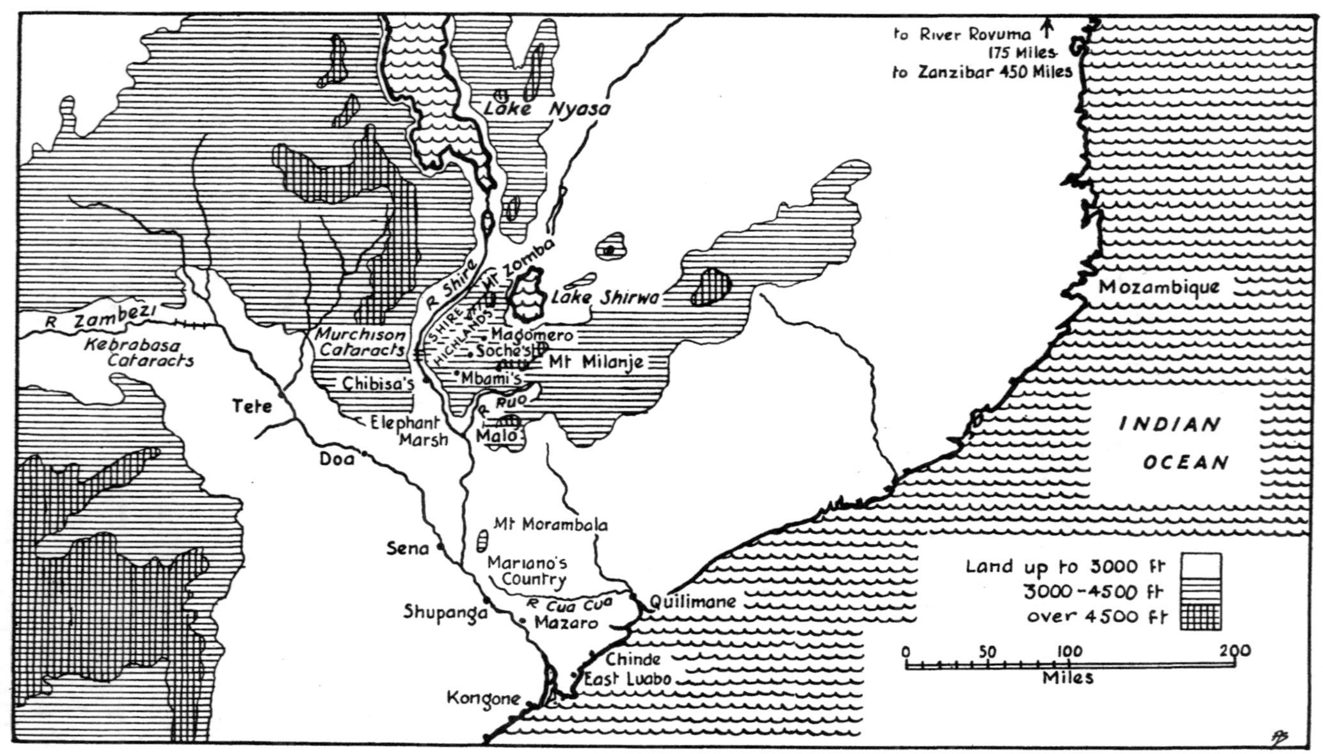

to River Rovuma
175 Miles
to Zanzibar 450 Miles
Lake Nyasa
R Shire
Mt Zomba
Lake Shirwa
SHIRE HIGHLANDS
Magomero
Soche's
Mt Milanje
Mbami's
R Ruo
Malo
Murchison Cataracts
Chibisa's
Elephant Marsh
R Zambezi
Kebrabasa Cataracts
Tete
Doa
Sena
Mt Morambala
Mariano's Country
R Cua Cua
Mazaro
Shupanga
Quilimane
Chinde
East Luabo
Kongone
Mozambique
INDIAN OCEAN
Land up to 3000 ft
3000-4500 ft
over 4500 ft
0
50
100
200
Miles

I

LIVINGSTONE'S PLAN

DURING the middle years of the last century British cruisers were engaged in a ceaseless watch upon the shipping round the African coasts. They were sailing and steaming—for these were the years of naval history when sail was still carried by steam vessels—to blockade the slave trade. In the Atlantic a squadron was still, in 1861, enduring disease, discomfort and danger in the effort to prevent the export of slaves to Cuba or Brazil. In the Indian Ocean, a smaller squadron had recently been reinforced by the Admiralty. For the British government saw reason to believe that the trade was growing, and that from East African ports like Mozambique, Quilimane and Zanzibar, an ever-increasing number of African slaves was being exported. Mediterranean ports like Tripoli and Benghazi, which not so long before had been used to bring slaves into the Turkish Empire, were now closed to the traffic; and hence the Arab traders of the Red Sea and the Persian Gulf were enabled to make quick profits by supplying the demand. Arab dhows or 'buddeens', little vessels of from 40 to 200 tons, and each capable of carrying from 60 to 300 slaves, came southward to the African coast at the end of the north-east monsoon, bringing dried fish and cotton which they traded for negroes. Most of them began to return about the end of March, at the beginning of the south-west monsoon.

The traffic was increased, though to what extent was in doubt, by a plan of the French government to import labour into the island of Réunion, a plan called euphemistically the Free Labour Emigration System. The French engaged the Africans upon proper terms of service, and managed the scheme with equity. But inside Africa the methods used to secure the required number of hands were not the concern of the French, and were as suspect as the dealings of any Arab trader. It was true that by 1849 nearly everyone had abolished the slave trade in theory. Even the Sultan of Zanzibar, the Persian government, and the Arab chieftains on the Persian Gulf had professed to restrain the import of slaves into their dominions. But the trade did not cease. Smuggling continued; and it did not appear to be in the interests of these various potentates that it should cease. The Sultan of Zanzibar was believed to be making large profits. The Imam of Muscat, who claimed to control part of the coast south of Zanzibar, seemed to be flourishing upon the trade. Some of the Portuguese in Mozambique were believed to be wealthier because they were ready to engage in the macabre commerce. And the only deterrent, apart from the remote and haphazard effects of public opinion in Europe, was four or five British warships, based upon the Mauritius and Seychelles, using Zanzibar and the Comoro Islands as their coaling-stations, and under the ultimate command of Rear-Admiral Sir Baldwin Walker at the Cape of Good Hope. The magnitude or hopelessness of their task may be judged by the verdict of the British consul at Zanzibar, Colonel Rigby, that 20,000 slaves were being exported annually through Zanzibar. The slave-trade was dying; everyone agreed that it was dying because everyone had agreed to abolish it. But the British government, and the British captains in the Indian ocean, could not help thinking that its death-kicks were violent and disgusting.

The naval officers did not resent their work. It was an interest out of the routine; if the actions were trivial, the actions of policemen rather than of seamen, at least they were actions. Modest prize-money was obtainable. The hazards arose, not from the brief scuffles which might be dignified occasionally by the title of fights, but from the difficulty of distinguishing the slave-trader from the legitimate seafarer. Arab dhows on honest purposes looked like Arab dhows on inhuman purposes. The dhow which was carrying slaves when captured was no problem. But dhows were rarely found to be carrying slaves. In the year ending 30 September 1862 the British cruisers captured twenty-two dhows, of which only three had slaves aboard (the three were carrying 289 slaves between them). In the year ending 30 September 1863 the cruisers captured twenty-one dhows —but they released only 123 slaves.[1]

[1] Cf. e.g. Baldwin Walker's Report of 17.11.63 in PRO Ad. 1/5822.

The captains argued that they could easily account for this curious discrepancy between the number of dhows destroyed and the number of slaves released. Their cruisers were big and heavy, and could not sail inshore with safety. The dhows, vessels of light draught, clung to the coast, took cover in the inlets and channels. To arrest them the warship needed to send out its pinnace and its whaler, and these were often too slow for effective pursuit. The crew of the dhow had time to run ashore, discharge their load of slaves and vanish into the bush before the British arrived. On 25 August 1861, for example, Lieutenant Ross of *H.M.S. Gorgon* (Commander Wilson), out with the whaler near Cape Delgado, rounded a promontory and found an Arab dhow running along the shore. On sight of the British the dhow bore towards the beach; and although Lieutenant Ross fired four or five rounds of blank cartridge, the dhow would not heave to, but ran aground. When the crew of the whaler boarded her, they found no one aboard, but water and rice and fittings for slaves below. An hour and a half later Ross chased a second dhow, with the same result.

To Rear-Admiral Sir Baldwin Walker and his officers at the Cape, this ease of escape sufficiently explained the discrepancy between dhows captured and slaves released. This opinion was not shared by everyone. The potentates of the Indian Ocean resented these proceedings, and claimed that British sailors frequently maltreated honest merchants and burnt their boats. The temptation to seek prize-money was a temptation to confuse the lawful trader with the villain. Lieutenant Ross and his crew were accused of stealing the sum of 3,480 francs in gold and 2,200 dollars from the first dhow captured, which was alleged to be the property of a French merchant at Zanzibar. The court of enquiry acquitted Ross, proved that the men of the whaler and pinnace had been searched (by way of routine) on their return to *H.M.S. Gorgon*, and that nothing had been found but twelve English sovereigns in the carpenter's tool-box.

On 19 March 1860, *H.M.S. Persian* (Commander Hardinge) had found a dhow of sixty tons, the *Meti Mengi*, off the coast of Johanna in the Comoro Islands, boarded her, found that she had no papers, and burnt her. To the vexation of the officers of the *Persian*, the British consul at Johanna reported the dhow to be the property of the Sultan of the Comoro Islands, that the Sultan had summoned him to his presence and said, 'It is not the value of the dhow I care about, but I feel too much shame, all the people of these parts will laugh at me and congratulate me on my having such good friends as the English.' The dhow was alleged to have been flying the Sultan's flag and the colours of Johanna, and to have been transporting a cargo of several thousand coconuts. Though it was true she carried no papers, she had been sailing round the island and had therefore sent the papers overland in a box.

Captain Crauford, of *H.M.S. Sidon*, sailing eastward from the Cape on 1 January 1861, was not to avoid troubles like these. Before the end of the year he had the diplomatic misfortune, on a clear moonlit night, to sail menacingly upon the French flagship, with the French admiral aboard, on suspicion that she might be a slaver. On 22 April he seized a vessel flying the Turkish flag; his boarding party tore up the flag and some of the sailors made themselves turbans out of it. The Turkish government claimed that so far from being a slave-dealer she was carrying a valuable cargo of spices and grain, she had only four Africans aboard her, all young boys and Arabic-speaking, and she had correct papers from the Turkish authorities at Jeddah. For Captain Crauford the year's cruise was to end in a court of enquiry and subsequent court-martial at Portsmouth. To crown all, the Portuguese vice-consul at the Cape of Good Hope protested that the dhows captured by *H.M.S. Sidon* were captured in Portuguese waters and therefore illegally.

Neither the British government nor the Admiralty was much moved by the clamours of petty despots along the African coastline. Some captured dhows carried neither slaves nor papers. But *H.M.S. Sidon* had also captured a dhow with 272 slaves aboard—and the vessel was furnished with a correct clearance from the Portuguese authorities at Mozambique.

The cruisers, it was plain, were saving only some 300 slaves annually, a tiny proportion of the negroes being exported. Their effect in deterring traders from engaging in the transport of slaves was greater than the little successes which their captains achieved. But it was apparent to all sensible Englishmen, and had been apparent for the last twenty years and more, that a blockade alone could not cure the slave-trade. The gains of success were too high. When a return of 200 per cent or 300 per cent was obtainable, merchants were not to be deterred by any blockade, certainly not by a blockade with four or five cruisers. They would smuggle the human bodies where once they had sailed them openly; and smuggled negroes suffered more risk, torment, and loss of life than had the negroes exported openly in the days before the British blockade. The slave-trade could not be destroyed by naval guns alone. It would only be destroyed if it became possible for African chiefs to sell something more profitable than human bodies. They could not heal the running sore from the sea. They could heal it only if they penetrated the interior of the country and transformed its economy as well as its morals.

* * * * *

When *H.M.S. Sidon* left the Cape on 1 January 1861, she was not only on her way to join the blockade of the East African coast. She was engaged in support of the venture which the British government had planned to penetrate the interior and transform the African economy by opening it to British trade. This venture was David Livingstone's Zambezi expedition. Every ship in these waters had received orders to help Dr Livingstone wherever possible. *Sidon* had been instructed to tow Livingstone's new river-steamer, the *Pioneer*, from the Cape to the mouth of the Zambezi.

* * * * *

Livingstone had emerged from the interior of Africa in 1856, bringing with him the accomplishments and the name of a great explorer and great missionary, the geographical discovery of the Upper Zambezi, and a passionate mystical selfless belief in the future of Africa, and in himself as the opener of its gates. In his triumphal progress through England and Scotland and Ireland in 1857 he had communicated the belief, and even something of the mystique, to huge cheering audiences. By the magic of his name and his achievement, by his ruggedness and simplicity, his absence of rhetoric, his sincerity and his passion, he interested not only the geographers and the missionaries, who might be expected to pay attention, but the merchants of the Manchester cotton exchange and the civil servants of the Foreign Office and the Admiralty. The government was assenting to its own inclination, as well as bowing to public opinion, when it announced a Zambezi expedition, to be led by Livingstone, who was created H.M. Consul for East and Central Africa outside the dominions of the Sultan of Zanzibar.

Livingstone, by his book called *Missionary Travels and Researches in South Africa*, as by his lectures and speeches during his stay in Britain, singly caused a revolution in the attitude of the British public towards the interior of Africa. His style was admirably adapted to convince. It was so plain and unadorned, there was so little pomp or artifice, so little apparent inflation, so little of the 'traveller's tale', that if he was not always cogent or uplifting by reason of any plan or coherence in arrangement, he persuaded by the unity of style and personality. The British public had supposed that Africa's coasts were fever-ridden and marshy, its interior a country of sand and desert like the Sahara or the Kalahari, infertile, waterless, inhospitable. Livingstone had shown them a land of promise, a land of fruitfulness and of minerals, a land which needed only white venture and white capital to make it flow with milk and honey. The British public had imagined Africans to be nasty, brutish, animal, squalid, to be nothing but savages. Livingstone had shown them that some of the savagery derived from their recent communications with the white man; he had drawn a portrait of upstanding men of honour and integrity, peoples of humour and friendliness, of faith and loyalty, needing only to be treated like human beings to respond as human beings. And this revolution in thought and sentiment had evoked in the public mind that latent altruism which thirty years before had driven the British people to the suppression of the slave-trade. Livingstone had recreated something of that old evangelical fervour of William Wilberforce and Buxton and the slave-emancipators. He had shown the villainy and horror of the slave-trade the more pungently and movingly by setting it off against a vision of what might have been and a future Africa which could be. He caused his readers and hearers to hate slavery the more because he believed so patently and sincerely in the African as a man, a friend, and a brother.

The slave-emancipators of thirty years before had believed that civilisation and Christianity must go hand in hand. It might be dubbed by the cynical as 'philanthropy and five per cent', but the ideals of men like Wilberforce or Buxton were above this kind of pettiness. They had seen that the body of the African needed redeeming as urgently as his soul. It was not enough to send a missionary into the country to teach him that he was a child of God. It was also necessary that he be taught to trade. He would sell human bodies until he learnt how to use those bodies in selling something else. He must therefore be shown how to farm according to the best methods, how to grow crops like cotton or coffee of which Europe had need; capital must be directed to opening the mineral wealth which was presumed to lie beneath the soil.

Livingstone inherited these ideals, or, more accurately, won through to them for himself. It was 'commerce and Christianity' together which should free the African. But his book and his lectures galvanized the British public because he brought forward the ideal no longer as an ideal or vague aspiration, but as a practical programme which could be realised within a few years. The mineral wealth was there—he had seen the coal seams near the Zambezi. The area contained much land that was excellent for agriculture, and uplands healthy for Europeans. The fertile hills and valleys waited only for the spade of the cultivator, the teeming population waited only to be helped by European knowledge and guidance, and offered an inexhaustible supply of labour. The time was ripe, not merely for the lone explorer, but for colonies of emigrants, with their wives and children, their ploughs and their seeds. Central Africa was a land of as wide an opportunity for the settler as Australia and New Zealand twenty and thirty years before.

To allow that Central Africa might be wealthy or fertile was not all. Commerce needs communications. The hypothetical cotton-fields of Central Africa would be as useless as swamps unless there was an open door for the export of the produce and for the import of goods and equipment for the hypothetical immigrant. Livingstone believed that he had discovered this open door. He had come down the Zambezi on his journey across Africa, with the exception of a short distance above Tete, and he thought that this was the door and the highway. For four or five months in the year, he wrote, a large vessel could sail up the Zambezi in 'abundance of water', and the months of low water 'still admit of navigation by launches, and would permit small vessels equal to the Thames steamers to ply with ease in the deep channel.'[1] Sea-communication all the way from London to Tete, some three hundred miles up the Zambezi, had been established. It was not Livingstone himself who originally described the Zambezi as 'God's highway for commerce and Christianity.' But the phrase sufficiently summarized the effect of his narrative upon the British.

Accordingly in 1857, the British government had constituted him the leader of a Zambezi expedition, the aim of which was to explore further the Zambezi country and prospect for a district where Europeans might settle and trade and grow cotton. This was the expedition which *H.M.S. Sidon* was sailing from the Cape, in January, 1861, to support. The *Pioneer*, which she was towing, was the little river-steamer provided by the Admiralty to replace the *Ma-Robert*, the first launch used by the expedition, which had begun to fall haphazardly to pieces until she disintegrated into a watery grave in the Zambezi below Tete.

* * * * *

Among the passengers upon the *Sidon* were missionaries for the Central African Mission—an Anglican priest named H. C. Scudamore; a young man named Horace Waller, who had been designated the 'lay superintendent' of the mission; a carpenter named Gamble and a cockney labourer named Adams; an African who had come from the Zambezi to the Cape, had there received an education in Christianity and the English language and would, it was hoped, serve the mission as an interpreter. *Sidon* was also carrying most of the mission's stores in her hold.

The Central African Mission was one of the three missionary plans issuing from Livingstone's impact upon the British Isles.

[1] *Missionary Travels*, p. 674.

Africa seemed to be opening its gates, the darkness of the continent was at last receiving shafts of light, and the evangelist must not be behind. Livingstone, in whose mind pioneering and mission were never sharply distinguished, believed that the missionary and the trader must go hand in hand into the interior of Africa, bringing the best of European morals with the opportunity for European trade. In his addresses as he toured Britain, before the cotton merchants of Manchester as before the dons of Cambridge University, he had spoken of that union of commerce and Christianity which should redeem Africa. Without the new moral tone and teaching, commerce would be impracticable; without the commerce the missionary would preach the word fruitlessly, battering in vain against the manacles and chains of the slave-dealer.

The Central African Mission, sent by the Church of England, had been designed upon the principle that Christianity and industry must go together. At great meetings, in the Senate House at Cambridge in December 1857 and in the Sheldonian at Oxford two weeks later, Livingstone had aroused the undergraduates to the needs of Africa. Bishop Gray of Cape Town, in the following year, had taken their smouldering enthusiasm and directed it towards the Zambezi. The Universities of Durham and Dublin had later accepted invitations to join with Oxford and Cambridge in the work, and soon the initials of the four participating universities, O.C.D.D., became a useful abbreviation to describe the mission. It was intended to settle a mission inland, up the Zambezi. The mission was to become as soon as possible self-supporting materially, by teaching the natives to cultivate their fields and to spin the cotton which (Livingstone had convinced himself and his vast public) would be growing ready to hand. Waller, the lay superintendent whom *Sidon* was carrying, had received elementary instruction in the cultivation and management of cotton. Alfred Adams, though in England he would have been called a labourer, was elevated for the African expedition to the title of agriculturist. They intended to found a little agricultural village which should show the natives how to export cotton, which should teach them the truths of the Christian religion and the moral consequences thereof, and display in its corporate life the model of a Christian and a civilized community; and thus, by their presence, their example, and their economy, would begin to destroy slavery.

The terror of any European expedition into Central Africa was fever. Fever had carried away far too high a proportion of the men of the Niger expedition in 1841, far too high a proportion of the missionaries and government servants at Sierra Leone. One of the other missionary ventures roused by Livingstone's speeches in Britain, a move by members of the London Missionary Society from the south to Linyanti on the Upper Zambezi, had just been tragically ended by fever—the news had reached Cape Town shortly before *Sidon* sailed. Livingstone faced fever with the same equanimity or contempt as he faced hostile spears. The west coast of Africa was being christianized and civilized, though white men died like flies; should the south and east hold back? Arab and Portuguese traders risked fever for high profits, was it a time for the evangelist and the lawful trader to remain behind? His enthusiasm minimized the difficulty. The expedition and mission were now going to thrust their way past the swamp-ridden mosquito-infested low-lying coastlands to the 'healthy highlands' of the interior. As soon as he heard of the tragedy at Linyanti, he sent an urgent message home to Lord John Russell. He had found, he claimed, the cure for African fever. He had discovered, or thought that he had discovered, the cure some nine months before—

> A pill of equal parts of Resin of Jalap and Calomel, Rhubarb and Quinine. For a powerful man eight grains of Resin of Jalap, four or six grains of Rhubarb, and four or six grains of Quinine, and make the whole into pills with tincture of Cardamoms.

This pill, Livingstone wrote to the Bishop of Cape Town, would cure 'the very worst cases in a few hours'. It rendered African fever, he believed, 'not a whit more dangerous than the common cold'. All the members of the missionary party thought, when they arrived at the mouth of the Zambezi, that the fever was no longer dangerous, that they might regard it with the same equanimity as a dose of English influenza.

On receipt of the prescription Lord John Russell broadcast it —to the Royal College of Physicians, to the Admiralty for distribution to its captains in African waters, to the French and Spanish and Portuguese, to British officials at Sierra Leone and on the west coast. It produced, Livingstone had written, 'a terrible row inside, but all the after-effects are avoided. A fellow with his head like to split, or another in a state of somnolency, is relieved in a few hours, so that we call them Rousers.' Not all the experts who received the news of this prescription were as enthusiastic as Livingstone. Spanish doctors questioned whether it was efficacious with all types of fever, and reported that where the fever was accompanied by inflammatory symptoms or dysentery, the proposed remedy would aggravate the case. The Royal College of Physicians reported that the cure was reasonable and normal provided it was not used in cases of diarrhoea. These hesitations of the experts were not known to Livingstone when the *Sidon* arrived at the Kongone. 'We can cure the fever,' he had written triumphantly. The Rousers had extracted the peril from African disease.[1]

* * * * *

Sidon reached the Kongone mouth of the Zambezi on 31 January 1861, and anchored uncomfortably outside the bar seven miles out in the open sea, with a heavy ground swell setting directly towards the shore. The *Pioneer* was brought riskily across the bar, to Livingstone and his party ashore, *Sidon*'s boats suffering a narrow escape from capsizing. The mission party and its stores were put ashore, and Livingstone met Scudamore and Waller. 'I hail their arrival with very great satisfaction,' he wrote to Lord John Russell, 'for they seem to have sound practical views of the work before them, and during our short intercourse have shown that they have no nonsense about them. It is so much strength added to our own mission . . .'

A week later, another cruiser of the blockading squadron, *H.M.S. Lyra*, arrived from Natal and anchored near *Sidon*. *Lyra* carried three more English, and two more African, members of the mission. The three English were the 'Bishop of Central Africa', Charles Frederick Mackenzie; a priest named Lovell Procter; and a deacon, Henry Rowley. These did not complete the mission party; it was intended that a second

[1] Livingstone 26.3.60 UMCA; cf. 8.4.60 UMCA; 25.3.60 copy LMS; FO 63/894.

detachment, consisting of a printer, a shoemaker, a doctor and perhaps another priest, should follow within a few months.

It will seem strange that there should be a bishop before any flock had been gathered from the mission field, before the missionaries had even discovered their mission field. The arrival of Bishop Mackenzie needs an explanation.

* * * * *

To send a bishop without first seeing that he had a flock to shepherd was a scheme disapproved by some of the leading churchmen of England. A practical and hard-headed administrator of missionary endeavour like Henry Venn, the secretary of the Church Missionary Society, regarded the plan for sending a bishop as a fanciful notion of high churchmen, and believed it likely to end in trouble for the mother church. When the first bishop of Melbourne arrived in his diocese, he found there three other clergymen. Was it not absurd to suppose that you needed one bishop to three clergymen? Was not this to create petty little sees and thereby to lower the episcopal office? It was not that he was immediately likely to ordain other men from the Australian frontier. For many years after his arrival he would need to depend, for the growth of clergy, on men summoned from Britain, men who could therefore be ordained in Britain.

The civil administration was equally opposed to the plan. Gray, the Bishop of Cape Town, had consecrated Mackenzie to be bishop in Central Africa against the decided wishes of the British ministers of state. Though they felt that they could not legally obstruct him, they would have preferred him not to consecrate. Was not the consecration of a bishop to a territory outside the British dominions equivalent to a quasi-claim over that territory, a method by which the church was leading the state towards more annexation of backward and expensive lands?[1] If a missionary clergyman were foolish enough to land

[1] Under the Act which created the see of Jerusalem in 1841, it was possible to consecrate a bishop for a see outside Her Majesty's dominions, but for the sole purpose of shepherding British subjects who might have gone there to reside. The Government had steadily refused to allow a bishop to be appointed to New Zealand so long as New Zealand was not a British possession. In 1853 a bill to legalise missionary bishops was introduced into the Lords and given a third reading; it was

upon a savage island and be speared, it was his fault. But if a bishop were to land and be murdered, the administrators feared a wave of public emotion and a demand for protection or reprisal, whereby the British would find themselves saddled with the responsibility, and the expense, of a punitive expedition, perhaps of an annexation.

Against these arguments of reason and practice, churchmen set the arguments of sentiment and of theology.

The United States of America had left the Empire because the mother country had neglected the aspirations of the colonies. Churchmen believed that the failure of the Government to provide bishops for the church in America was the most fatal among all the various neglects. They were determined that

not even debated in the Commons. The immediate and ostensible object of this Bill was to legalise a bishop for Borneo. Rajah Brooke had by 1847 carved out a principality for himself in Sarawak, and had opened the door to Christian missions: and by 1852 four Anglican missionaries were working in Sarawak, supported financially by S.P.G. and politically by Brooke. Many members of S.P.G. were convinced that so isolated a mission needed a bishop. But Borneo was not British territory. The difficulty was circumvented by creating (1855) a Bishop of Labuan, an insignificant island off the coast of Borneo which by Brooke's agency had been ceded to the British government a few years earlier as a coaling station. In the same way a bishop had been consecrated for Hong Kong (1849), not only because Hong Kong needed a bishop, but because this seemed the only legal way of creating a head for missionary enterprise in Southern China. It was once suggested to Bishop Selwyn of New Zealand, who was trying to make Patteson a missionary bishop for the Pacific Islands, that the only legal way to do it was to sail out beyond territorial waters and consecrate him on the ocean.

Some people thought that the system of titular bishops was the right one. It was suggested for example that the Archbishop of Canterbury should consecrate a titular bishop of Cambridge (on the ground that Cambridge was one of the important towns of England still bishopless) and send him out to the heathen (cf. *Chronicle of Convocation*, 1860, pp. 284–5; and 1859, pp. 15, 16). *The Times*, which disliked these theories, thought there was no difference in principle between consecrating a bishop for islands in the Pacific outside British rule and consecrating a bishop to evangelize Spain. The contemptuous talked of 'ambulatory bishops' (cf. A. Ollivant, Bishop of Llandaff, *A Few Remarks on the Missionary Bishops Bill* (1853)).

Gray of Cape Town pressed the Colonial Office until they withdrew their opposition. In November 1858, Lord Carnarvon told Gray that though the law officers of the Crown held it to be doubtful whether an English bishop could legally consecrate another bishop for a country outside the dominions of Her Majesty, no opposition would be offered if he did so, but any bishop so consecrated would not be able to perform legal acts of an episcopal nature within the Queen's dominions (*Life of Gray*, i, pp. 438–9). But he was then told that he might not consecrate on British territory. This restriction was grudgingly withdrawn by May 1859. Cf. also *Chronicle of Convocation*, 1861, p. 361.

never again should colonial churchmen be left without an episcopal ministry, never again should Anglican clergymen travel wearily across the ocean in search of ordination. That there were only three clergy in the diocese of Melbourne when the first bishop arrived was a vain and foolish argument. Those priests needed supervision, their people needed confirmation, their churchyards needed consecrating. The church of Victoria, though it was diminutive, was a church nevertheless, and it could not be 'the church in its integrity' (as the catch-phrase went) unless a bishop presided at its ministrations. It was the entire ark, not scattered planks and timbers, which floated Noah and his family into safety. Did the apostles plant churches 'by driblets, fragments, instalments'?

The bishop, therefore—if the argument is pursued logically—should not be the last stone to be inserted, the keystone of the missionary edifice: he should be the first, the foundation-stone. Instead of being sent afterwards to supervise the various congregations collected by his forerunners, he should land in the first boat, himself the evangelist-in-chief.

There was much in it of the Oxford Movement; of the attempt by Newman and Keble and the others to teach the bishops that they were 'apostolic men'. England was accustomed to bishops who were 'grandees', who rode in carriages and mingled easily with dukes, churchmen of dignity and smooth hands. In 1854, Bishop Selwyn had arrived home on leave from New Zealand and had profoundly influenced the popular notion of the episcopal office. Selwyn, navigating his little boat through the Melanesian islands, wearing seaman's clothing, sleeping in the open, cooking his own meals, hauling on cables, digging with his spade, jumping ashore upon islands where no white had landed before, landing without knowing whether he would be greeted by curiosity or a bludgeon—this was the portrait of a 'missionary bishop', this was indeed a planting of the church 'in its integrity'.

And thus the founders of the Central African Mission thought it not absurd, in creating an English settlement far out of reach of regular English aid, to send a bishop to be the leader of the community which was to be a church. Samuel Wilberforce of Oxford, in making a generous contribution to the funds, stipulated the condition that a bishop should lead the enterprise.

Hence the arrival of a bishop at the Kongone mouth of the Zambezi, though the mission had not established itself. And when some critics, confronted by disaster, argued that the mission should never have been established at all and reproached Livingstone for securing its establishment, they should not have forgotten that Livingstone's pleas for Africa were not alone in drawing the mission, like a magnet, to the Zambezi route. It so happened that he was appealing for a mission in the Zambezi country at the moment when Bishop Gray of Cape Town, a man resolved on grounds of orthodoxy to send forth a missionary bishop, was looking for suitable territory in Africa where that bishop might evangelize. Gray was determined on an example of the 'true' kind of mission; within a few years he would in any event have created one. Livingstone's cries for the Zambezi gave Gray's endeavours a direction, they were not the cause of those endeavours.

* * * * *

Livingstone, before he had even met Bishop Mackenzie, was glad that a bishop should be coming.

Until 1856 Livingstone, the Scottish Presbyterian from Blantyre, had been a missionary with a stipend from the London Missionary Society. Then the directors, who supposed that he was confusing exploration with evangelism and did not feel under any obligation to support an explorer, severed the connexion. Livingstone had remained in spirit, and would remain to the end of his life, a missionary. Everything—exploration, commerce, natural history, geographical enterprise—was subordinate to the higher end of bringing the African to the God of the Christians. But though he remained a missionary, he was an unusual missionary. He had no interest himself in building up strong congregations, in gathering a nucleus of faithful men, in creating the first beginnings of a church. He believed in the diffused influence of a white and Christian civilization as the christianizing force in Africa; and he conceived his own travels as the opening of gates for the spread of that influence. He was ready to allow that the building of congregations was necessary, that Christian pastors must settle and teach the people. He eagerly called the Scottish ministers or the undergraduates of the English universities to that type of work. But he was sure that it was not his work. With these conceptions he was wholly devoid of narrowness, perhaps at times even of definiteness, in religious thinking. Though the notions or prejudices of his upbringing were still strong within him, he had nothing of a sectarian spirit. Provided Christianity was taught to the African, what did it matter who taught it? From the Shire highlands north of the Zambezi valley he had written to Henry Venn, the secretary of the Church Missionary Society, appealing for a mission from the Church of England. He thought that the Church of England had been backward in missionary endeavour, and should now put forth all its strength for Africa, like a giant aroused from sleep. He had not expected the mission to be headed by a bishop. But he was pleased to hear the news. His journal shows that he was curiously gratified by the dignity thus conferred on his expedition. His clear practical vision saw that the eminence and prestige thus given would ensure a readier support from home.

The alliance between an English bishop and a celebrated Presbyterian of strong opinions might have contained the chemistry of a rare explosion. For the Zambezi expedition, in its course since 1858, had discovered, in addition to vital information about African geography, that Livingstone was no commander of white men, and that his relations with white colleagues were likely to engender friction if not strife.

Livingstone could handle Africans. He treated them with a patience, an honesty, and an absolute fearlessness which won their respect and turned them into disciples. The simple sincerity of his spirit, and the manifest unity in his person of courage with faith, his entire lack of self-seeking, captivated their allegiance. These are the qualities by which men become disciples, and white men as well as black came under the unselfconscious spell of his personality. But not all white men. Finding himself to his surprise a government official and the commander of a government expedition, he also found himself to be uneasy and embarrassed. His natural dourness had been deepened into the silence of men who have lived solitary, and he had a little of that fear of men which the creatures of the solitudes shared. He knew that his vocation was essentially a lonely vocation. He distrusted this paraphernalia of consulates and equipment and naval officers with which he was now, willy-nilly, surrounded. He was often at loggerheads with the engineers or the navigators of the expedition. By the time Bishop Mackenzie arrived he had driven away three of the five leaders of the expedition, and the fault was by no means always theirs. He was so harsh with himself that he was sometimes harsh to other white men; he could not sympathize with them if they did not attain his almost superhuman standards of endurance and doggedness, or if they did not seem to share his absolute self-dedication. He sometimes shrank into a kind of shell, the self-concealment which springs from an inner diffidence and fear of social relations. Uncertain of himself, he was inclined to regard discussion as insolence, disagreement as incipient mutiny, inefficiency as criminal negligence, prudence as cowardice. But this did not mean he was a martinet. On the contrary, he was the most easy-going of commanders. It would have been easier for his subordinates to bear if his severity with them had been a consistent severity. The worst was that the discipline was liable to fits and starts, almost to moods.

The only two officers of the expedition who had survived the earlier expulsions, Charles Livingstone the brother of David, and John Kirk, were men of opposite characters and yet had remained in the expedition for more or less the same reasons. Kirk, the botanist and doctor of medicine, was a friendly man of ability and level-headedness. By February 1861 he was well aware of David Livingstone's limitations as a commander. And yet even those who saw these defects to the utmost could not help admiring Livingstone—and more, liking him. In the midst of every kind of vexation and irritation, Kirk still saw that Livingstone had courage and perseverance of a rare degree, and he still believed in the vision of a civilized Africa which Livingstone had seen. Under diverse temptations to abandon the work and go home, Kirk stayed because he was a man of loyalty, because he was interested in his work, and because he believed in the expedition.

Charles Livingstone had been a pastor in America and had

been summoned by his brother to join the expedition as the Moral Agent; the man who should take charge of the secular and moral side of any station which might be formed. The virtues of Charles were the family virtues. He was in the expedition mainly out of loyalty to his brother, though it was a different kind of loyalty from Kirk's, deriving from a strong sense of family affection. He was a calamitous choice. Among a crew liable to bouts of fever along the river, and the irritability which fever always brought with it, he was the spark which ignited the fuel of bad temper. More than anyone on the river-steamer he longed for home, for his wife and family. He would brood over photographs of his wife and children with an intensity of home-sickness, he dreamt of them at night, their images kept recurring to him in the day. Like his brother, he was unsuitable as an officer of the expedition; but his nervousness of colleagues, instead of driving him into a shell, rendered him aggressive. He concealed his uncertainties by a veneer of roughness, self-elevation, truculence, dogmatism and assertiveness. And on occasion this irritability could flare up into wild storms of rage and resentment. Less intelligent and innately less humble than his brother, he seemed to more than one observer to be the evil genius of the expedition, and even David Livingstone once admitted that selecting him had been his greatest mistake. But family ties were still strong. Though he saw Charles' weaknesses and limitations, he still felt able to overcome the barrier of personal relations with him as with none of the other whites on the ship. He listened to what Charles the Moral Agent told him, accepted his often inaccurate and sometimes unbalanced judgements on persons and situations, took note of his gossip about the crew; and thereby committed some of his mistakes.

Into this little party of men with strong opinions and vehement disagreements the battle-cruisers *Sidon* and *Lyra* now discharged a bishop, three clergymen, a lay missionary, and some artisans. Livingstone had asked the Church of England for a mission, and the mission had arrived.

The alliance was put to the test at the first meeting.

II

THE WARS

Livingstone had fixed the destination of the mission. During 1858 he had further explored the Zambezi and discovered how severe an obstacle to river communications was formed by the Kebrabasa Rapids. He had therefore turned to the chief tributary of the Zambezi, the Shire, had discovered Lake Nyasa and walked through the Shire Highlands to the south of the Lake. Here, in the highlands, he believed that he had discovered the site for his immigrants, his colony, and his mission. Two hundred miles above the junction with the Zambezi, the Shire is broken by falls which he had named the Murchison Cataracts, in honour of the president of the Royal Geographical Society. With the exception of these cataracts, which, he thought, could be by-passed along a road easily built, there was easy communication by sea from London to Lake Nyasa. He had written home in glowing terms of the land which now he had found—highlands two and three thousand feet above sea-level where Europeans could work in health and comfort, where water was plentiful and the soil fertile, where cotton would grow in profusion, where the land was only waiting for the European cultivator. He wrote that this land might rapidly become 'the counterpoise to American slave labour', for it would produce cotton abundant and cheap enough to undercut the American market. Plant an English settlement on the highlands, he believed, and it would soon be self-supporting, it would open commerce for the African labourer, transform the economy of the region and so suppress the slave-trade.

The Zambezi expedition, then, claimed to have fulfilled one of its objects. It had aimed at prospecting for a site for an English colony; and Livingstone asked for a mission to be sent to the Shire highlands south of Lake Nyasa. Bishop Gray of Cape Town had accepted the information and directed the Universities Mission to this destination. At the cathedral in Cape Town, he had consecrated Mackenzie, who could scarcely be given his title from a see, to be 'Bishop of the mission to the tribes dwelling in the neighbourhood of Lake Nyasa and the River Shire.'[1] The mission intended, with Livingstone's help, to sail easily up the 'highway', the Zambezi and Shire, to a point near the Murchison Cataracts, and then carry its loads overland and uphill to settle somewhere in the mountain country immediately to the south of Lake Nyasa. When the party arrived at the Kongone, in *Sidon* and *Lyra*, they had no inkling that the plan was liable to be changed.

Before Livingstone had even met the Bishop, he had determined upon a different plan. He intended now to explore the River Rovuma, 450 miles to the north, and finding the missionaries arriving at the Kongone, he resolved to take them with him. He had not lost his faith in Lake Nyasa and the highlands thereabout. He had partially lost his faith in the Zambezi-Shire route as a means of reaching the agreed destination—and this in spite of the arrival of the *Pioneer* which had been expected to make it easier to sail up the Zambezi and Shire.

The chief reason for the decision, a decision so awkward for Mackenzie to meet, was the Portuguese.

Livingstone, always ready to believe the best of Africans, never quite so happy with Europeans, had been forming unfavourable opinions of the Portuguese. It was true that the Portuguese record in the government of East Africa was not creditable. The colony was used as a variety of penal settlement, the whites were always few and occasionally villainous; some of the officials went out for a period to make a fortune and returned successfully. The country was neither healthy nor attractive, and only a special reason could persuade white colonists to settle there. Once, in the sixteenth and seventeenth centuries, there had been Jesuit and Dominican missions up the Zambezi, but these had been withdrawn long ago, leaving no trace but the ruins of a few chapels. There were Portuguese forts up the Zambezi at Sena and Tete, mainly for the supervision of the ivory trade. But it appeared to others besides

[1] The title worried some churchmen at home unable to conceive a bishop without a see. There was a rumour that Mackenzie's title was Bishop of Quilimane, Woodcock to C. F. Porter, 20.5.62 UMCA.

Livingstone that the Portuguese colony could never be the power to open and redeem Africa. There was more than a suspicion that some Portuguese officials were not above engaging in the slave-trade. Some of them returned to Lisbon more enriched than would be possible from the ivory traffic or the salary of a civil servant. The white citizens of Portuguese East Africa were still slave-owners (though slavery was due to expire in 1878); and men who owned slaves could hardly be expected to be alive to the immorality, as well as the illegality, of the slave-trade.

But the Portuguese claimed the Zambezi, the intended highway to the interior, and an unspecified area of hinterland. Livingstone was convinced that they could have no possible claim to the Shire highlands; but they controlled the access to it. For a time he wrote urgent letters to the British Foreign Secretary, begging him to secure freedom of navigation on the Zambezi, until he learnt that the plea was hopeless. To Livingstone it seemed that the Portuguese possessed the key to Africa but were refusing to use it—a 'dog-in-the-manger policy' which he kept denouncing in his letters home.

This dark impression which Livingstone formed was to be, in a roundabout manner, the cause of one of the disasters of the mission. But, immediately, it led him to seek an alternative route to Lake Nyasa. He must find a highway which did not run through Portuguese territory. The Rovuma River appeared to him, as early as March 1860, to be probably the right alternative. It flowed into the sea at a point where the Portuguese were admitted to have no control, and it was believed to rise within easy distance of Lake Nyasa. He was confirmed in this decision by seeing a new fort built at the Kongone. It was a mixture of fort and customs-house, about twenty feet by thirteen feet, of poles mounted with a thatched roof of coarse grass, and staffed by five coloured men and an officer named Mesquita, who had been born at Plymouth of an English mother. Living stone believed the fort to be the Portuguese answer to the British plan of opening Africa through the mouth of the Zambezi. The difficulty, which Livingstone at first had minimised but now saw as the greatest of the stumbling blocks, had not been missed in England. The Prince Consort had refused to be patron of the Universities Mission because he thought that it could only lead to diplomatic friction with the Portuguese.

Another route must therefore be found. The Rovuma promised the free access which Mesquita and his five soldiers denied.

The Bishop, then, landed at the Kongone intending to take his mission up the Zambezi and Shire. Livingstone sailed down the Zambezi to the Kongone intending to take himself and the mission to the Rovuma.

* * * * *

On 9 February, the Bishop and Captain Oldfield of the *Lyra* crossed the bar of the river, which effectually prevented ships of any size from coming inshore, and stayed two nights on the *Pioneer*, to which Livingstone had already transferred his party. On the 9th and 10th[1] they discussed and argued. In the early morning of the 11th, about five a.m., the Bishop and Oldfield went out to the *Lyra*, and the Bishop drafted a letter refusing to go with Livingstone to the Rovuma. On the 12th, the two Livingstones and Kirk came out to the *Lyra* and the argument was thrashed over again.

Livingstone, with his usual and immovable tenacity of purpose, was determined to go to the Rovuma. He had not been responsible for the detailed plans of the mission; he had earlier written to the London headquarters of the mission that he planned to go in the *Pioneer* to the Rovuma, but the letter was sent too late for Mackenzie to receive it. He had only learnt that a bishop was coming when a mailbag was washed ashore from a boat which had capsized in trying to cross the bar. But he could not simply say that if the Bishop determined to ascend the Zambezi and Shire he must be left to shift for himself. He believed that he and Kirk knew how to manage African fever and African natives, and the Bishop had no knowledge of either. He was clearsighted enough to see the menace to his own

[1] On 10th the Bishop also bathed. He went into the space under the paddle-box of the *Pioneer* for the purpose. The paddle-wheel started suddenly to turn, and he was 'like a squirrel in a cage, his clothes all went and his cassock, he rushed out without clothes crying to the (seamen) to save the cassock.' The same night Scudamore was badly bitten by mosquitoes under his net, because he had failed to arrange it properly. Charles Livingstone to his wife, 11.2.61 RL.

expedition if an inexperienced but obstinate bishop ended his life uselessly among the mangrove swamps. He was aware that the Bishop needed his help to establish the mission; and therefore the only question for Livingstone and Kirk was how to persuade Mackenzie to bring his party to the Rovuma. They had one other card to play. In his earlier ascent of the Shire, Livingstone had been befriended by a chieftain named Chibisa, the head of a village some twenty miles south of the Murchison Cataracts. He had written home that Chibisa was a chief with whom a mission might safely settle. Chibisa would also provide labour and porters if the mission wished to ascend the Shire highlands and dwell there. But Chibisa had lately moved to a village named Doa on the Zambezi. Livingstone argued that the mission would no longer have its friend up the Shire, might meet hostility from the natives, and might fail to get its stores and equipment carried.

Mackenzie disliked, thoroughly disliked, the proposal, and so did all his party except Waller. He had been sent to evangelize, not to explore; and he thought, as the directors of the London Missionary Society had thought before, that Livingstone failed to distinguish between the character of a missionary and the character of an explorer. He had not acquired, he was not possessed of the sort of nature that could acquire, a universal suspicion of the Portuguese. His mission had been given letters of recommendation from the Portuguese government, he had no expectation of hindrances from the local officials. He thought it bad for the spirit of his party that they should delay, perhaps for several months longer, before embarking on their proper work, while they engaged as additional and unnecessary hands in an unexpected voyage of exploration. The road had been represented as so easy. It was not his business to discover a settlement or the road to that settlement. He had been told that Livingstone had found this already. He was reluctant to turn aside from a route which he still believed to be easy, and which Livingstone still confessed to be possible, for the sake of finding a new route which might prove a cul-de-sac. And as for fever, it was true that they lacked a doctor—Mackenzie despite anxious appeals had not been able to find a volunteer in time—but they knew that a doctor from Gateshead, by name John

Dickinson, was on his way by the next party to come out. Nor did the naval officers encourage the Bishop to agree with Livingstone. Captain Crauford of the *Sidon*, the senior naval officer off the Kongone, believed that the Rovuma was navigable only for forty-five miles, and then only for boats. He was astonished that Livingstone, the moment he was equipped with the *Pioneer*, which had been designed for the Zambezi and Shire, should be turning aside, because little Portuguese forts had appeared at the Kongone and (so Livingstone told Crauford), at the confluence of the Zambezi and Shire. Crauford was a 'poor little man', at loggerheads with his crew and nearly everyone else, and no one took much notice of what he thought. But Captain Oldfield of the *Lyra* said to Mackenzie, 'I am clear you ought to go to the Shire, only don't shut your eyes to the responsibility involved in your acting contrary to Livingstone's advice.'[1]

Nevertheless, in the debate and the conflict of wills which always remained friendly, the Bishop must give way. Livingstone was the expert, he the novice. Livingstone had summoned the mission, Livingstone must plant it. Mackenzie was carrying in his pocket a letter from Bishop Gray of Cape Town to Livingstone, telling him that the missionaries arrived with 'an anxious desire to be guided by your knowledge and experience, and will only be too thankful to be directed by you.' It was probable that the success of the mission depended upon the support of Livingstone, and that must mean initial dependence. And it was too easy to imagine what the British public would say if the Bishop rejected Livingstone's advice and then ended in the disaster which he half-predicted. Mackenzie did not think he needed to go to the Rovuma; he realized that he needed to obey Livingstone.

* * * * *

Nearly three months later, on 1 May, the *Pioneer*, with expedition and mission both aboard, re-crossed the Kongone bar into the River Zambezi. In the meanwhile, they had succeeded in sailing some twenty miles less far up the Rovuma

[1] FO 63/894, Crauford's letter of 28.2.61; Mackenzie to Strong 14.2.61 *et seq.*, UMCA; Waller's opinion of Crauford W 29.12.60, 5.2.61.

than the pessimistic Captain Crauford had prophesied. The explorers had lost little by the delay: they had been continuing to do their proper work. The missionaries returned to the Zambezi in less good shape than they sailed from it. All of them except Rowley had suffered from fever, some severely. They had tried the Rousers and, as Mackenzie said amusedly, in his experience the cure was worse than the disease. But the real calamity was the loss of the main part of their stores and equipment. The *Pioneer*, in taking aboard enough coal to steam beyond the treeless delta area of the Zambezi, was overloaded enough, and could carry only a limited portion of the mission's goods. *Lyra* and *Sidon* had disappeared northwards on the blockade. Two-thirds of the stores had to be left in the old hulk *Vega* beached at the Comoro Islands, and were fated to rot or be loot. Livingstone consoled Mackenzie with an assurance that he would have no difficulty in helping them to bring up their stores for the second year which would later arrive at the Kongone. With that consolation they must be content. Rowley described the voyage from Johanna in the Comoro Islands to the Kongone. 'Fever still prevailed among us, and from the foul and crowded state of the little ship, this was not to be wondered at. At most there was but healthy accommodation for twenty people on board the *Pioneer*, and there were forty-eight, with an amount of baggage etc., disproportionately large. The deck was blocked up with boxes, bales, and sacks of coal. The saloon and after-cabin were offensive with the odour proceeding from the mass of stuff stored in them. For three days, when unwell and unable to remain on deck, I lay up in a corner of the saloon with my head close to a number of sugar-cane tops which were fermenting and developing vinegar, while piled about me were reams of paper, containing between their leaves botanical specimens, many of them imperfectly dried and rotting. Indeed, every available space in the ship, fore and aft, was blocked up with stores, baggage, and natural history specimens, not only preventing a free current of air, but poisoning what we had.'[1]

The original plan was now to be executed. They planned to ascend the river swiftly to Chibisa's village, some miles below the lowest of the Murchison Cataracts, there disembark the

[1] R 42.

mission, and carry its goods into the highlands to the north-east. Livingstone calculated that they would reach Chibisa's in less than three weeks.

These expectations were disappointed. They sailed easily, apart from one breakdown of the engines and three days stuck fast upon a sandbank, to the confluence of the Zambezi and the Shire. But once inside the Shire, the difficulties began to multiply. The *Pioneer*, having used her coal, had to stop for wood; and the time taken in cutting wood upon the bank was almost equal to the time taken by the engines in consuming it. The river proved, at that time of year, to be too shallow to be satisfactory for any vessels but canoes. The *Pioneer* had been intended as a vessel drawing not more than two and a half feet; she was found to be drawing four and a half. She dodged and twisted her way up the river, from side to side, and sandbank to sandbank, with the maximum strain to the tempers of all on board. In the Elephant Marsh they took twenty-four days to cover twelve miles, now repairing a smashed or bent paddle-wheel, now pulling her with hawsers fore and aft, now trying to ward off obstacles with poles, now looking for a passable channel, now manufacturing substitute capstans, and most of the time stuck upon sandbanks. They went ashore upon one more sandbank than necessary because the Bishop, who was being instructed in driving the engines, put them inadvertently into forward gear instead of reverse. Once, after steaming with delight and surprise for six or seven miles without a stop, they ran into a barrier of sand reducing the depth of the river to three and a half feet at the deepest point. The anchors were taken out beyond the bar and then the ship hauled up by the capstan. But the ship was too heavy when loaded. All the stores had to be disembarked, the boilers emptied, and the process reversed when the ship was over the bar. It took them eight days to cross that sandbank. The three weeks which Livingstone had predicted turned into more than two months. They reached Chibisa's village on 8 July, and Magomero, the site which they found in the highlands, not until 19 July.

They whiled away the time when they were not working as stokers or anchor-haulers in a variety of pleasant devices. They bargained and bartered with villagers on the bank. They studied their appearance and their customs, eyed with repugnance the lip-ring as large as a napkin-ring worn to puff out the upper lips of the women, watched with amusement or astonishment their music and their dancing. They shot crocodiles (which for some time they thought were alligators) basking in their hundreds on the sandbanks, they were amused by a hippopotamus which shattered the Bishop's sermon one Sunday with huge snorts and guffaws, they admired the hornbills and the guinea-fowl, the divers and the bitterns, and the hollyhocks flowering amongst the rushes. They read books from their little library—Moffat's *Missionary Labours*, Stephen's *Essays in Ecclesiastical Biography*, *The Life of Henry Martyn*, Samuel Wilberforce's *Addresses to Ordination Candidates*, and (unexpectedly) Darwin's *Origin of Species*. On 31 May, aground somewhere in the Elephant Marsh, Mackenzie, as Bishop at last within his own diocese, swore Procter, Scudamore, and Rowley as his clergy. They took the normal oaths of allegiance taken by English clergy, and Waller witnessed the oaths as Registrar.[1]

All the time they were growing to know each other. It was impossible to live together when the *Pioneer* was fast on a sandbank, and amid heat, mosquitoes, frustration and monotony, without becoming intimate friends, or intimate enemies.

With one exception, they became friends.

Among so many forcible characters aboard, and with the potential disturbance of religious difference superimposed, it might have been expected that relationships would become strained. Mackenzie, in his different way, possessed as strong a will as Livingstone. But tension there was none.

Troubles there were. Under the irksome conditions there might have been trouble with any commander. The grumbles of the crew against their officers became at one point so articulate as to imperil even that tempered disorder which passed for discipline on the *Pioneer*.[2] The Africans whom the Bishop had brought from the Cape displayed signs of tantrums. But these troubles were not between the leaders of the expedition and the

[1] W 31.5.61.

[2] 'On principle,' Livingstone wrote, 'I abstained from multiplying orders, believing that it is more agreeable to men to do their duty in their own way' LJW i. 164 (13.5.60).

leaders of the mission. With the single exception of Charles Livingstone, behind his barrier of moods, they formed a happy group, and even Charles Livingstone enjoyed the company. The Zambezi Expedition lasted for more than five years, from 1858 to 1864; and in spite of the exhaustive scope for irritation offered by the River Shire, the officers of the expedition were more harmonious now than at any other time during the five years.

Anyone who seeks to discover the springs of this harmony needs to look first at the character of Mackenzie.

* * * * *

Mackenzie had taught mathematics in Cambridge, at Gonville and Caius College, where he still held a Fellowship. After combining his Fellowship with a curacy at the village of Haslingfield near Cambridge, he was moved, partly by a friend, and partly by the visit of Selwyn of New Zealand to Cambridge, to offer himself for missionary work abroad, and had spent a few troubled years as archdeacon in Natal. Bishop Gray of Cape Town had contemplated using him for one of the new missionary bishoprics which he planned to create in South Africa, and to this end Mackenzie had found himself in England during 1859, at the time when the Central African Mission was being constituted. He was seized upon by the promoters to be its head.

He was the simplest of men, if the epithet *simple* is used in its complimentary sense. Though an able mathematician, he was in a manner an unlearned man. He was content with a simple, practical faith. He barely felt the need of philosophising about faith, of studying Christian history or Christian thought, he was uninterested in theological argument and believed himself incompetent, he took no pleasure in metaphysics. His was the logic of the heart, not of the head. Do we need oratory, or eloquence, or erudition? Like several of the mid-Victorian leaders of religion, he could not find the sparks to kindle truth in the volumes of systematic thinking which burdened the shelves of libraries in English vicarages. Dogmatic theology was necessary but arid. It was poetry and sermons which guided his mind in the apprehension of Scripture; not the intellectual, but the evocative which watered the channels of a living faith without which dogmas and articles were but a cheerless and infertile desert of prose.

He was simple in not romanticizing himself or his mission. No thought crossed his mind that the venture was heroic. The African needed christianizing and civilizing—few people would or could go out to do it—he had better offer himself in default of better men. It was impossible for him to dramatize himself. It was therefore impossible for him to be eloquent, rhetorical, imaginative.

He was simple in not possessing tact; or, if tact be admitted to be a complex quality of diverse components, in not being able to be diplomatic. He had no guile, and no capacity for compromise. He said what he thought when he thought it. He could not say what would please, if he did not think it to be true. His mind was as limpid to the beholder as a deep pool in the mountains. He was so little conscious of himself that he could not ask himself the question, what will others think of you if you do or say this? In consequence, he was able to speak to others on religious subjects, and the deepest matters of the heart, without embarrassing them and without being himself embarrassed. It was as natural for him to speak about God as about the next meal, and his hearers accepted it as naturally. It was natural for him to speak about God because he lived in a world where God was as real as the capstan on the ship. But if he had no tact, he had grace. In another man it might have been called charm; but the word charm has a ring of veneer, of polish, of cultivation. In Mackenzie, it was an open-hearted friendliness which seemed to issue from the inmost sanctuary of the soul. Men disagreed with what he said, they did not resent the way he said it. He possessed that rare faculty of being outspoken without being aggressive.

He was not naturally efficient, brisk, punctual. It was somehow characteristic that he should have driven the *Pioneer* on a sandbank. He suffered from an unusual ability for losing himself on journeys. He was a poor planner, he would have made a regrettable head of a house of business. He saw what was to be done at the moment and did it: it was right now, the future could look after itself. And as the logistics of the Zambezi mission were to be of a complexity far beyond what had been expected or predicted, the deficiency would become important.

His mother had died when he was an infant, leaving him the youngest of twelve children, and he had been brought up by his two eldest sisters. Being nurtured by sisters is in some ways comparable to being nurtured by aunts, but there was nothing fussy or drooping or precise about Mackenzie. He was tall and muscular, a powerful walker with an athletic frame and a slight Scottish accent which was more marked when he was excited, and he was certainly manly. Yet the feminine education had left its mark. He was possessed of the kind of tenderness of which only women are normally capable, he could nurse the sick with a delicacy and a self-giving beyond the crude courtesies and sympathies of the average male, he looked upon little children and babies with an interest and a compassion that was almost feminine, he had that sweetness of temper and temperament which is more often found in women than in men. He expected two of his sisters to join the mission in the course of the next year. Indeed he had refused to accept the headship of the mission until he was assured that his sisters could follow him in perfect safety.

This was the man who was now thrown into the ship's company of the *Pioneer*, as seaman, stoker, amateur engineer, and chief pastor. Three of those who knew him on this expedition, independently use the analogy of sunlight to describe him. His face seemed so constituted as to be physically incapable of scowling or frowning. You might dissent from his judgement, you might question his competence, you might be amused at his directness, but whatever else you thought about him, he was a man, as Rowley put it, 'to rob you of your heart'.

Mackenzie was far removed from Livingstone in upbringing, education, and outlook. Livingstone was dour, Mackenzie the opposite. Livingstone was solitary, Mackenzie gregarious. To Livingstone the highest moments of religion were those when a man was prayerful with his Bible in his loneliness, Mackenzie could conceive no worship higher than the liturgy of the church. Livingstone would turn aside from the world into his personal sanctuary and commune with his God like an Elijah in the wilderness. Mackenzie seemed to carry with him wherever he went, whether he was praying or building huts, the consciousness of the everlasting arms. One of Mackenzie's sisters compared him to the water-spider which carries its own stock of air within so as to be able to breathe within the stream of a river, living as though it were in a diving-bell. 'He mixes with the world because he must, and he leads such an active life as would be distracting to most people; and yet he carries his own heavenly atmosphere around him, and breathes the air of heaven as freely and purely as though he never went down into the water at all.'[1] And yet the two men were oddly akin. In both of them was a rare combination not often seen in human nature. They were vacillators, and yet they had wills of iron. They were vacillators in practical life, chiefly because they were diffident of themselves and liable to be moved by the last opinion which they heard. In the conduct of an expedition, or of a congregation in Natal, the same shifts and twists and turns are to be seen. But move from immediate decisions of expediency to principle, and in both men the sense of uncertainty vanished altogether. In the pursuit of the vision which they had both seen for Africa, there was but one course open—to go onward, recking nothing of the obstacles in the immediate path, confident that they were instruments of a high cause, forgetful of planning or of prudence.

They found that they admired each other. 'Quite a brick of a bishop' was how Livingstone described Mackenzie in a letter[2] to Sir Roderick Murchison. He admired his straightness and his common sense, his readiness to turn a hand to any job, and his participation in the mystique of affection for Africa. Mackenzie, who in any event liked everyone, liked Livingstone's plainness and unpretentiousness and honesty, enjoyed his unmalicious humour and his wide knowledge of men and books. The most interesting outward sign of the harmony was the common participation in religious interests.

The delight, or the recreation, of the harassing voyage from sandbank to sandbank was religious discussion. Charles Livingstone discovered that Rowley the deacon was a high churchman, even for those days an extreme high churchman, certainly the highest on the Zambezi, and that if given a glass of gin his

[1] G 171. [2] Cf. 23.9.61 CAA.

tongue could be loosened to heated argument. He had been a Baptist and a Quaker, tried various other expedients, and had then reacted against the past and become a dissenter against dissent. When they wanted an evening's entertainment, someone would make an outrageous pronouncement denouncing King Charles I, or extolling Oliver Cromwell, and the consequences were 'rare fun'. It amused the Livingstones to discover that they could in these ways set the missionaries by the ears; for Waller, if confronted by some extreme statement from the high churchmen, rose to the bait as if magnetized and upheld an equally extreme proposition to the contrary, against infant baptism, or apostolic succession. Rowley, pretending to be shocked, would become more and more vehement and combative until the Bishop would bring his torrent to a sudden halt by digging him in the ribs. The Livingstones found to their surprise that even Mackenzie was a believer in the divine right of kings, and it amused them to entangle the Bishop in knots over the divine right of Chibisa and what duty of obedience the Englishmen owed him in passing through his village. It struck them as eccentric that he should hold these high views of authority and be so strict a disciplinarian in theory, and yet be so 'liberal and very lax in his control in practice'.[1]

Mackenzie lent Livingstone his favourite book of devotion outside the Prayer Book, Keble's *Christian Year*, and Livingstone professed to like it. The arguments never transgressed the limits of friendly provocation; and the harmony which prevailed was ascribed by more than one, in retrospect, to Mackenzie's character and attitude.

The two Livingstones and Kirk came with the sailors to full Morning and Evening Prayers on Sundays, and to the brief daily prayers, consisting of ten or twelve verses and a few collects, on weekdays. Fever prevented the celebration of Holy Communion for the whole party until the Sunday after Easter. During the week before, Mackenzie went to both Livingstones and to Kirk and asked them if they would come, and they all replied that they would. But on the morning of the service Kirk came to Mackenzie and said that he had never been confirmed, and that he wondered whether he ought for that reason

[1] Charles Livingstone to Mrs Fitch 9.1.62 CAA; W 12.5.61; LJW i. 189.

to refrain from coming. Mackenzie said that on this occasion he ought to carry out his intention, and that they would talk it over later. He then told Kirk that 'in the case of any Europeans living for a time in our neighbourhood, willing, and in the habit of coming to our services, though not members of our church, nor confirmed, but belonging to some other communion—I will admit them to our communion if they wish to come, provided always they are not receiving the communion from anyone in this district not a clergyman of our church.' Kirk was grateful for the attitude. And he told Mackenzie that he felt it a great privilege to be enabled now to communicate. Mackenzie understood him to say that he had had no previous opportunity of receiving the Holy Communion for six years, and was astonished to learn that Livingstone himself had not consecrated bread and wine since the beginning of his expedition. The Bishop was pleased at the way in which Livingstone supported the Anglican ordinances—'reading his Bible in the saloon here every morning before breakfast, kneeling at our prayers, and supporting our position and authority every way he can.'[1]

We should be careful not to exaggerate the harmony on the ship. We are told by Procter that no one liked Charles Livingstone. He said that even Mackenzie, 'who tried to like everyone, was obliged to confess that he failed in that case, even after trying.' The remark rings true—what Kirk had found on the Zambezi, the missionaries found on the Shire. He was too unpredictable, too liable to gusts of irritation, too apt to magnify trivialities into mountains of stumbling. But it is observable from the papers of Charles Livingstone that he liked the Bishop and Scudamore and enjoyed their company, had (at this time) a respect for Rowley and Waller, and was contemptuous only of Procter.[2]

* * * * *

Even at this early date divergent attitudes towards David Livingstone can be faintly seen within the little company of missionaries. Waller and Rowley were at opposite poles, not

[1] Mackenzie to Gray, Shire 8.6.61; Bishopscourt.
[2] SJW 120; Charles Livingstone to Mrs. Fitch, 9.1.62 CAA.

only in churchmanship. They were beginning to react differently as they came to know Livingstone more intimately.

Livingstone had prophesied that they would steam up the Shire in three weeks, and they had taken more than two months. The Shire was not deep enough for the *Pioneer*. Any other commander, perhaps, would have abandoned the attempt a hundred miles before they reached Chibisa's. Waller felt all his regard for Livingstone confirmed—the doggedness of the man, his incapacity for knowing when he was beaten, his faith that he would overcome. 'Never shall I forget the untiring patience of the Doctor at this time—always cheerful, never tried with the hundred and one questions put to him by those who were bored with the monotonous laying out of anchors.'[1]

Rowley had a harder head. He agreed in regarding Livingstone's unbreakable power of endurance with admiration. But his clear, unsentimental mind began to be naggingly critical. This mission had been founded on Livingstone's invitation and his word that the country was ripe for a mission—a safe and healthy place with a friendly people was awaiting them in the Shire highlands, the *Pioneer* would maintain regular communications every three months down the high road of Shire and Zambezi to the sea, the mission would rapidly become a source of commerce and render itself self-supporting by its export of the produce of the area . . . Whether the place in the Shire highlands was safe and healthy and whether it was the home of a friendly people remained to be seen. But Rowley was beginning to worry over the remainder of the programme. If the *Pioneer* took two months each time it ascended the Shire, communications between the future station of the mission and the sea were going to be neither easy nor frequent. How were regular supplies to come up? Still more, how were the products of the colony to go down? Rowley had felt the first touch from the chill hand of scepticism when he was still aboard *H.M.S. Lyra* off the Kongone mouth. Because the mouth of the river was blocked with the bar of sand, the ships had to lie seven miles out to sea; the naval officers thoroughly disliked the station; every time a small boat crossed the bar it crossed at the risk of life—what sensible merchant, wondered Rowley, would invest capi-

[1] Cf. W 22.6.61.

tal in a venture where the communications were so uncertain and so perilous? Livingstone had encouraged them to come by telling the world that the highway for commerce and Christianity was open; and they seemed to be in the predicament of men who have been invited to travel along a fair main road, and thereupon discover that the expected road is nothing but a rough and exhausting track through potholes and ravines.

Already Rowley was ceasing to share Waller's uncritical devotion to Livingstone. He had begun to think that Livingstone was not quite so reliable a guide to Central Africa as everyone had supposed. Livingstone, by reason of his innate modesty, could not see that what was possible for him, a lone and tenacious explorer, might not be possible for a stream of merchants, missionaries, artisans, most of whom would possess but a normal gift of perseverance. And Rowley was beginning to see, for the first time, that Livingstone still retained something of the preacher. Despite the sobriety and the lack of artifice and rhetoric, despite that want of adornment which had so captivated his English audiences, his words must sometimes be taken, not as the words of the cautious observer, but as the cry of a preacher who had seen a prospect of redemption for Africa and was calling others to his own way of dedication. Rowley did not question that Livingstone had been right to summon men to the work. But a faint query was beginning to enter his mind, whether, if Livingstone was blinded, by his humility and his high prospect, to the practical difficulties which confronted the programme, he might be endangering English lives, or, at least, might be summoning men to waste their endeavours in a work which was not yet possible.

But, even in Rowley, the most critical of the missionaries, these questionings were faint. The morale on the *Pioneer* was high; partly because Livingstone never wavered in a cheerful belief that they were acting sensibly, and partly because Mackenzie (as Rowley remarked) 'was not only the most hopeful, but the most hope-inspiring man I have known.'[1] Here providence had brought them, here they were sent, here they must stay and leave the problem of communications to be met later.

* * * * *

[1] R 84.

They had determined to settle in the Shire highlands. They selected the village of Magomero, not because it was the most suitable and healthy, but because it was easy to defend and Livingstone thought the missionaries needed to live in a fort. The missionaries had been told that their lives and their property would be secure. The need for the fort arose because the climb to the highlands had not been accomplished without excitements.

At Chibisa's, as Livingstone foretold, they had not found Chibisa. But they had found an embassy of Manganja tribesmen, from Mount Zomba, who were on their way to ask Chibisa for help against their rival tribe the Ajawa. They claimed that the Portuguese were supplying the Ajawa with guns and so enabling them to sell the Manganja as slaves to the Portuguese. The Bishop sent Rowley, with William from the Cape as his interpreter, to make the ambassadors a present of cloth and to give them the mission's sympathy and support. Rowley told them[1] that God was angry with warriors who burnt their villages and kidnapped their wives and children to be slaves; that the missionaries were English who had come to teach the Manganja how to be a better and a happier people, to teach them about God; and that the mission was going to live near Mount Zomba and would help to bring peace to the land. Rowley recorded that 'the gratitude of these poor fellows seemed great, tears rolled down their cheeks, and on receiving the presents they prostrated themselves on the ground.' He did not realise at the time how easily a simple and savage mind, accustomed only to white men as slave-dealers, might construe a message of sympathy into a suggestion or promise of warlike support.

On 15 July, with a long train of porters and sixteen Makololo whom Livingstone had brought from the upper Zambezi, they set out from Chibisa's for the highlands. Mackenzie carried a can of oil in front, a bag of seeds at his back, in one hand a crozier, given him by the clergy of Cape Town, and in the other hand a double-barrelled gun, loaded. The crozier, though designed for liturgical use, certainly inflicted various jabs and pokes with its butt end upon a lazy and grumbling porter from

[1] R 97.

Sena who had refused to carry a heavy load and who too frequently sat down upon the path. The Africans believed the crozier to be a new kind of musket.

The double-barrelled gun had been the subject of argument aboard the *Pioneer*. Though the Bishop had bought a gun and ammunition from Captain Oldfield of *H.M.S. Lyra*, he had wanted not to take guns with them from Chibisa's to the highlands. They should go, it was said, as men of peace, and command the respect and obedience of the native tribes by their defenceless courage. To the contrary, it was suggested that though they themselves ought not to use guns against human beings, they were engaged to found a civilized, as well as a Christian, community in Central Africa, and that this aim could not be attained unless the means of order lay to hand—unless for example they could arm the weaker villages against marauding savages who were intent only on the kidnapping of women and children. Livingstone, backed by Charles Livingstone and Kirk, said that he would have not the least hesitation in lending guns for these protective purposes. He thought it better to lend only guns, and keep the ammunition in order that the guns might be used only for licensed campaigns. He imagined the mission station, which they were to found, as a kind of 'arsenal for ammunition' to which right-minded Africans might apply.[1] He had said, 'By all means take them [the guns] and if necessary use them. But if you take them, there will be no need to use them, for they are the greatest pacificators in the world if you have peaceful intentions yourself. The Ajawa and all other tribes, knowing you to be well-armed, would assist you, for the natives will never dream of attacking you unless you are defenceless.' With this view everyone but the Bishop agreed. Several of them said that it would be wrong and un-Christian to kill in self-defence: but if one of their friends, still more one of their future flock, were being attacked and his life in imminent peril, ought not even the Christian minister to do whatever could be done to save life?

Mackenzie, overruled by Livingstone and by his own clergy and people, gave way, and so it was that he carried gun and crozier together. Once reconciled to the unusual juxtaposition,

[1] W 7.7.61: cf. P 28.5.61; 8.7.61.

he was amused and half-edified. 'I thought,' he said, 'of the contrast between my weapon and my staff, the one like Jacob, the other like Abraham, who armed his trained servants to rescue Lot.'[1]

On Tuesday 16 July, a march of three hours in clear sunshine, with low ground mists slowly creeping up the mountain-sides, brought them to Mbami's village, three thousand feet above sea level, commanding a magnificent panorama of the Shire valley and the wooded plains and marshes. Livingstone had a fit of vomiting on the marsh; and as the porters refused to go further, they determined to halt for the night and hire porters from Mbami. The Bishop, with Procter and Scudamore, went down to a stream to bathe.

About noon, a slave-party under the guard of six armed African drivers came winding down the slope into the village, the drivers blowing long tin horns to warn the people of their approach. The drivers came into the village treading jauntily like lords of the universe, carrying muskets, one with a scarlet Arab-looking cap. The moment they saw Englishmen, four of the drivers ran away. The two Livingstones recognised one of the two remaining drivers as Katura, a household slave belonging to Senhor Tito, a high Portuguese official. Katura had been lent to them as their cook and steward when they were in Tete. One of the Makololo gripped his hand and stopped him.

David Livingstone stepped forward in his blue jacket and peaked cap. The slaves, eighty-four men, women and children, sat or crouched on the ground, their hands tied, the necks of the male adults in wooden slave-sticks, manufactured of a thick piece of wood about six feet long with a fork for a neck at each end, the neck being imprisoned by an iron pin through the ends of the fork.

'Did Senhor Tito send you?' said Livingstone.

'No, Senhor.'

'Did the Governor of Tete?'

'No, Senhor.'

'Did Candido?'

'No, Senhor. We came away secretly.'

[1] G 323.

'Well,' said Charles Livingstone, 'let's cut the slaves adrift at any rate.'

At once their men (Waller using his fishing knife) started cutting the hard bark and grass cords from the necks of the emaciated women and children. It was more difficult to free the men's necks from the slave-sticks. Rummaging among the Bishop's baggage they found a saw. While the 'liberation' was in progress, the slaves clapped their hands rhythmically and continuously—a loud solemn sound, a hymn of gratitude, as Waller fancied. Katura and the other remaining driver took the opportunity of this business to bolt into the bush.

Livingstone told the released people that they were now 'free' (that was what he intended to tell them, but what the native interpreter, William, said is not known—years later it was found that there is no word for 'freedom' in the Manganja dialects since the idea did not exist) and that they could either go to Tete or go back to their homes. No one seemed to show enthusiasm for either of these courses. They were all almost naked, so the English gave them cloth and then told them to eat the food which some of them had been carrying. One released lad said, 'The others starved us, you cut off our cords and tell us to eat, where do you come from?' As a symbolic act, the English made them collect the thongs and slave-sticks and use them as fuel for the fire to cook their meal.

Enquiry elicited something of their past. Some had been stolen; some sold by their relatives; the children were nearly all orphans. Two women had been shot on the way because the drivers said they were trying to escape; one mother had seen her sick baby's brains dashed against a rock because she could not carry it fast enough.

The Makololo and the Sena men viewed the incident with pleasure, since they divided the spoils between them—a hundred hoes, some cooking pots, cloth, beads, brass rings, mats, spears, bows and arrows, and four guns, two of which could not be fired.

The English viewed the incident with a unanimous pride, each in his different way. David Livingstone thought of it as plain, unexciting duty, Charles Livingstone like a half-detached observer. Kirk, in his moderate way, thought the action 'well-considered'. Waller was excited and fervent beyond measure, his heart swelling with gladness that he had been enabled to share in the first great blow for freedom in the land—'as the half-starved, hard-travelled limbs unconsciously nestled up to my old Highland cloak, it seemed indeed as if nothing kept us now from the brotherhood God would wish to see again on earth.' He thought of the deed as 'a perfect picture of high-minded humanity, painted by His hand on the dark terrible land man has made . . .'

Bishop Mackenzie arrived back from his bathe to find himself with eighty-four protégés, already clothed and cooking 'as composedly as if nothing had happened'.

It crossed his mind to ask whether the action was right. Was it proper to use force? If it was proper for Livingstone, himself a missionary, to use force to free slaves, was it proper for a bishop? It seemed to him, after hesitation, that Livingstone had done right, and therefore that a bishop, placed in a similar situation, should have acted similarly. The next day he wrote a note to Rowley, who had been left at Chibisa's in charge of the remaining stores, 'I am clear that in such cases it is right to use force, and even fire, if necessary, to *rescue captives*. I should do so myself if necessary; but I think it more becoming our office to see the guns in the hands of others. Do you as you think best.'

Mackenzie was aware, even at this early moment, that the action could be misinterpreted. A bishop with a gun? Missionaries seizing the weapons of others? He was sure now, in his own mind, that Livingstone had been right. The black baby's smashed head had changed his outlook. 'Surely,' he said, 'all will join in blessing God that we have such a fellow-countryman.' No doubt, as he had said to Rowley, it was more becoming to see the guns in the hands of others than missionaries. But what if there were no others?

Livingstone offered him the freed people, as his first congregation and his first school. Mackenzie accepted the charge willingly. He told Livingstone that he had doubted whether it was right to interfere, but doubted no longer.[1]

[1] The incident is exceptionally well documented by eye witnesses: R 112–3; W 16.7.61; Charles Livingstone's Journal 16.7.61, RL; K 16.7.61; Livingstone's *Narrative*; Livingstone to Lord John Russell 10.11.61, FO 63/894; LJW 1.182, (16.7.61); Mackenzie to Samuel Wilberforce, July 1861, G 323.

Scudamore and Procter were left in charge of the freed slaves: and on 17 July the long caravan proceeded through the mountains to Soché's, the next village northward. They heard of other slave-parties in the neighbourhood, and felt that, once begun, they ought not to do the thing by halves. They sent a little band of armed men off the path to liberate eight more slaves (five women and three girls) at a nearby hamlet. They heard of a big party of perhaps a hundred slaves on their way to Tete, and Kirk with seven Makololo was sent back to warn the ship's crew to intercept them on the River Shire. The remainder divided into two columns which went northward by different routes, each column headed by a Livingstone. Charles Livingstone seized six more slaves (three women and three boys) at Mongazi's village, and told the tipsy old chieftain that if they found him selling his people they would burn his village and drive him from the land.

Nor was this the only force which they found it necessary to use. When Livingstone and the missionaries arrived at Magomero, they found the countryside in a state of terror and turmoil, in the belief that the Ajawa were close at hand, burning and killing and enslaving as they went. On 22 July, therefore, Livingstone and Mackenzie sallied out with most of their party, the Makololo and some Manganja, went towards the rumoured Ajawa, and found that the report of burnt or deserted villages was true. The crops of maize, white beans, and sweet potatoes were standing in the fields ungathered, because their owners had fled for their lives. At noon they encountered a party of Ajawa on their way back from raiding a Manganja village. They could see the smoke of a village burning in the distance, and behind the raiding party came a column of captives, weeping and bearing the plunder. The Ajawa failed to see the English until they were upon them. Then they came menacingly forward, shouting and dancing. Livingstone shouted that he came to talk, and that it was peace. They shouted to him that it was *Nkondo! Nkondo!* not peace but war, and took cover behind the trees and the rocks. Johnson, the black cook whom the mission had brought from the Cape, thinking that he saw a man aiming at Livingstone (according to his own account later) fired at him. And then the poisoned arrows began to fly.

The Ajawa doubtless saw how few were the English and came rushing down shouting 'derision' and charging 'like demons'. Livingstone gave the order to fire. The charge 'was met with a few well-directed shots from the rifles; they halted, and returned to cover. But at last they were forced from their stronghold, and their camp destroyed and burnt. The captives escaped during the fight; they threw down their burdens and fled into the bush. None of the English was hurt; one Manganja was killed, and another had an arrow through his wrist.'

The Bishop went through the middle of the fighting. He was carrying a gun but he did not use it. 'Seeing Livingstone without one, I asked him to use mine, rather than that I should—on the principle that I *preferred* not to use it, and that I thought it more seemly that his finger should pull the trigger than mine.' The shouting, the threats of defiance and of vengeance, reminded Mackenzie irresistibly of the Homeric battles. If he had but closed his eyes he could have imagined himself wandering among the combats on the plains of Troy.[1]

It seemed strange to begin their missionary endeavours with a pitched battle. They regretted the necessity of the action, they did not regret the action. Minds unfamiliar with the rigours of the slave-trade boiled when they saw its outward signs. 'Logic,' wrote Livingstone in retrospect,[2] 'is out of place when the question with a true-hearted man, is whether his brother-man is to be saved or not.'

For the mission the battle entailed momentous consequences.

At Livingstone's earnest recommendation, the mission chose Magomero as the site for its settlement. Mackenzie had wanted to choose one of the attractively sited villages, perhaps Mbami's, through which they had passed on the climb from the Shire. Livingstone pressed on him that his camp ought to be defensible. Magomero was built upon a peninsula formed by a stream, and therefore possessed attractions if a man was looking for a fortress. It suffered from the disadvantage that it lay in a hollow into which the surrounding hills drained, and Rowley's heart sank when he compared its amenities with the clean breezes

[1] Mackenzie to Gray, 4.11.61 UMCA; LJW i. 184; Charles Livingstone's Journal, RL; R 111–13.

[2] *Narrative* p. 357.

and distant views of some of the highland villages through which they had come. Magomero was the village of a minor chieftain named Chigunda, a Manganja who told them that he and his people would flee from the Ajawa unless the mission stayed with him. The peninsula was eighty yards by three hundred; and across its neck Waller who, though the son of a London stockbroker, showed surprising competence in these practical matters, directed the natives in building a stockade. For the first few days they expected attack from the Ajawa and maintained sentries to meet it. Livingstone conceived of the fortress as near enough to the Ajawa to be a city of refuge for oppressed peoples. It might be the beginning of pacification for the whole region.

On 25 July, Livingstone invited the chiefs to meet him at Magomero. When he had gathered a small group of them, he made them a formal speech.

'You have seen us only as fighters. We have not come for this. We have come to teach you about God, and to promote peace. But finding men (the Ajawa) murdering, burning, and selling men, we went to stop them. If they profit by this lesson, and will live at peace, we shall rejoice and be all friends —if not we shall look after you again.[1] I am going, but some will stay. They will stay here, and make a strong place to which women and children may flee in case of attack.'

The chiefs said, 'Selling people is bad.'

Livingstone said, 'You have sold also, the only difference is that the Ajawa murder and steal and then sell.'

The chiefs did not deny the impeachment. They said, 'Let the English settle at Chinsunzi's; *he* will not be pleased else.' Chinsunzi was the greatest of the near-by Manganja chiefs who had sent representatives to the meeting.

Livingstone said, 'This place is better. It is far to carry goods to Chinsunzi's.'

[1] So Mackenzie's Journal, the only first-hand record. But when public controversy arose, it was queried whether Livingstone had said this. Rowley appealed to the evidence of the Journal. But Waller, the only other member of the mission to be present beside Mackenzie (Rowley was still at Chibisa's), denied that he meant it, and said that he (Waller) had not this impression of the speech. Accordingly Rowley omitted the phrase from his later account of the speech (R 114) and made Livingstone say simply, 'If they would profit by the lesson they had received and would live at peace, he and his friends would rejoice, and be friends with all.'

The chiefs assented and said they thought Chinsunzi would consent. Livingstone said, 'You must cultivate cotton, we will buy that.'

'But where shall we get seed?'

Livingstone distributed seed to about fifty people. The chiefs said that Chinsunzi himself was too old to come so far, so Mackenzie gave them a present for him. 'Before two o'clock, however, Chinsunzi himself came—old man—pleasant expression—brass earrings, necklace, a single string of red beads—a native cloth six feet each way, a large ivory bracelet two inches broad, and a very dirty cap on his head. A long discussion as to whether we shall build here or at his place. He urged us strongly to come: how could we say we loved him, if we would not come and live beside him? If we stayed here we should get news of his death—in fact he was dead already (a strong form of the idea that he was broken-hearted). Livingstone took his bow and arrows, saying that if he was dead he would of course let *him* have them. (A laugh.)

'Livingstone said, "Well, if you do not want them to stay here, you had better say so."

'To this he gave some vague answer. When they rose to go, Livingstone said, "Well, we shall build here," and he made no answer.'[1]

* * * * *

At the end of July, Livingstone left Magomero, to return to the *Pioneer* and his work of exploration. He had done what he could for the mission, left them and their stores in the place which he had designated for them, and all this with surprisingly little disagreement or friction. Before he left, he was asked what they should do about the conditions of warfare in which they found themselves. He advised the Bishop to beware of joining in any tribal war—'You will be oppressed with requests but don't go'—and to make Magomero a refuge for the oppressed. The advice was equivalent to recommending that they use their weapons in defence but not in attack.

[1] Mackenzie's Journal, 25.7.61, UMCA.

In these circumstances, the distinction between defence and attack appeared sometimes to be hard to discover.

* * * * *

The English had said they were friends of the Manganja. They had said that the Ajawa were wicked in burning and killing and enslaving. They had established a stockade at Magomero, near the scene of warfare, as a refuge for the oppressed. They had attacked and driven away a plundering band of Ajawa. They were living in the same village as men engaged in war with the Ajawa. To the Manganja tribes around them it was clear that the English were not only good men but allies in their resistance to their enemies. No sooner had Livingstone departed than embassy upon embassy came to Magomero to plead for English help against ravaging and murdering assailants.

On 9 August, a deputation of the highland chiefs arrived at Magomero.

'The chiefs were assembled close to the Bishop's hut. Chinsunzi and Kankomba were there. They were the two greatest men in the land. . . . On the right sat Chinsunzi alone; on the left sat Kankomba alone; in front of all squatted Chigunda, and he acted as spokesman. Behind these illustrious three, sat about a hundred and fifty others, most of them men having authority—the governing body of the hill Manganja, in fact. The Bishop, and those with him, sat on a mat facing this imposing assemblage, and William acted as interpreter and spokesman.

'There was much deference paid by the subordinates to the two great chiefs. They themselves said but little, the subordinates much. One after the other got up, and after bowing reverently to their great men, commenced their orations by saying, "I follow my lord Chinsunzi," or Kankomba, as the case might be. They were encouraged in their speeches by a regular chorus of ejaculations, now high, now low, now long. When each had done, Chigunda repeated what had been said, commencing with *Arti* (he says), and his faithfulness in repetition was rewarded by approving remarks. All speeches were uttered in a high-pitched voice—intoned in fact, for they intone all their speeches and prayers. The purport of all the orations was to enlist the sympathy and the aid of the English against the Ajawa. They pictured the happy state of the country before the Ajawa came, its misery and desolation now that they were here. They spoke of villages burnt, of brethren slain, of wives and children carried away; and they concluded by describing the happy state of things that would again exist, if the English would only help them against their cruel enemies . . .

'After hearing all they had to say, the Bishop told them that in three days he would give them an answer.'[1]

Truly, the relations between church and state are complex when there is no state for the church to have relations with. A year before, Henry Venn, the able Secretary of the Church Missionary Society, who by no means approved of the design and constitution of the Central African Mission, had drafted some notes for the guidance of his own missionaries upon their political relations. In heathen countries, he told them, the activities of the missionary could not avoid political consequences. They elevated the social position of the converts, instructed them in the principles of justice and humanity, and thereby quickened in their minds the sense of the wrongs they might suffer through oppression and misgovernment. They taught their people obedience towards their earthly rulers, but at the same time obedience to a law hitherto unknown to them, the law of God, and this obedience might conflict with the institutions of the country, or the custom of the tribe. The missionary, in so far as he is successful in his mission, soon becomes the friend, the guide, the father of his people. If therefore he won their confidence, he looked to them for advice, for assistance against injustice and wrong-doers. And the difficulty is admitted to be multiplied when the missionary is working among uncivilized peoples. 'The injunction to abstain from all interference with political affairs is obviously not applicable when the native government is mixed up with national superstitions and social institutions which violate all justice and humanity; when the magistrate's sword is in the hands of every petty chief, or self-constituted oppressor . . .'[2]

[1] R 123–4.

[2] William Knight, Memoir of Henry Venn (new ed. 1882), appendix E, wrongly dated.

Venn had written this with one eye upon the Maoris. But no one can be sure how such principles will work out in peculiar circumstances. The mission to Central Africa, on Livingstone's initiative, had taken under its protection a group of the oppressed. Was it not also logical to think of the village immediately in its neighbourhood as also under its protection? Was it possible for an Englishman and a Christian to sit down and fold his hands while people in his vicinity were being carried off into slavery or murdered? They had come professing to teach principles of peace, to show the tribes a better way than that of the slave-trade. They had selected their position with the special object of stopping traffic in human flesh. What would their flock think of them if they refused to help the sheep against the wolf? Would it be possible to hold a Christian mission of any kind in the area unless some measure of pacification was achieved, and was it not therefore their duty to achieve the pacification?

After Holy Communion on Sunday, 11 August, they held a solemn discussion, and agreed without a single dissentient that they would be right in helping the Manganja against their oppressors. The group was working, thinking, and deciding as a group. Those who watched the mission from outside, like Livingstone and some of his men, thought later that Mackenzie was not giving them enough of a lead, that he was not decisive enough, that he was too humble to assert his own mind, that he presided over a friendly democracy. This was not the view of the missionaries under him. Rowley expressed his admiration for Mackenzie's qualities as a leader thus: 'He had the power of harmonising diverse dispositions, and keeping men at one who naturally would be opposed. I have never met with another who so quickly disarmed opposition as he; no man obtruded his own opinions less than he, and few men were so likely to carry what they advocated.'[1] At the moment there was no disagreement on what must be done.

The reasoning of the discussion had run upon these lines. Suppose that they had been, not a mission, but a party of English lay settlers who had come to cultivate land among the Manganja—they would have been justified in allying themselves

[1] R 156.

with the Manganja to drive off marauders. If this was true of English settlers, nothing could make it untrue of English settlers who were clergymen. In Europe it would be inappropriate for the clergy to do the work because there were other hands to do it. But here there were no other hands. It is inappropriate in civilized countries for bishops to haul on anchors, carry oil-cans sixty miles, and build houses, for in civilized countries bishops have other duties which they ought to be performing. But the Bishop in Central Africa had already been engaged on all these tasks. And if it was argued that it must be wrong for a bishop to go out fighting, it was replied that it must be wrong for a Christian to go out fighting—but there are sometimes circumstances when a fight is the lesser evil of the two. If you do not fight, you watch while your congregation is murdered or sold into slavery. 'Livingstone is right,' Mackenzie had written to Bishop Wilberforce of Oxford, 'to go with loaded gun and free the poor slaves; and there being so few English here, we are right, though clergymen and preachers of the Gospel, to go with him, and by our presence, and the sight of our guns, and their use if necessary (which may God avert), to strengthen his hands in procuring the liberation of these people. . . I believe some will blame Livingstone, and more will blame me. But I can only act as I think right . . .'

The prayer to which he continually resorted for guidance was the Prayer Book Collect for the first Sunday after Epiphany —'Grant that thy people may both perceive and know what things they ought to do and also may have grace and power faithfully to fulfil the same . . .' Waller, unlike Mackenzie, had no qualms at all. He found himself on a crusade of liberation, a member of the first band to strike a blow against the slave-traffic, and he rejoiced whole-heartedly.[1]

On Monday 12 August, therefore, they forced the Manganja chiefs to an oath no more to engage in the slave-trade, and thereupon agreed to help them against the Ajawa. On 14 August the Bishop, at the head of a thousand Manganja, marched through beautiful country with glimpses of a sunlit Lake Shirwa, a country of such smiling peacefulness that Rowley dotted it in his mind's eye with a happy people of the

[1] G 328; W 24.7.61.

future, though at the moment it was dotted with burnt and deserted villages. Mackenzie had resolved that he could not fight until he had conferred with the Ajawa and sought to persuade them to retire peaceably. But a conference was not easy to achieve without the death of a bishop. Mackenzie summoned all the whites round him, and while they knelt upon the grass, he prayed that God would be with them in what they were about to do, that he would incline the Ajawa to go away peaceably; 'If not, that he would protect us and give us the victory, and that he would, for Christ's sake, forgive the sins of those who might fall that day, whether white or black, friend or foe.' Mackenzie later took Waller, Charles the Cape interpreter, and a Manganja, and walked ahead, unarmed, to the Ajawa encampment. The Ajawa saw them approaching and began to utter blood-curdling war cries and run hither and thither to arms and to cover, reminding Rowley of nothing so much as a nest of hornets. Waller was to wave a white handkerchief if the conference was successful and the Ajawa agreed to obey, a red handkerchief if it was war, and the Manganja force would at once advance down the slope.

The unarmed quartet went towards the camp and met several Ajawa, one with a gun and the rest with bows and arrows. They looked threatening. Waller caught himself several times telling himself that his duty as forthcoming leader in the fight was to stay behind. The Bishop spoke in English, Charles translated to the Manganja, and the Manganja translated to the Ajawa. The moment the Ajawa heard that they were English, they said, 'We do not want anything to do with the English; they help the Manganja against us', and they began to come menacingly forwards. Mackenzie held up his hands to show that he was unarmed and asked them to stay where they were. The Ajawa stopped; and then Mackenzie told them that 'he came with a message of peace, but if they would not listen to it it would be war.' The Ajawa made it plain, or seemed to the parleyers to make it plain, that it would be war. So the four returned, at first walking away, followed by the armed Ajawa, drums sounding continuously in the valley below, until, as Mackenzie expressed it, 'the thought of a musket-ball in their rear had had time to produce a certain amount of nervous irritation', and they began running. Waller arrived back panting, 'It is war! They will not have peace! They will have nothing but war with us!'

The battle was soon over. The Bishop asked Waller to take command, 'thinking it more seemly, and also believing that his character—prompt and instinctive—as well as his previous habits (among sportsmen) would make him a better general than myself.'[1] One of the seamen, Rowe, nevertheless thought that the generalship in the battle was non-existent. Another of Livingstone's blue-jackets, Hutchins, afterwards claimed that he burnt more Ajawa huts than anyone else. The Ajawa fired at them a few times and then ran away, frightened by the long range of the rifles. The Ajawa casualties probably numbered about five. This time the Bishop carried his own rifle and used it. 'In this fight I used my gun to the best of my skill, as did all the rest. We were only *ten* guns, and I thought it right to do all I could to rid the country of robbers and murderers . . . It is right to take up arms at the command of the civil magistrate. It was the cause of mercy to free the captives who might be in their camp. It was striking a death-blow to the slave-trade at its heart. It was not till after some deliberation that we came to this conclusion. I do not doubt now that it was right.' Two or three villages near Mount Zomba were burnt, no member of the mission was hurt, and the Bishop returned wearily towards Magomero.

He saw a little boy, obviously very ill, nothing but bones and skin, sitting in the doorway of a hut in a deserted village. The Manganja said it was no use carrying him, as he would soon die. But the Bishop insisted that they bring him with them. At nightfall the child was dying. The Bishop took him into his own hut, forced brandy vainly down his throat, and seeing that it was of no avail, determined to baptize him. With Scudamore and Rowley as his godparents, the little African was baptized under the names of Charles Henry, died two hours later, and was buried next morning in a shroud of calico rolled in a sleeping mat, the Bishop reading over his body the burial service in the Book of Common Prayer. Livingstone, when he heard the story,

[1] Mackenzie's Journal, 27.8.61; *Guardian*, 1862, p. 687; cf. K 8.11.61; Mackenzie to Gray, 4.11.61, UMCA.

was puzzled. It seemed to him an odd form of the Bishop's high churchmanship.

The Second Ajawa war, as Mackenzie came later to call his expeditions in mock imitation of the three Punic wars, put the number of dependants in Magomero above 160, mainly women and children. He was confident that the expedition had done what it set out to do; that it had pacified the whole area of country to the south of Lake Shirwa, and incidentally had compelled the Manganja chiefs to agree to abolish slavery. The day after he returned to Magomero, further deputations of Manganja began to wait on him, all with agonizing stories of the slayings and burnings in their immediate neighbourhood.

Mackenzie did not believe them. He sent out a scouting expedition and discovered that an Ajawa village was living not far from a Manganja village with every sign of peaceableness, and that the Manganja chief was lying. On the arrival of further embassies he discovered that the Manganja were themselves retaining captives as slaves, and refused to have further dealings with embassies until the captives were delivered to him. He himself went out on reconnaissance and discovered the Manganja to be, at least, exaggerating grossly. He arrived at a village which its chief had tearfully and heart-rendingly declared to be razed to the ground, found it peaceful and flourishing, and met there the chief, who did not even blush but offered him a drink of pombi out of a pot.

One evening he paraded all the refugees in Magomero and discovered to his astonishment that three-quarters of them were Ajawa. (The Manganja were long-headed, the Ajawa round- or broad-headed, and the tattooing marks were distinctive.) Instead of being, as the whites had supposed, Manganja who had been captured for the slavers by the Ajawa, he found that they were Ajawa who had been captured for the slavers by the Manganja. And the Ajawa, instead of being ruthless invaders, were discovered to be fugitive tribes, fleeing southward from barbarians in the north.

But of one village, that of the chief Nampeko, which lay forty miles to the north, there seemed no doubt. The Bishop's reconnaissance proved that Nampeko was being ravaged and oppressed, and his people in danger of murder and enslavement

A new station for trade with Portuguese slavers had recently been built nearby. The missionaries were not quite unanimous. Rowley doubted whether, with so much work about them, they were wise to send out pacifying expeditions to villages forty miles away. But for the rest the hatred of slavery, and the sympathy with the innocent, was an overwhelming argument. If Nampeko's story was true, they must as Christian men go to his help.

They were not encouraged when Nampeko was discovered to be lying about the destruction of his village, and appeared to be smilingly impenitent about so venial a sin. Mackenzie shook his fist in his face, and broke up the conference. But within a fortnight the chiefs were creeping back. On Sunday 6 October they reappeared at Magomero.[1] Mackenzie told Johnson, the black cook, to put a quarter of a goat extra in the pot for dinner, and invited the five squatting chiefs to dinner. There was no room for five extra inside the hut, so their portions of goat were sent outside to them; a fortunate expedient as there was not enough plum pudding to go round, and the chiefs were never aware that the whites had eaten a second course. Mackenzie did not encourage them to start supplicating. But all that day they went on squatting inside the gate of the stockade, and were still there next morning. At three p.m. they sent a message that they wished to speak to the Bishop, and the conference ensued.

Nampeko: 'I come to tell you that I am much ashamed of myself for the lies I told you. I ask you to forget them, and promise that all I shall say for the future will be the truth.'

Bishop: 'The more you speak the truth now and for the time to come, I will forget about this lie more and more.'

(Later, looking back on the conversation, Mackenzie decided that the idea of an increasing oblivion was so awkward as to be impossible for any interpreter to translate.)

Bishop: 'I do not wish to attack the Ajawa if I can help it. I should like to send a message to the Ajawa to say, "Do not attack the Manganja. Go into the desolate country

[1] Mackenzie to Goodwin, 14.10.61, UMCA.

behind you and pluck and reap there. If you attack the Manganja, I will attack you. If you are not away out of this country when the next harvest comes in, I will drive you all away." '

Manganja: 'All right. Only do not lose time sending the message.'

Bishop: 'Will you send it? Is there anyone that knows the Ajawa well enough to go to them?'

Manganja: 'There is no one that dares to go.'

Bishop: 'Well, I'll try and find some of my people to go. If not, you must send some of your own people to catch one or two of the Ajawa and send the message by them.'

Manganja: 'A message given by us to the Ajawa would not be believed.'

Bishop: 'Well, bring the captives to me and I will talk to them.'

Manganja: 'We are afraid to go.'

Bishop: 'What, are there not thirty Manganja willing to undertake so small a risk for the sake of their country?'

(Much silence and shaking of heads.)

The Magomero people proved to be equally reluctant to risk their necks by bearing the threat to the Ajawa. In the end, Scudamore and Livingstone's doctor, Meller, who was staying for a time in Magomero to recuperate his health, went off to Nampeko on a further reconnaissance. The result was the Third Ajawa war, in which there were no casualties to either side, a camp was burnt, a large barracoon for slaves destroyed, some Manganja plunder rescued, some captives released. Here is Mackenzie's description in his Journal:

16 October: 'Up at 3.30 a.m., breakfast, loading Manganja guns [about thirty of the Manganja had guns] and off by 6 . . . More than 1,000 of the allies. Nearly ten o'clock we got to the river Mingole. [I repeated to myself several times, "The Battle is the Lord's, and he is the Governor among the people." As on former occasions we the Christians stood together to ask him to direct all things according to his will.] Adams saw three men on the opposite side, two of whom had guns. He [i.e. Adams] fired at them and we never saw them nor any other male Ajawa all day—crossed unopposed—burnt huts, from which the people had fled—Adams pursued till he could see over the hill northward, Scudamore and I and others turned soon on hearing that the Ajawa men had gone out on a raid and might return soon. We assembled in the central space of the village—great confusion—men pouring through in crowded streams, loaded with grain as booty—a number of women in the middle who had been taken. [It was not pleasant to see men bringing . . . booty into this place, and then looking round at the women as if they were so many cows captured.] These we took under our guardianship, till they could say where they would like to go. We had agreed they should all be free, and not be captives of war. I offered them to take them in sight of their countrymen and let them all go—but they refused saying they would rather be with the English—more women and children were continually brought in till there were about 400.

'There was a rumour of the approach of the Ajawa. We took up our guns and went down to meet them, but could see nothing so we returned—tried to send the women off under the charge of one of Nampeko's men. He said he would take them, but soon slipped away, and we did not see him again. [It is most annoying the way in which these people leave you in the lurch. . . . There is no court that will take notice of breaches of contract.] This lost us an hour. We tried to arrange for the women to cook—giving them water was a long operation—after two hours' delay it was evident they were not going to cook. (I don't suppose any of them had broken their fast that day, and cannot tell why they would not cook.) Finally Scudamore impressed me with a sense of the unpleasantness of sleeping there, and being perhaps alarmed in the night by a cry of the return of armed Ajawa. It is clearly unwise to arrange to sleep in an open village in an enemy's country, without, at least, a friendly chief and his retinue, the latter to look out and he to advise. So about five o'clock we determined to return on our four hours' march. We all left the village, after setting it on fire, and set off. [What man in England would start on a five hours' walk, with women and children like this, who had eaten nothing since ten certainly and probably not since the previous evening . . . I kept behind for a good while with Scudamore to see that no helpless people were left behind.] It was painful to see weak women carrying children or others with bad ulcers on their legs, on such a walk. We tried to get some of the men to relieve such—but before we had got halfway it was clear they must camp out and come on in the morning. *We* quickened our pace and got back tired just as it began to lighten, and rain heavily on the poor unsheltered captives.

17 October: 'It rained piteously till about 3 p.m. No food to be got. Three goats we had set apart for the people had been stolen—some of the captives came in last night, most this forenoon—children cried—no fires could be lighted outside, and the huts were all filled before half were housed—how to get them disposed of so as to secure their liberty was now the difficulty. We gathered them and the chiefs together—asked where they wished to stay—they could not make up their minds, how could they? They did not know the nature of the choices they had, to go with the English or with the Manganja. Some made choice, and were put aside.

'It began to pour: all ran for shelter, and confusion followed. At last those who declared for us were got together, and put into their huts. I wanted to see the rest have their choice with whom they would go—but at last came to the conclusion that if I pressed this point they would all be starved with hunger, and so there would be nothing left to contend about. Went away with the full belief that Nampeko would allow his friends to take such as they liked, who would have them as slaves, to pay debts with and suchlike. But we had done our best—we returned to Nampeko's to sleep, and with difficulty got enough kassava roots to feed them.

'I do not think I ever spent a more miserable day: wet through, urging the chiefs to do something but not succeeding, quieting the crying of the children, feeling for the hunger of our freed people, which I could ill abate by two or three fowls among 60 or 70—and finally doubting whether on the whole we had done much good by our fighting, as we had been the means of 400 women and children being severed from their relations, of whom only fifty ultimately would be free.

'But I tried to lay the burden on Him whom I knew I was

anxious to serve. When we got home, found we had added forty-eight to the number of our dependants—chiefly old women and children.'

Rowley had warned him before the expedition marched that they might not be able to feed another mouth, and looked perturbed and depressed as the new refugees, soaked driftwood of humanity, walked or limped or tottered into Magomero. Mackenzie saw his face and said, 'Look at them, you old grumbler, and tell me if you could refuse them!'[1]

The missionaries were aware, with a nagging and half-secret fear, that these proceedings would seem odd to some, perhaps to most, of their backers at home. They were also convinced, in frequent meditations upon the theme, that they were doing right, that they could not do otherwise. They were heartened by remembering that Livingstone had seemed to encourage them in this path and to begin the policy which they had continued, and they still looked upon Livingstone as the expert, whose opinion carried the greatest weight in all matters, and upon whom the mission was more than half-dependent—physically as well as mentally, since their life-line to the outside world seemed to depend upon the *Pioneer*'s presence on the Shire. They admitted that they had behaved in an 'unusual', even an 'extraordinary' manner for missionaries, and they were continuously uneasy; but they were content with the answer that their situation was extraordinary. Just before the expedition set out for the Third Ajawa war, Rowley (who was indefatigable in maintaining his journal even under the most uninviting conditions, so much so that Meller formed the opinion that he was too often to be seen writing when he should have been out working) wrote:

'I own all this appears very inconsistent. Good folks at home will be greatly shocked, I dare say. I advocate to-day what I disapproved of a few days before [i.e. the expedition to Nampeko's]; and I must confess it is more feeling than reason which inclines me to do so; but it is not possible to be the cold-blooded thing which would sit down quietly unmoved, when

[1] Bishop's Journal, UMCA (spelling slightly altered); additions from Mackenzie to Goodwin 14.10.61 *et seq.*, UMCA; R 183.

you know that you have but to move in order to stop the horror and bloodshed described by Scudamore.'[1]

They were perfectly correct in prophesying that their supporters in England would think these proceedings extraordinary. They supposed nevertheless that their supporters would not cease to support. In this they were mistaken.

[1] R 181.

III

THE MEETING AT THE RUO MOUTH

THE missionaries had other things to do than fight. Behind their stockade they were engaged in creating a Christian community out of their dependants, the flotsam and jetsam of the slave-trade.

The community was distorted in regard to age. On 2 October 1861 it contained seventy-eight men and boys and seventy-nine women and girls; but of the males only twelve or thirteen were adults, whereas forty-five of the women were adults and most of them had been married. About half the population was aged ten or under. They had to build a village and organize a school with ten whites (including Dr Meller, Rowe the quartermaster from the *Pioneer*, and Hutchins the blue-jacket, sent to Magomero for their health), four Makololo, four Africans from the Cape, and such assistance as they could command or persuade from the dozen adult Manganja. One of the whites, Gamble the carpenter, proved to be incompetent. Almost everything constructed by him collapsed.

They built huts, six men being able to complete a single hut in two days. By the end of September they had completed the Bishop's Palace, a somewhat larger hut with thatched roof and inner walls of entwined bamboo, Mackenzie being architect as well as the most hard-working among the builders. It looked like 'a large roughly-built cow-house, or as some say like an old haystack with the inside eaten out.'[1] But the new refugees from the Third Ajawa War had to be housed in it until new huts had been built for them, and the Bishop did not move into it until 8 November. He and the clergy slept in the Palace on wooden bedsteads, and ate their meals off a table which Gamble the carpenter had erected after prolonged effort and which was

[1] W 22.8.61.

therefore wobbly. 'The Bishop was very proud of his house, and proclaimed it an end to all our discomfort. But alas for his anticipations! It rained for a few hours during the night, and at once found out the weak places in the thatch. On waking, I found Scudamore placidly sitting up in his bed under an umbrella; puddles were everywhere; and the Bishop looking comically aghast. This was the first heavy rain we had had.'[1] Waller objected, not so much to the rain, as to the rats and cockroaches which cruised about the hut during the night.

On 1 October, the anniversary of their farewell service in Canterbury Cathedral, they erected with due solemnities the first pillar (intended as the north-east corner of the chancel) of St. Paul's Church. The pillar was a big tree cut down by Scudamore, who in spite of his absent-mindedness and inconsequential humour proved to be a master of the axe. A bottle containing a commemorative paper was buried at the base of the pillar. But St. Paul's Church was destined never to be finished.

Adams, though brought as an 'agriculturist', proved to be a more capable carpenter than Gamble. He constructed a 'night-house' for the goats, and then turned his hand to building a coop for the hens. Johnson the Cape African, who was chief cook, supervised the building of a kitchen. The worst deficiency was in accommodation for their black dependants. At one time, before building had far advanced, twenty boys were sleeping in a hut not more than ten feet in diameter. The whites soon discovered that the perils of overcrowding were not only ill-health and discomfort. Mackenzie wrote home urgently to his committee in London applying for '200 blankets (7 foot by 3½ foot), as much a means of morality among the people, to prevent them huddling indecently together at night as for their warmth and comfort.'[2] He summoned the population, and told them that henceforward the men were to live in huts on one side of the village, the women in huts on the other. 'This astonished them not a little, and they asked if it were the English custom for the women to live away from the men. They were told that it was not the English custom for men and women to live as they had been living until they were married.' The Bishop

[1] R 188. [2] R 146; Woodcock to Atlay, 12.8.62, UMCA.

made a public assumption that they were all unmarried, and told them that if a man wanted to have one single woman for his wife, and she was willing, he would allow it, but he must first be told.

'A day or two after this, a young man came to us while we were at dinner. He sat at the door of the hut, and to our enquiry, said he came to talk: but he did not talk, we could not get him to talk, it was the last thing he seemed able to do, but at last he informed us that he wished to have a certain woman for his wife. Upon our asking him if she wished to have him for a husband, he held down his head, and softly said: "She says so." And there was no doubt about it, for when he fetched her, she did say so. And then the Bishop, William acting as his mouthpiece, spoke to them very gravely upon the duty of husbands towards their wives and wives towards their husbands; made the man promise he would have no other wife, made the woman promise she would have no other husband; and that they would be kind and faithful to each other. Then he said they were man and wife, and pointed to a plot of ground outside the stockade where he intended the village of the married people to be. We were now in no fear of the Ajawa, and so were no longer obliged to keep within our barricades.

'Next day five men wished for wives, and appeared with *six* women. There was no difficulty with three of the pairs, all their arrangements being satisfactory; but in the fourth instance the woman refused at the last moment to marry the man, who then went away, and to prove he was not such an undesirable fellow, came back shortly afterwards with two women, both of whom were anxious to be his wives; in the fifth case the man did not exactly want to marry the woman he had brought with him, but wanted to have another. Of course we did not let the man have two wives, and we made the other business comfortable for all parties. And after this marriages became popular until all the men were provided for. Unfortunately we had more women than men: quarrels therefore occasionally took place; the wives began to get jealous of their prerogative, and would not allow any to share their husbands' affections with them, though up to this time they had been accustomed to the arrangements of polygamy. But in the end these people lived happily in that condition we had brought about, and, as a rule, they were kind and affectionate one to another, and faithful. It was thus we attempted to lay the foundation of a Christian community.'

This was not, however, the end of matrimonial troubles. Damanji, the man who had wanted to marry two wives, had only been permitted to marry his first preference. When the second saw the first established in Damanji's newly-built hut, she was inconsolable, and 'rushed about like a mad woman, talked frantically about killing herself, and seemed utterly wretched because she had not the half of a husband . . . She rushed at the wife, and would have been sadly handled, for she was excited, while the wife was cool and also the stronger.'[1]

The matrimonial affliction which beset the Bishop most severely was nearer at home. Johnson the cook was found to be the father of a forthcoming child. 'I should not mind,' wrote Mackenzie, 'discouragement among the heathen; but it is among our Cape Town men. God help us all to grow in grace, and them especially in the grace of purity . . . I feel these sins in themselves as wounds to our Saviour and breaches in the walls of our Zion, and as positive hindrances, so far as they go, to our work, by lowering us among the heathen.'[2] Johnson offered to marry the girl. Mackenzie was too sensible to apply the custom of home to the predicaments of Magomero. He foresaw that the 'marriage' could not last, and discouraged it. Nothing shook his affection for the Cape men, and yet their conduct (for Johnson was not the only one so guilty) pained him deeply, he felt it like a personal stain. It was fortunate that he never seems to have discovered that Livingstone's quartermaster, the whiskered, porter-drinking Rowe, also begot a child while he was staying for his health at Magomero.

* * * * *

The day's programme followed a regular pattern prescribed by the Bishop. Johnson the cook called them at six; after private prayers, washing in the river, and making beds, the

[1] R 147–8, 170.

[2] G 385; cf. Tozer to Samuel Wilberforce, 23.7.63, and Tozer to Gray of Cape Town, 31.10.63, both Bishopscourt.

whites (with a rare, stray black from time to time) attended Morning Prayer—that is, the full office according to the Book of Common Prayer of 1662—at seven o'clock; breakfast at eight, in the Bishop's hut, usually goat-meat or chicken, vegetables (yam or sweet-potatoes, beans or peas) and 'porridge of ground Indian corn. Once or twice a week we have a loaf. We drink coffee or tea, and have one goat in milk. Our plates and cups belong to a canteen for sick persons, bought in London. They are iron, enamelled inside, and don't break.' Meanwhile, Charles the Cape man assembled the entire population, and they called the roll, each person answering his name with *kuno* (here). The Bishop then made a speech, interpreted by William, arranging the work of the day—clearing undergrowth outside the enclosure, cutting wood, bamboo or grass for building. The boys were taught in school all the morning, after a period of drill by Scudamore, who taught them to march and plunged them by numbers into the river, 'a shoal of bronzed mackerel diving and splashing and ducking each other'. The water was necessary: many of the children slept almost in the fire at night and were coated in ash. The school was divided into three classes according to age and taught by Procter, Scudamore, and Rowley; though, since Rowley as deacon had charge of all stores, buying goats or fowls or vegetables (for lengths of white calico, occasionally for coloured beads), bartering, and the commissariat generally, the Bishop frequently needed to take his place in teaching the youngest class. Rowley also conducted a class in 'music'. They dined at one o'clock, waited upon by one of the liberated boys named Wekotani; conducted classes for adults from two to three; were free from three to six for their own affairs, learning the language, visiting other huts, constructing houses. At six they had tea (porridge with nuts or eggs), followed by a time of leisure until evening prayer at eight, after which they inspected their little domain and went to bed by the light of oil lamps. The Bishop fell asleep with his double-barrelled gun and a revolver, both loaded, above his head; and above them a shelf of books—the Bible, Keble's *Christian Year, The Imitation of Christ,* Wordsworth's commentary on the New Testament, Trench (probably his most celebrated and popular book, the study of the parables), Archer Butler's sermons, and one or two others. On one wall hung a photograph of Bishop Gray of Cape Town.

Waller, who had some amateur knowledge of dressings and first aid, began by taking charge of the medicine. But Meller the doctor from the *Pioneer*, was staying at Magomero from 16 September, 1861. There were the normal, and terrible, ulcers, especially on the legs and feet of the children. The day after he arrived, Meller diagnosed small-pox, from which six children quickly died. A child in a neighbouring village was killed because playing children knocked over a loaded gun which Seseho the Makololo had left leaning against a tree, another died because when they found her she was already too emaciated and starved and ravaged by disease, a third because being an infant it rolled into the fire while asleep and burnt itself irrecoverably. A child named Meri, aged three, 'was very emaciated, had a large head, and a wild hungering look was ever on her face. I gave her thrice the quantity of food the others had, but no sooner had she eaten than she was groping among refuse for raw vegetables that might have been dropped, or for bones that might have been thrown away.'

Rowley, more than any of the others, had the faculty of standing back from circumstances, however tragic or emotional, and looking at them with a half-amused and half-whimsical eye. It interested him that the Manganja medicine men seemed more successful than the English doctor in curing the ulcers.[1] Their methods were often painful. 'In cases of severe fever, they take the sap of a trailing, climbing plant, called by them Candanarubi, wood-ashes, and castor-oil, mix them well together, make a few gashes with a knife in the body of the patient, and rub the compound in through the wounds.' Rowley respected their skill in herbs and their knowledge of practical remedies. Some of them indulged more in magic than others. One of them told a sick girl that 'her enemy, whoever it was, had bewitched her and caused a land tortoise to enter her mouth while she was asleep, and it was then eating away her heart'—and charged fees for the magical aid to its removal. Moloko, one of the three leaders among the Makololo, was later gored and tossed by a wounded elephant which spotted him

[1] R 164, 220–1.

among the long grass by his white feathers. His suppurating wound was given all the medical treatment known to the whites, and his condition steadily deteriorated until they despaired of him. His companions, seeing that he was at the point of death, insisted on removing him from white care and trying their own remedies; from the moment of his removal he began to recover. Rowley, when he came to know the Portuguese at Tete, discovered that they often seemed to prefer African cures to treatment by their own doctors.

Sometimes, in the suffering, the outward expression of gratitude or affection could be moving. There was a dumb idiot girl, who clapped her hands whenever the Bishop passed, walked up to him and patted his hands, followed him everywhere like a dog. He would take her into his hut and show her a large coloured picture of the raising of the Shunammite's son. 'She pointed to some limb, and then pointed to the same part of herself. I have followed this hint, and each time we have gone through every part. We are keeping patiently to the one picture. There are four figures, which is variety enough. From the earnestness with which she does this I am sure it is a pleasure to her, breaking in on the vacuity of her mind. I do not know anyone of my charge with so gentle, manageable, and amiable disposition; and that is better than all brightness of intellect, or keenness of perception. I do not know that she ever had a name; but the one by which she commonly goes is *Kana nena*, "she cannot speak".'

One night when the Bishop and Scudamore were away on a reconnoitring expedition, Rowley was woken by a dismal wailing and, going out, found the dumb idiot girl crouching over the embers of the kitchen fire. She was missing the Bishop, who had allowed her to sleep covered by a blanket in his hut, and was wretched in a hut under the care of the Manganja women. She tried to fight Rowley, and each night till the Bishop came back he had to carry or drag her to her hut. She spent the day quietly sitting by the gate in the stockade, waiting for the Bishop's return. On another of the Bishop's absences, she crept away to a deserted hut and lay down. Rowley, who had fever, did not miss her for several days. When he was fully out of bed again, he missed her one day at a distribution of food, and at last found her corpse, several days old, in the hut where she had crept away to die.[1]

Demonstrative and dependent affection in children can look like sycophancy when it is found in adults. One observer who, much later, entered Magomero in company with Rowley, was repelled by witnessing his reception, and compared it to a cat rubbing himself against a man's legs.[2] It could not be helped. The attitude of the destitute to the wealthy is not always as manly as the wealthy would like. It was not only the contrast between the grim poverty which scrabbled for food among the roots and looked only for warmth from the proximity of a human body, and the riches represented, to simple eyes, by an apparently unlimited supply of calico and beads. The white men possessed magical instruments, like telescopes, which could transport a man standing a hundred yards away to within a few feet. The affection, inevitably mingled with a lively expectation of favours to come, was also tempered by fear.

The attitude was less marked in the children. 'Scudamore and Waller thought to surprise the children with a kite. The kite was made, the children assembled to see it ascend, but the kite was ill-made, was lop-sided and heavy, would not go up, and the children made merry thereat. Said Waller, "You have never seen anything like this before, have you?" Said a little urchin in reply, "Oh! yes, we have, though. We have seen them, but ours were different to yours. Ours went up, yours go down." '[3]

Many secrets may be suspected of those who know the magical arts. At first, it was widely believed that, when white men went into church for Mattins according to the Book of Common Prayer, they were engaged in brewing or in imbibing their war-medicine. It was a notion that sorcerers need human flesh to eat, and several women fled from Magomero because they believed a story that the English were fattening them for consumption and that the tins of preserved meat were tins of human flesh. It was a popular fear that the ship was lying at Chibisa's for the purpose of removing Africans to a distant and unknown land of slavery. At first Mackenzie had not dared to make a list of the women's names, for this was the habit of slave-

[1] G 350–1; R 163–4, 253–4. [2] SJW 102. [3] R 205.

traders. It was difficult for the Africans to perceive any rational motive which should persuade the English to maintain and feed so many unproductive, and some sick, children, and for a time they believed that gunpowder was manufactured from the substance of infants' brains. But one by one these timidities faded away, before the kindness, the even-handedness, and the frank consistency of the English 'government'.

The missionaries were perplexed whether they should teach religion. It might have been thought that the answer to the problem was obvious, and there were times when elementary teaching was perforce given, and given urgently. The chief of a Manganja village died, and one or more of his wives were to have their legs broken and be buried with him. Procter went to the village with the interpreter William to see if he could save her life. They received him as a friend; but when he asked them why they were going to kill the woman, they replied simply, 'It is the custom of our country.' Procter asked the crowd, 'Do you know what becomes of people after death—not of their bodies (that, we know, goes into the grave) but of their spirits?' They said that they knew not. Procter told them that the missionaries knew, 'because we had God's word, which He had given to us in order that we might know what great love He had for us, how far we had fallen away from Him by wicked works, and what we must do in order to please Him here, and to go to Him when we die . . .' And he told then that God was angry with those who killed, and that in their future life they would be punished or rewarded as they had obeyed His will or not in this life.

They were astonished, and remained silent. At last one of them said, 'it would be a bad thing to make God angry with them; they should be sorry to do that, and if it would make God angry with them if they killed the woman, they would not kill her, they would let her come and live with us if we would permit her. Ready consent was given to this, and they went at once to the place where the woman was (she was in the stocks, not far from the dead body of her husband), unloosed her, and took her to Procter, who brought her to our station, and she lived with our people.'[1]

[1] R 231: P 28.7.62.

Not all their successes were equally dramatic; but the encouragement was more than sufficient to inspirit them, even though the 'teaching' was purely ethical. One of their protégés had been sold into slavery away from her child of two years old. 'For some time she could learn nothing of her child, but at last she heard that a Manganja man named Kankadi, who lived about a mile away . . . had lately bought it for three baskets of corn. We knew this man. He was a big-boned, knotty-browed, savage-looking fellow, and bore no good character, for he had been guilty of several deeds of violence, it was said, and was generally feared. We sent to Kankadi, and told him to come to us on the next day, and bring the child with him. He came, armed with his bow and poisoned arrows, and his old mother came also, and she brought the child with her. The child was a pretty little thing, in good condition, and had evidently been well-supplied with food.

'As soon as he fully understood our object in sending for him, Kankadi assumed an insolent attitude, and spoke out boldly and defiantly. The child was his, he said. He had gone down to Soché's village, where he saw a man who said he wished to sell her for food. He had no wife, he had no child, he wanted a girl to grow up in his hut to grind corn for him, and fetch his water; and so he brought the man to his hut, and gave him three large baskets of corn for the child. The child was his, and if the English wanted her, they must buy her as he had bought her; and he did not care to let the child go at all.

'Kankadi had been with us on all our expeditions; he had agreed to the conditions proposed by us before we consented to aid the Manganja against the Ajawa—conditions which made it a crime for all there, and all whom they represented, to buy or sell man, woman, or child again—and the chiefs had promised to punish the criminal. So we desired Kankadi to follow us down to Chigunda. Chigunda . . . had been ill, and we found him outside his hut, surrounded by his wives, and submitting to the operation of cupping. He had been taking our medicines, but did not give up his own remedies, and cupping is most popular for many sicknesses among the Manganja. The Sinanga (medicine-man) made a slight incision with a native razor just above the instep, and then produced a goat's horn, the root end of which he dipped into water and placed over the wound. The top of the horn was cut off; he applied his mouth to the orifice, and sucked away until he had exhausted the air, and then cleverly stopped the hole with wax. The horn stuck fast to the foot. While this was being done, William declared to Chigunda the particulars of the case between us and Kankadi. Chigunda was not so fluent of speech as usual. He paused some time before he made any remark, and when he did speak, his speech was destitute of the fire and force which generally marked his pronouncements. What he said amounted to this:

' "I have never broken my promise. I have not bought or sold people; I have been faithful to my word, and will always be faithful. I knew nothing of what Kankadi had done, and if I had I could do nothing, for though Kankadi lives near me I am not his chief—he comes from a long distance and is a stranger. I have no power, therefore, to make him give the child to its mother, or to punish him. If I were to do so, my friends would go away, and I should be left alone. I think he ought to give up the child. All that the English have said and done is quite right. All that Kankadi has said and done is quite wrong. Let the English do as they please; they will be sure to do right."

'Poor Chigunda! He was a mouse of a man, and a powerless chief, and was afraid of Kankadi, who did not seem in the least afraid of him. We then asked Kankadi if he had anything more to say. No, he had nothing more to say. The child was his, and he meant to keep it. We told him that the child was not his, but its mother's, and that he must at once give it up to its mother, and pay a fine for having broken the covenant he had made with us. On hearing this, the expression of Kankadi's face was diabolical; it looked like murder; and he relieved his hot wrath by fiercely plucking up the tufts of grass around him, and at last said: "It's a lie! I never promised not to buy a slave. All I promised was not to sell to the slavers. I have not done that, and I have done no wrong. I bought the child for myself with my own corn. I will not give her up. The English are strong; let them take her, but . . ."

'What the "but" meant William could not say; that it meant mischief was certain, for in his wild mood he looked like Cain, and I think he felt like Cain, for he fingered his bowstring spitefully, as though he would like to twang an arrow into the hearts of some of us.

'The attempt to influence this man for good seemed hopeless for a time. We might have taken the child from him by force and driven him out of the village, but that we did not wish to do; we wished to develop some better feeling in the man; and though I was hopeless of being then able to do it, Waller was not. He pictured to him the sorrow of the poor mother, her heart yearning for her little one, and trembling with anxiety for fear it would not be returned to her; he told him of the sorrow desolating the hearts of many poor mothers in that land, through their children being sold from them. And while he spoke in this way a better spirit came over the man; his face assumed a milder expression; he ceased to speak or behave insolently; and when Waller said, "Supposing you had a child, and it was stolen and sold away from you, would you not think it very cruel, very wicked of those who took it from you? Would not your heart feel as sorry as this poor mother's here?", an expression of pain passed over the man's features. He did not reply for some moments; he was much agitated; but at last he said, and while he said it he was almost choking with emotion: "It is true I should feel it. I should feel it here", laying his hand over his heart, "and my heart tells me it is a cruel thing to take the children from the mother. Take the child; give it to the mother; I will keep it no longer. I don't want anything for her, I give her up freely." '[1]

* * * * *

The problem of religious teaching was more domestic. Should they baptize infants, or prepare children for confirmation? Should they introduce the teaching of Christian doctrine into their adult classes? The aim of sending a bishop before a flock was gathered was to plant 'the church in its integrity', to convert not by the distribution of a Bible but by gathering the heathen into a Christian community with a sacramental life. Rowley, the highest churchman in Magomero, thought at first that they ought to be preparing the boys for baptism. Mackenzie

[1] R 256–9; P 5.2.62

argued to him that though the settlement was beginning to look permanent, they could not yet be sure that savages, pestilence, or famine would not force them to move and that they might then have to leave baptized children behind. He thought that until they were certain of remaining, they should baptize only the infants on the point of death. The second to be baptized was the little child which rolled into the fire and lived for a few hours afterwards.

Every day the whites recited Mattins and Evensong. Every Sunday and Saint's day the Holy Communion was celebrated, with a collection for the church in other lands, each missionary taking his turn to name the charity, at home or overseas, to which the little offering should be sent. There were no sermons at any service, but Mackenzie conducted a seminar for the study of the Bible after lunch on Sunday. By December, there was none of his party with whom he had not conversed privately about the growth of the soul. Some of them were glad of the opportunity, none resented it. It was impossible to resent Mackenzie.

At first the Africans were puzzled that the English refused to buy food, or to work on a Sunday. Soon a Sabbath rest had been established, and the Manganja were aware that this unusual custom was part of the white relation to the spirits. But to teach them openly seemed to Mackenzie to be as yet impossible. He would not teach until he knew the language. Scudamore and he rapidly began to pick up the names for physical objects from their pupils and from the chief Chigunda, and to understand elementary phrases. By December. they could both speak simple and intelligible sentences, and grasp part of what a Manganja said. But he was frightened of planting into the heads of the Manganja crude ideas which would be received erroneously, be incapable of correction, or be more difficult to rectify than a state of bare ignorance. He thought it perilous, on the basis of a vocabulary quarter-learnt, to fit Christian religious ideas to a language bearing primitive religious ideas. The whites did not yet comprehend it and could not yet perceive how far the ramifications were corrupt, barbaric, immoral, or misleading. Nor would he teach religion through an interpreter. William's Manganja was fluent, his English deplorable; Charles' English was excellent (he had been twenty years at the Cape), but his dialect was Makoa and he could hardly understand the Manganja and the Ajawa. And the Cape men, as Mackenzie soon discerned, were so ignorant, and (as Rowley put it with meiosis) their 'spiritual susceptibilities' were so dull, that it seemed better not to teach at all than to teach through trumpets which gave such uncertain and discordant noises. For a conversation about building a hut, or cooking a meal, they were passable; for a conversation about God they would not do at all. And so the missionaries did not teach. The most which they tried to do was to relate their moral judgements to the absolute law of a God above. They tried to establish that lying, stealing, murder, and adultery were not merely inconvenient to the community, but condemned by the mightiest of spirits.

Slowly and gently they were displacing confidence in the medicine men, breeding confidence in their own government and justice. Gradually they found that they could introduce something like equity and even like a trial by jury in the settlement of disputes. 'Some corn had been stolen from the garden of one of Chigunda's people. The owner complained to the chief, who employed the services of a celebrated medicine-man living near. The people assembled round a large fig-tree just outside our station, and the magician, a wild-looking individual, who seemed exceedingly uncomfortable when we appeared, commenced proceedings. First of all he produced two sticks, about four feet long, and about the thickness of an ordinary broom-handle; these, after certain mysterious manipulations and utterings of unintelligible gibberish, he delivered, with much solemnity, to four young men, two being appointed to each stick. Then, from his capacious and greasy goatskin bag, he brought forth a zebra-tail, which he gave to another young man, and after that a calabash filled with peas, which he delivered to a boy. The medicine-man rolled himself about in hideous fashion, and chanted an unearthly incantation; then came the man with the zebra-tail, followed by the boy with the calabash, moving, first of all, slowly round the men with sticks, but presently quickening their pace, and shaking the tail and the calabash over the heads of the stick-holders. For a time nothing came of these proceedings; but ere long the spell worked. The men with sticks were subject to spasmodic twitchings of the arms and legs. These increased rapidly, until they were nearly in convulsions; they foamed at the mouth; their eyes seemed starting from their heads; they realised to the full the idea of demoniacal possession. According to the Manganja notion, it was the sticks that were possessed primarily, the men through them; it was the devil *in* two sticks . . .

'The men seemed scarcely able to hold the sticks, which took a rotary motion at first, and whirled the holders round and round like mad things. Then headlong they dashed off into the bush, through stubborn grass and thorny shrub, over every obstacle—nothing stopped them; their bodies were torn and bleeding; round to the gaping assembly again they came, went through a few more rotatory motions, and then, rushing along the path at a killing pace, halted not until they fell down, panting and exhausted, in the hut of one of Chigunda's slave wives. The woman happened to be at home, and the sticks were rolled to her very feet, and by so doing denounced her as the thief. She was brought before the now excited assembly, and to their indignation denied that she was the thief. The medicine-man was appealed to. In triumph he was smoking his pipe under a tree, and the only remark he vouchsafed was: "The spirit has declared her guilty; the spirit never lies." But the woman vehemently declared that the spirit did lie, that she was innocent, and to prove her innocence said she would take the muavi [a test of drinking poisoned water, which the guilty swallowed to die and the innocent vomited to live] . . . The muavi was produced; but as corn-stealing from a garden was, according to the Manganja code of laws, a petty offence, and she was connected with the chief, she was allowed to take the muavi by deputy. She ran home, came back with a fowl, a cock; this bird's mouth was pulled open, the deadly stuff was poured down its throat, and the expectant congregation looked on, with greedy eyes, to the issue. It was this: the bird, after struggling for a few seconds, threw up the poisoned water, lay quiet for a minute or two, and then, hearing a lusty challenge from a rival bird in the village, stood upon its legs, flapped its wings, and crowed. It was evidently none the worse for the ordeal it had gone through, and all the people pronounced the woman innocent. She carried off her cock in triumph. The medicine-man shrugged his shoulders, and disappeared . . . In the end we succeeded among our own people in establishing trial by jury instead of these objectionable, and in most cases unjust, proceedings; and our method of proceeding so commended itself to the pockets . . . as well as to the good sense of the natives about us, that before we left the country one or other of us had to sit in the administration of justice almost every day.'[1]

* * * * *

So long as their money—that is, their calico and beads—lasted, they seemed to be secure. In the autumn of 1861, it was easy to buy goats, or hens, maize, yams, sweet potatoes, peas, beans, salt, cassava, pumpkins, or pombi (beer) from the surrounding villages, and occasionally fish from the fishermen of Lake Shirwa. The agricultural methods of the Manganja appeared to be advanced, and the Bishop felt that even his 'agriculturist' Adams had nothing with which he might instruct them. The two difficulties in the way of becoming self-supporting were, first, that the disproportion of age in the community and the quantity of 'unproductive heads' was likely to mean an inadequate contribution from the Magomero allotments, or 'gardens', to the total stock of food; and, secondly, that until the crop could be gathered in February or March they were producing almost nothing and were having to buy almost all their food with cloth.

The country came short of their expectations. From Livingstone's warm-hearted descriptions they had formed a vague but roseate picture of a country across which the game was ranging, and had supposed that a skilful marksman would be able to keep them amply supplied with the meat of buck or buffalo. Livingstone had told the undergraduates of Cambridge University that a missionary might earn his living with his gun. But, said Rowley sadly,[2] 'the vast plains covered with deer, the herds of eland, buffalo, and gnu, which we dreamed would be always within reach of our rifles, we never found . . . One unfortunate eland strayed down to the neighbourhood of

[1] R 218–20. [2] R 143.

Magomero . . . and a whole army of natives turned out after it.' Game, they discovered later, abounded in the Shire valley, but not upon the highlands.

In his letters from the Shire to England, Livingstone had proclaimed the discovery of what he believed to be the greatest cotton-growing area in the world, the counter-poise to the slave-labour of the United States. One village his party had earlier nicknamed 'the Paisley of the hills'. This was the productive commerce which the community of Magomero expected to be able to develop and export, this was to raise the standard of life for the African and teach him that industry was more profitable than the selling of human bodies. On this principle, Waller had received instruction in the superintendence of cotton. On this principle, Livingstone sold to Mackenzie a second-hand cotton-gin, of an antiquated pattern, manufactured by Jameson of Ashton-under-Lyme; and this lugubrious machine was carried by bearers up the mountain paths from the Shire to Magomero, the presumptive spearhead of Lancashire industry in Nyasaland. Even when it arrived, they knew it as 'the poor cotton-gin', and it became at once the most forlorn object in Magomero.

For when they looked for cotton they found none. In the valley of the Shire the inhabitants grew a little, manufactured a few cloths from it—but not in the highlands. During their time at Magomero they were offered only one small bundle of cotton, and then at a price higher than they could have sold it in Manchester. In a moment of gloom Waller told a visitor, 'You cannot get as much cotton as would fill your hat though you were to travel for days.' Commerce and Christianity? Waller could find no commerce to inaugurate or superintend.

* * * * *

In October and November, 1861, Mackenzie was optimistic that they were succeeding in establishing the station at Magomero. The country round them was pacified, the Ajawa tribes were no longer raiding, the Manganja villages were cultivating their ground in quietness and peace, the campaigns seemed to have achieved their purpose. He began to think hopefully of the time when the ladies should come. He had accepted the headship of the mission only after receiving an assurance that his sister Anne might follow him, and the more he saw of the morality and customs of the Manganja women, the more he thought their presence indispensable. Before he left the Cape, he had arranged that Anne and another unmarried sister, Alice, should join him wherever he should settle.

Nearly everyone except the Bishop disapproved of these arrangements. The committee of the mission in London disliked the additional cost to the funds which they expected, and the risk of disaster, from fever or from barbarism, to the delicate sex. Mackenzie had even agreed with a gunmaker of Handsworth, Mr John Crofts, that he should come out with a wife and six young children between the ages of five and fifteen. The committee refused to send his family. Crofts, possessing a letter from Mackenzie appointing him and summoning him and his progeny to London to be examined by a doctor, talked of suing the committee, and they had to buy him off with a compensation of forty pounds. Waller, always prone to vehemence, was vehemently against the plan. Livingstone, whose dourness made him superficially unsympathetic in the presence of either death or marriage, and who could express himself caustically, thought that the Bishop was psychologically in need of a feminine personality on whom he might rest. He did not dislike the notion that Mackenzie should bring his sister to Magomero. But he disliked any suggestion that family ties should interfere with a man's work, and he expressed himself hardly when he heard that Mackenzie intended to leave Magomero in order to meet his sisters and escort them. 'He seems,' wrote Livingstone in his journal, 'to lean on them. Most high church people lean on wives or sisters . . . I hope the Bishop will remain at his post; if he doesn't, he is a muff to lean on a wife or a sister. I would as soon lean on a policeman.'[1]

Mackenzie was unmoved by such arguments against the presence of women as reached him. He even thought that he could encourage Procter to bring his fiancée from Natal to the Shire, and suggested that he should marry them himself in the chapel at Magomero, though he saw complications about securing the legal registration of the marriage in England. He

[1] LJW ii. 213, 30.10.61.

believed that the women would set the African women an example for which their clumsy male guidance could never be a substitute. The Manganja had proved to have repellent or unedifying rites connected with the puberty of girls and with tattooing, and regarded promiscuity with equanimity. In the same week that Livingstone was committing his reproaches to his journal, Mackenzie was writing home that he 'longed' for the women. 'It is not a week since we got an increase of fifty people, only ten boys and no men. Here is more work for them. It is impossible for us men to do what I trust God will do by them. The women are some of them wild and rude, and some of them worse, but I hope the influence of our ladies will tell upon them.'[1] Livingstone was being less than just to him when he charged him with fetching his sisters because he leant upon them. Livingstone had himself encouraged his wife Mary to join him upon the *Pioneer*, and the same vessel which was expected to bring the Mackenzie sisters was believed to be bringing Mrs Livingstone also. Yet the criticism was thus far just. Mackenzie was allowing a personal relationship to enter his public plan. Though it was true that Anne Mackenzie believed herself indispensable to her brother, it was less true that Mackenzie wanted his sister or sisters as a prop and a stay. But he knew that his sister Anne needed him, that he was the happiness and the haven of her life. And therefore he was doing what Livingstone would never have done. He was allowing his affection to divert him from the ruthless path of duty, or, more accurately perhaps, was persuading himself that the path of duty and the path of affection were the same.

The women, with the supplies of the second year which Livingstone had promised to bring to Chibisa's, were expected at the end of the year 1861. Late in November, the builders of Magomero, after finishing two storehouses, a hen house, and a big dormitory for the boys sixty feet by fifteen, began to build a large hut to house the ladies when they should arrive.

* * * * *

On the afternoon of 12 November, they received to their surprise a letter, a ewe, and a pair of turkeys, from Livingstone. He

[1] G 350.

had returned to Chibisa's from his exploration of Lake Nyasa, and wrote that he was going down river immediately.

The letter was odd, or seemed to the missionaries to be odd. He had heard of the Second (though not yet of the Third) Ajawa war, and appeared to approve . . . 'You were quite right to identify yourselves with the interests of your people . . . I sympathize with you in all your difficulties: act with a determined vigorous will . . .' They were glad of his approval. But the rest of the letter was not so palatable. Mackenzie had written to him proposing that Procter should go down the river in the *Pioneer* to meet the ladies at the Kongone and escort them up. Livingstone refused to give him a passage on the ship. He gave as the principal reason, or pretext, that the missionaries ought not to diminish their numbers at Magomero by a single man. Not being able to penetrate the secret meditations of Livingstone about clergymen who depend upon ladies, they found this reasoning strange. It seemed to Procter that he had evidently written while 'out of sorts and out of temper, as the letter had a sharpness of tone and decision quite unusual in the Doctor'. It contained a severe sentence: 'This is not a passenger ship, and members leaving the mission will generally meet with a different reception from those joining it.' And it contained calamitous news. Livingstone confessed that the *Pioneer* was drawing too much water for the Upper Shire, and that therefore he would not be able to fulfil his promise of bringing the stores of the second year to Chibisa's. He thought that the highest point to which the ship could bring the stores (and the ladies) was the confluence of the Shire and the Ruo; and he recommended the Bishop to reconnoitre an overland route from Magomero to the Ruo mouth. 'You will now' he wrote bluntly, 'see the necessity I have so often referred to, of having a steamer of your own'. He asked them to meet the ladies and the stores at the Ruo mouth on 1 January.[1]

Mackenzie hurried with Meller to Chibisa's (seventy miles in thirty hours). At a conversation on the ship Livingstone insisted on his plan. They agreed to meet at the Ruo mouth on 1 January.

At Chibisa's, Mackenzie found to his astonishment an English missionary, the first reinforcement, Henry de Wint Burrup.

[1] Mackenzie's Journal, 12.11.61; R 189; P 12.11.61.

Burrup was a clergyman who had married a charming young wife two days before he left England, and had deposited her with friends at the Cape, with the intention that she should sail to the Kongone with the Misses Mackenzie. He had travelled from England with the doctor whom the London committee had at last found, a Durham graduate named John Dickinson, and with two more artisans, a printer named Blair and a shoemaker named Clark. In addition, Clark had received a training in the process of tanning, so that he might be able to tan the hides of the supposed herds of eland and antelope. Blair had fallen ill and been sent back to the Cape from Mozambique. At Johanna they had liquidated the bulk of the mission's stores which had been left in the hulk of the *Vega* and which the *Pioneer* had been unable to convey. Part of the stores had been looted, nine-tenths of the remainder had rotted and were thrown into the sea, the remaining tenth was sold to ships then in the port. Burrup arranged for a Portuguese escort to take him up the Zambezi, and then hired discontented African paddlers to canoe him up the Shire, a journey and a physical feat which Livingstone, of all men the most competent to judge physical endurance, never ceased to admire. Mackenzie and Burrup arrived at Magomero on 19 November, Dickinson and Clark (with the letters from home) on 29 November. Before Mackenzie left Chibisa's he had given Livingstone three rousing cheers from the bank as the *Pioneer* gingerly began to sail its tortuous course through the sandbanks down the river.

To Rowley's eye, Mackenzie seemed to be losing some of his optimism and buoyancy. He was worrying about communications. The *Pioneer*, Livingstone had told him, could no longer help him; he must have a steamer for himself. He did not believe that the mission could afford a steamer, nor did he want to superintend the crew of a steamer; yet he could not see how they could survive at Magomero indefinitely without one. 'I think,' said Rowley, 'he was greatly troubled at the difficulties opening out . . . Though he was always full of faith, he seemed to lose much of that bright hopefulness which had distinguished him above all other men I ever met.'[1] Mackenzie's papers begin to show the signs about a month after Rowley noticed it,

[1] R 193.

or supposed that he noticed it. Towards the end of December a melancholy note began for the first time to creep into his tone. Partly he had been weakened in health by the forced rush to Chibisa's; partly he had discovered the promiscuity of, at least, one of his Cape men, and was distressed to the depths of his soul at what he felt to be the stain on the Christian community for which he was responsible. On 22 December he was writing home in language that was new to him. 'I have much at times to depress me; more than ever I had. But I expected it, and must not complain. The Dean of Cape Town, in his sermon at my consecration, told me I should. But the work is God's.'[1]

* * * * *

In his gruff way Livingstone had said that he could only transport the stores (and the ladies) as far as the Ruo mouth and that they must be responsible for the rest. By enquiry from Chigunda they found that there was an overland route to the Ruo mouth which they estimated at 130 miles.[2] The Bishop selected Procter and Scudamore to lead an expedition which should establish the route, make friends with the chiefs of the villages, arrange porters for the stores, and so create a stable road of communication to the Lower Shire and the Zambezi. Procter and Scudamore were accompanied by the interpreter Charles, eight Manganja as porters, and an Ajawa boy named Nkuto.

The expedition left on 2 December. Five days later, on 7 December, Charles limped into the camp alone, with fixed eyes, 'haggard and worn, his feet lacerated and swollen, the very picture of a man who had been hunted for his life.

' "All are gone—I alone am left—not one besides myself has

[1] G 384–5.

[2] Livingstone had suggested a route more or less parallel with the Shire. Mackenzie preferred a route with a wider arc; partly because the information available from Chigunda suggested that this was the normal route, and partly because Livingstone had said (in a published letter to Sir George Grey, 1 July 1859, Monk's *Dr. Livingstone's Cambridge Lectures*, 1860), that there were only thirty miles between the navigable part of the Ruo and Lake Shirwa. Waller had argued with Kirk when sailing up the Shire that this might well prove to be the better route in view of the Shire sandbanks. But though Mackenzie was partly guided by Livingstone's estimate of distance, he recognised that it was a distance which might need correction. Cf. Mackenzie to Gray, 4.11.61, UMCA; W 4.6.61.

escaped!" said he, and then sank down and burst into tears.'[1] He had eaten nothing for two days. After he had recovered a little, he said that Procter, Scudamore, and the porters had been killed or imprisoned at the village of a chief named Manasomba.

'Twice,' said Charles, 'was I surrounded. I hardly know how I broke away from them. And when I was about a hundred yards off I heard two shots fired. I fear this was all Mr Procter and Mr Scudamore could do before they were overpowered. The natives were all around them firing at them with their bows and arrows.'

They gave Charles some soup and then went into the little makeshift church, 'in prayer for them,' as the Bishop said, 'whether in suffering or in fear, wherever they might be, that God would be their support and strength; and for ourselves, that we might have wisdom to act with thought and charity towards the persecutors, and yet for the safety of our brethren.' Waller thought that he had never before seen Mackenzie faltering. They then sat down to a consultation.

They must plainly send an expedition to rescue Procter and Scudamore. Yet they had few white men in Magomero. Rowley was down with dysentery, not all the others were fully fit, and it seemed imperative to leave enough whites to defend the city of refuge against any sudden or marauding band of Ajawa. The best African fighters in the vicinity were Livingstone's Makololo, whose conduct or misconduct on the *Pioneer* had caused Livingstone to dismiss them from the ship and leave them at Chibisa's. They were tough, were contemptuous of both Ajawa and Manganja, and had guns. Two of them were believed to have killed two Ajawa in a recent brawl at a village not far from Magomero. They would gladly accompany any expedition where plunder was probable. They were somewhat uncomfortable allies, Mackenzie perceived, for an expedition of rescue. But they were the only allies available. Job, the Cape man, must be sent to Chibisa's to fetch them.

'This settled,' wrote Mackenzie, 'the sorrow, and the trying to be simply trusting in our Father, returned as before . . . I could not drive from my imagination the picture of what I saw in August—a man in the act of being stabbed to death.'

[1] R 234; cf. G 377 ff.; W 7.12.61.

A few moments later, Winapi one of the women, ran up to the door of the hut where Rowley was lying and talking to Johnson, clapping her hands and exclaiming 'Johnson! Johnson! Anglesi! Anglesi!' and she pointed to the path. Procter and Scudamore walked into the camp, obviously weary but unhurt and apparently in better shape than Charles. The revulsion of feeling in the minds of the whites was intense, and the Africans seemed to be as relieved as the English. After they had been fed, and had worshipped in the church, they told their story.

The expedition had made excellent progress through the mountain meadows gay with flowers and beneath ravines of the Milanje mountains, until it arrived at a village, fortified with hedges and thorn, on the steep right bank in a horseshoe bend of the River Ruo, beneath a high craggy hill. They were then some eighty miles from Magomero, and believed themselves to be fifty miles up the Ruo above its junction with the Shire. On entering the village, they thought the conduct of the villagers, who showed a different appearance and tattoo from the Manganja, suspicious.[1]

Charles, while looking about the village, was accosted by a man who offered slaves for sale and asked whether the white men wished to buy some. Charles said that they had not come to buy slaves, that they were English, and that the English set their faces against the slave-trade and would not buy.

'Well then, what will you buy?'

'We are only passing through to look at the path, and are anxious to lose no time that we may meet our friends at the mouth of this river. Where is the chief?'

'He is coming. You must wait for him.'

'Very well: only we want to get on to Tombondira's to-night.' They waited for an hour or two. The chief still failed to appear, and the conduct of the people still seemed unfriendly. So they packed and set off again. When they told their guides, the guides refused to go further with them, became insolent, and demanded twice as much cloth as they had agreed to take for their day's march. Procter and Scudamore therefore left the

[1] This account of the Manasomba expedition is a conflation, mainly verbatim of the four accounts in G and W and P and R; R is the most coherent.

village without paying them anything. The villagers were enraged, and abused them as they went, declaiming against the meanness of the English, who bought nothing, and gave no presents. They were followed out of the village by a number of men with bows and arrows, who started calling loudly and threateningly:

'Stop! you must stop! Come back! Where will you go? You cannot cross the river without canoes, and you must cross it to get to Tombondira's, and no one has canoes but us.'

Procter, indiscreetly, fired at some guinea-fowl, perhaps with the intention of showing that they were not defenceless. The tribesmen thought that this was done to threaten them, and one of them called out:

'Do you think you can do anything with your guns? You may kill one or two, but after that, what will you do? We are not afraid of them.'

They then divided into two parties, one band a little in front to the right, another a little in front to the left, and they shouted to others working in the fields to join them. About two miles from the village, Procter and Scudamore became seriously alarmed that fighting would break out. They sat down under a tree and invited the tribesmen to come and talk the matter over. They explained that they were in a hurry to reach the mouth of the River Ruo. Thinking that they might have infringed African etiquette by their impatience in not waiting to see the chief Manasomba, they asked if he had arrived. The villagers pointed to an old man standing a little distance off. They decided to return to the village, greet Manasomba formally, cook a meal, and then set off again.

Manasomba was an old man, once a very powerful man physically, but now feeble-bodied. He walked a little way in front of them as they returned to his village. There he welcomed them civilly, offered them beer and food, and asked to trade. Procter and Scudamore bought what they wanted for their Manganja. It seemed little enough; and Manasomba's people saw the extent of the calico which they were carrying for their journey of three weeks (about 140 yards), and evidently thought themselves ill-treated in not getting a larger share of it. Manasomba insisted that they accept his hospitality and stay the night, and said that in the morning he would send a guide with them to Tombondira's village. It seemed better to accept. They dined with Manasomba, who brought forward his wives and explained to them why the white men used knives and forks. But the people looked less agreeable than their chief.

Towards evening, Procter and Scudamore went down to the Ruo to bathe. When they returned to the huts, Charles said that he had heard from one of the Manganja bearers about an impending attack. One of the women had told the Manganja that in the night the English hut would be fired and the English killed as they tried to escape. Looking around, Procter and Scudamore saw that sure sign of imminent violence, the women busy removing their household utensils and carrying them out of the village. The men were sitting round their huts, with bows and arrows lying at their sides. The missionaries determined to set off at once. They tried to collect their Manganja bearers unnoticed; and while the bearers were packing the loads, they went to Manasomba and occupied his attention by making him a present of a fine bright-coloured scarf. He was not to be distracted. At the news that they were going to leave, Manasomba gave a shout, the men in the open space of the village were alert, and crowded before the English party as they made for the entrance in the thorn hedge. The crowd gave way whenever the muzzle of a gun was brought to bear upon them, but they tried to block the gate by their numbers. Charles ran at them; they gave way and started to scatter, and Charles escaped outside into the bush.

Scudamore and Procter were following close behind with the bearers. One of the crowd was bold enough to catch hold of Procter's gun, but it was readily wrenched out of his hands; and like the others he drew back in alarm when it was pointed at him. As soon as the bearers were outside the gate, the crowd attacked them, seized their loads, and started to ransack them. The pause enabled Procter and Scudamore to move right away from the village, though thirty or forty men, armed with bows and arrows, followed them closely, shouting *Nkondo! Nkondo!* War! At last two or three of them sprang upon Procter and snatched at his gun. In the struggle he fell upon his back, still holding his gun and trying to bring it to bear upon one of the assailants, and pulled the trigger. The ball passed under the man's arm. Scudamore fired at the leading assailant and also missed. At the two shots they all left Procter and fled. Procter again fired; and as he turned round, he heard a smart pat at his side, and found a poisoned arrow sticking fast in the stock of his gun.

They at once turned off the path and took shelter in the scrub to the left of the path. In a minute or two they stopped, deliberated, and prayed for guidance, and then set off homewards. They went about twenty miles that night, guided by a fire on the Milanje mountains to their right. They reached the River Rikania not at the ford. Procter could not trust himself to swim. Scudamore, who was a good swimmer, stripped and tried three times to find a crossing. Twice he was carried downstream by the current and driven to land on the same side. At the third place he was successful; and they carried their clothes in a bundle above their heads to keep them dry. It took them three hours to cross. About sunrise they rested for half an hour, half-dozing on the top of an ant-hill, concealed by the bushes which grew upon it, and debated whether they should hide there till nightfall and travel only under cover of darkness. But they came home, avoiding villages on their route, and reached Magomero after using their handkerchiefs as currency to buy food.

Six days afterwards six of the Manganja bearers had also dribbled into the camp.

It was now a puzzle to know what to do. The first judgements of decision had vanished. There were still two Manganja bearers and the young lad Nkuto missing. If it had been right to collect an army to rescue Procter and Scudamore, it was presumably right to collect an army to rescue three others who were on the same mission. They were bound, as they kept reminding themselves, to eschew every thought of revenge. If all the bearers had returned safely, they believed that it would have been mistaken for them, as a missionary body, to go out with arms simply for the sake of teaching Manasomba a lesson in how to behave to travellers. Waller, who in normal circumstances was more likely to be hot-headed than cautious, thought it wrong to denude Magomero of effective protection and leadership while so many went out to find the two Manganja and Nkuto. And yet it seemed plain that the servants of the English ought to be protected by the English. The wives and families of the missing men clamoured for their rescue. Moreover, they were the sole representatives of law and order in the Shire highlands. They had to show the Africans, they reasoned, that they stood for fair dealing, peaceful travel, honest hospitality, and that treachery and robbery must pay the penalty. They were, in the end, so convinced of the rightness of the expedition that Rowley, who had disliked the three Ajawa wars more than anyone else at Magomero, bitterly regretted the dysentery which prevented him marching on the campaign.

It is improper, in civilized countries, for the injured party to be also the judge and the executioner. They looked around, in accordance with Chapter 14 of the Epistle to the Romans, for a 'ruler ordained of God,' and found that the nearest approximation to it was Dr Livingstone, who, at least, held a commission from Her Britannic Majesty. Mackenzie debated whether to ask Livingstone to act, and knew that the suggestion was fanciful in the moment when he propounded it. Livingstone was engaged upon a task of exploration. He had more urgent problems than travelling far across country to a distant village in order to rescue two Manganja porters and an Ajawa boy. Mackenzie thought it might be better to wait for Livingstone's approval before he embarked on his expedition. But he could not receive Livingstone's approval without also receiving the ladies whom Livingstone was probably bringing, and he thought that the arrival of the ladies would make punitive expeditions impossible. And so he concluded that he must act at once, and act on his own responsibility. 'We believed that being the only power in the place that could do it, *we* were ourselves God's ministers for the purpose.'[1]

They gathered their little army. Fourteen Makololo came up from Chibisa's (after at first refusing because they suspected the mission of kidnapping Zomba, a Makololo who had temporarily disappeared), but only ten travelled with the expedition. 'Moloko had a tender foot, Ramakukan would go nowhere without Moloko, and the other two wished to remain behind.'[2] Chigunda, the chief at Magomero, assembled some

[1] G 410. [2] R 243.

twenty men, and on 23 December, Mackenzie, Scudamore, Burrup, and Waller set out with Chigunda's band, the ten Makololo, and William the interpreter. They intended to recover their lost men, either by negotiation or by force if necessary, and then to carry out the original plan of going on from Manasomba's village down the Ruo to await the *Pioneer* at the meeting of Ruo and Shire. Mackenzie would have liked to confront Manasomba, persuade him to acknowledge his crime, beg pardon, and accept whatever penalty the English might decree. But he was not sanguine that Manasomba would agree to this method of justice without a fight.

On 22 December, they celebrated the Holy Communion, with a collection for the consumptive hospital at Brompton, and on 23 December, they started. It was an uncomfortable journey. On Christmas Eve they arrived at a little village—'a disgusting hole, the people all starved out and a tremendous row about a bag that they said one of our men had stolen on entering the place. The rain poured, the huts smelt like a Covent Garden drain, the bugs were in myriads . . . and we were annoyed and soaked, making it a hard Christmas Eve.'[1] They were wet to the skin almost throughout the expedition, and the forgetful Scudamore had not brought anything into which he could change round a fire at night, and sat dismally shivering. On Christmas Day, after marching all day, 'we had our evening prayers,' wrote Mackenzie, 'followed by Communion. I thought there were innumerable Christian congregations joining in Communion, but probably none so far from the centre of earthly communion, I mean none in so out-of-the-way a place. How wondrous the feeling of actual instantaneous communion with all you dear ones, though the distance and the means of earthly communion are so great and so difficult! . . . December 27, St John's Day . . . It is strange passing these holy days in this secular way. It makes me often review my position and say, "If it feels strange to be on such an expedition on a saint's day, is it right to go on it at all?" and the result is that I always feel that it is.'[2]

He tried to explain to Chipoka, the chief of a village immediately before Manasomba's, that he was no man of war but a

[1] W 24.12.61. [2] G 389.

man of peace. It was put to him that he would more easily catch Manasomba and kill all his people if he came on him in the night. Mackenzie said, 'I think it is right to punish such a man; so we will go together; but do not suppose that I am always going about with my gun to kill men ("hear! hear!" from Chigunda); my children came down peaceably to this place, but were detained and attacked by Manasomba. I live quietly at Magomero. Our wish is to do you good by exchanging cloth, beads, and other English goods for your goats and corn, ivory and cotton: and what is more than all, we come to you from God, of whom we have a better knowledge than you, whose laws we know, and we want to teach you these things. (All the chiefs said to this, "That is good.") So do not think I like bloodshed; but this man must be punished, and we must get back the three that are in his hands.'[1]

On 29 December, they crossed the Rikania stream and moved towards Manasomba's village. 'We stopped to pray for God's blessing, professing that we were not going in private revenge, but to free the captives, and to punish the robber and would-be murderer, in God's name (having the good word . . . of the chiefs around, and their approval of our going[2]), and then I told them all I wanted was to get my children back, and the stolen property (more than 100 yards of cloth, besides change of clothing, food, pots, and pans, etc.); that I did not wish to kill anyone, only to get these things, and to burn the village, that Manasomba might learn not to do so again, and others might fear; that if they defended their village we would drive them out, but on no account take women or children, or hurt them; that I wanted none of the plunder we might get, but they must bring it all together, and I would give shares of it.'

During the prayers the company was bowed to the ground round Mackenzie, who was standing upright with his eyes shut. Ten minutes after they started again, they saw a large band of men, armed with bows and arrows, coming towards them. Mackenzie called out (on this occasion he had not thought it right to deliver the command to Waller), 'Walk on, do not

[1] G 394; somewhat different version of speech in Waller, Mss. Afr. 3. 16/4 (9).

[2] The best that could be done, in the circumstances, to secure approval by 'the State'.

stop.' It proved to be Manasomba and his men, who had come with the intention of holding a conference, though Mackenzie did not at the time know Manasomba to be there. Hearing that they wanted a conference, Mackenzie told William the interpreter, to shout that the chief and four others might come forward. But the conference was ruined by that section of the Bishop's army which preferred battles to conferences—the Makololo. Two of the Makololo dashed out at a straggler in front of Manasomba's men, who had halted on and round a huge ant-hill nearby. They pleaded afterwards the excuse that they had wanted to make him a prisoner so that the Bishop might use him as a messenger to the rest. Manasomba and his men supposed this to be the beginning of a charge, and ran, together with the straggler who had wrested himself from the clutches of the Makololo, into the bush. 'So we resumed our march, expecting to find the village defended: but when we got there, we found the entrance where the bearers some weeks ago had thrown down their burdens, and where Scudamore and Procter had had such a tussle, unguarded; and on passing through we found ourselves in a fine, but deserted, village. I stayed at the centre, telling the rest to search the huts and bring everything to the centre. There were some fine Muscovy ducks, about half a dozen sheep and goats, and a little corn; of our own goods we recovered our valises,' which were empty, 'a pair of shoes, two or three pots, two tins of preserved meat, and a piece of soap. Then we set the huts on fire, most of the party carrying out the plunder.'[1]

Nervous of a counter-attack, knowing that Manasomba's men were near and perhaps watching, they drew off from the village within half an hour. Mackenzie divided the goats and sheep between his allies. But the goats and sheep refused to be driven in the direction of the retreat, and between the straggling of the band and the slow speed of the live plunder, they seemed to offer defenceless targets to anyone with courage and a poisoned arrow. Waller, whose nerves were on edge, became irritated, and eventually forced the Bishop to leave the 'abominable' sheep and goats behind. Even so Waller's forebodings were in part justified. As he and Burrup and Scudamore were

[1] G 396–7; R 251; W 31.12.61; K 27.2.62.

leading their party through 'a narrow muddy place between masses of reeds', they were fired on by a gun and a bow almost simultaneously, the shot passing narrowly between the heads of Waller and Scudamore and the arrow sticking into the pit of the stomach of an old Manganja bearer. They borrowed Waller's clasp-knife and cut out the arrow-head on the spot. 'After this we tried to keep our party a little more in hand; but this was not easy, for after I had cut the sheep and goats adrift, the men would delay to kill and carry them . . . a time of no small anxiety . . . However, at last we got into order, and went on slowly. The wounded man could not walk fast, and at last had to be carried We were thankful to find the tree-bridge across the Rikania tree . . . The day had been got through, to which we had looked forward with much doubt as to how we were to act. We had indeed failed to get back our people . . . but we had punished the robber, and had returned safe. We had vindicated the English name, and had shewn in this neighbourhood that it is not safe to attack an Englishman; and I hope the lesson may not be thrown away on these people.' The wounded man died next day.

On Sunday 31 December they stopped (*rested* would be the wrong word since there were alarums of war, sentinels, and reconnaissances), to discuss where they were now to go. Livingstone had said that they were to be at the meeting of Shire and Ruo on 1 January. They could not be there in time; but the best chance of keeping as near to the appointment as possible was to follow out the original plan of finding the direct route past Manasomba's country to the lower Ruo. Mackenzie, believing that they were safe from future attack and could go through Manasomba's country without trouble, thought that this was the right plan. Burrup supported him. Waller, still nervy and irritable after the experience of retreating for continuous hours as a target for unseen arrows, was convinced that it was now madness to seek to find a road through Manasomba's country, and that the only safe course was a return to Magomero followed by the normal route to Chibisa's and the Shire. He thought the Bishop and Burrup were 'infatuated' to persist in their plan. Scudamore, who was becoming desperately feverish, supported Waller.

Mackenzie resolved, like King Solomon, that each party must be given half of what it wanted. He and Burrup would go to the Ruo. Scudamore, it was plain, must get back to bed at Magomero as urgently as possible and Waller should look after him. But the decision was taken out of his hands by Chipoka, the nearby chieftain. Chipoka would not supply bearers or guides to go through Manasomba's country. He said, 'All that country is occupied by Manasomba's friends. You will be killed if you go, and then the English who are behind (at Magomero), will come and blame me and burn my village. If you want to go back, I will give you guides and bearers; but forwards, I will not.'

The whole party was therefore forced to return to Magomero, the Bishop much against his will. 'Waller and Scudamore both said strongly, it was much better . . . Waller said we had had enough of fighting: and that going down that way was only provoking more, and would make it more difficult for us to assert our character as ministers of the Gospel of peace. I said I did not expect any more fighting: my party would be too strong to allow them to think of touching us . . .'

They reached Magomero on 2 January, at about two p.m.

It was a constant nagging spur to Mackenzie that he had to reach the meeting-place on New Year's Day. He felt that at once he must start again, this time by the Shire route, to keep the assignation. He was suffering from diarrhoea, as was Burrup. He had hoped to pick up a strong fresh man who had not suffered the exhaustion and strain of the journey in the rain to Manasomba's, but he found not one of the whites at Magomero fit to travel. It seemed therefore, if not the best, at least the only course that he and Burrup—the two whose ladies were believed to be coming—should set out to meet Livingstone. Both the Bishop and Burrup, wrote Rowley 'were strong men. But neither took care of themselves; the Bishop because he was always caring for others, and Burrup because he failed to understand that he could possibly need care.'[1]

In pouring rain, over swollen streams, and with the stalwart Makololo as their bearers, the two tired men set off for Chibisa's and the Shire. They were in wet clothes five days and four nights, from Magomero to the river. At Chibisa's the sun came

[1] R 253.

out; Mackenzie's spirits rose and his normal optimism and buoyancy returned. 'This is a very beautiful place: a village perched on the top of a cliff of red clay overhanging the stream, which is now swollen much, and commanding a view of the valley of the Shire, or at least of its lowest level, extending four or five miles to the eastern hills . . . All looks bright . . . God gives us bright spots in our life at the darkest—and how often bright tracts stretching over much of it!

'I am all this time stopping to shew my watch to some of them, and to explain to another that if we do not agree on the price of his meal we need not quarrel; on which he comes back to take what I offered, and I give him a little more. But I must stop now. Thank God for this day.'[2]

Next morning Burrup seemed unfit, and would eat hardly any breakfast. After breakfast Mackenzie read him a hymn from Keble's *Christian Year*; a hymn based on a parable of the morning sun shining out upon the dewy grass, and yet the wary traveller is not yet sure that the brightness will last through the day. Mackenzie admired the last verses. They told of the glory that transcends death, and Mackenzie knew and expected his danger:

'The promise of the morrow
   Is glorious on that eve,
Dear as the holy sorrow
   When good men cease to live.
When brightening ere it die away
   Mounts up their altar flame,
Still tending with intenser ray
   To heaven whence first it came.

'Say not it dies, that glory,
   'Tis caught unquenched on high,
Those saint-like brows so hoary
   Shall wear it in the sky.
No smile is like the smile of death,
   When all good musings past,
Rise wafted with the parting breath,
   The sweetest thought the last.'

[2] G 402–3.

Mackenzie's own perturbations now seemed to be more mental than physical. He was worried at being late to meet Livingstone. The worry was beginning to take on almost obsessive force, and no doubt was a symptom of the physical exhaustion beneath the surface. On Livingstone, and Livingstone's steamer, the mission was still so dependent for its life-line and its survival.

* * * * *

Taking three volunteers, two of them after much difficulty, from the Makololo—Zomba, Charlie, and Seseho—they set off downstream on the afternoon of 9 January, in a canoe borrowed for a few days from Chibisa's people. 'It was delicious, the floating down that broad green-backed river.' They spent the night at a village called Magunda's, and, though Burrup was still unwell, canoed again early next morning. They were now entering the Elephant Marsh, the most unhealthy region of the Shire: and one of the reasons for Rowley's growing scepticism of Dr Livingstone had been his astonishment that Livingstone should have chosen the Ruo mouth, as mosquito-ridden a spot as it was possible to find in the land, for a rendezvous. That night they landed on the bank, made fast the canoe to the grass, and ate some cold goat. The mosquitoes gathered round their prey; and the three Makololo were unprotected by mosquito-curtains. Mackenzie lent them two pairs of trousers and a blue coatie, and wrapped his own head and shoulders in his mosquito-curtains. He was just dropping off to sleep when one of the Makololo said, 'We are going on.' They could endure it no longer, and told him that they preferred paddling in the moonlight to being eaten by mosquitoes on the bank. Within a minute they were again in the canoe, sailing down with the Shire current under the stars. Mackenzie sometimes lay down in the bottom of the canoe, sometimes sat up and watched the tricky piloting of the canoe down a narrow winding channel; for they had left the main channel of the river when they went towards the bank at night-fall.

The Makololo Zomba guided the steering of the canoe from a post in the bows, Charlie and Seseho paddled it from the stern. At a sudden turn in the channel which Zomba failed to see the canoe ran aground on a point where the stream parted into two, and the stern started to fill with water. Charlie and Seseho jumped out and stood up to their waists in water. Mackenzie followed, and then Burrup. But the canoe continued to fill with water. They began to pull out their goods. A case which contained all Burrup's luggage was washed overboard at the stern. The properties which they salvaged they laid out in the long grass on the bank, though the long grass was growing out of two or three feet of water. They raised the canoe and baled it out. Then they put all their soaking properties back—'guns, powder-flasks, bags of sugar and coffee, books, mail-bag, watch, etc.'—all of which had been lying in the shallow marshy water which was called a bank. They climbed back into the canoe, wet through to the waist, wringing the water out of their trouser-legs. It seemed impracticable to go on now. All five men clambered back into the canoe and lay down to try to get some sleep. It was ten o'clock, as Mackenzie later judged from the time at which his watch had stopped, on account of its soaking.[1]

The mosquitoes were if anything more numerous and more persistent here than at the earlier stop on the bank. Burrup said that he did not mind mosquitoes, and uttered no word of complaint. Mackenzie took Charlie under a corner of his mosquito-curtain. The others could be heard through the night switching themselves from time to time. Mackenzie himself was surprised at his success in sleeping under these conditions.

Before the sun came up they were off again down the river. Not until they had travelled some distance were they aware of the full extent of their loss. Burrup's case, lost overboard, had contained not only all the spare powder, but all the medicines which Dickinson had given them, except a few sodden Rousers in Burrup's pocket.

About nine a.m. on Saturday 11 January, they reached the point where the clear waters of the Ruo flowed into the muddy currents of the Shire, and landed at the village on an island there named Malo. The chief's name was Chikanzi. They asked whether anyone had seen Dr Livingstone or the *Pioneer*. The villagers had seen the ship. She had chugged past, only a few days before, *travelling downstream.*

Livingstone, it was clear, had been fast on a sandbank, or

[1] G 404–6.

perhaps several sandbanks. He must have had as much trouble in handling the ship down the river as in handling it up. He was later in keeping his programme than the missionaries. The rush, at such cost, to the Ruo had been vain.

* * * * *

Mackenzie and Burrup discussed what to do. They enquired if Livingstone had left a letter for them. There was no letter. They determined to abide by the agreement and wait for him to return as soon as he could. It would hardly be less than a fortnight.

Five days later, on 16 January, though Burrup was still ill, Mackenzie seemed to be recovering a little. He wrote a letter on that day to Strong, the secretary of the committee in London, and told him, 'I am myself, thank God, in almost perfect health, and only regret, on my own account, the loss of the little packet of drugs, inasmuch as I shall probably have a touch of fever soon for want of quinine.' And his buoyant spirits were making new plans. Mackenzie always possessed the strongest trust in an overruling Providence. If Burrup and he had missed the *Pioneer* by a few days, this apparent disaster must have been designed for some good purpose. Perhaps they were intended to begin missionary work at Malo and along the river. 'May not our stopping here and making friends with this *island* chief be of importance, greater than all we might have done if we had been here a week earlier?'[1]

The circumstances reconciled him at last to Livingstone's view that the mission must possess, and could possess, a river-steamer. In the long and fruitless discussions of the subject which they had conducted at Magomero ever since Livingstone had unexpectedly told them that the *Pioneer* could no longer help them, Mackenzie could not reconcile himself to the idea. It seemed scarcely thinkable that the mission could afford either the capital expenditure on purchase or the high annual cost of running year by year. But he had too sanguine a temperament, or lively a faith, to base his opposition on this ground. He was afraid of a crew of seamen. He conceived of the white men under the mission's control showing forth the

[1] G 411–2.

Christian way of life to the African, and he could hardly bear the idea of men being associated with the mission, even as experts, who were not personally consecrated to the aims of the mission. It was this attitude which caused him such profound grief when the Cape interpreters, nominally Christians, misbehaved themselves at Magomero. He did not see the incompatibility between this concern and the policy of 'commerce and Christianity' which many supporters at home believed the mission to represent. Commerce would mean white civilization bad as well as good. Mackenzie longed that the African should receive and appropriate only the good. When he had written home for artisans, he had declared that he would rather have no house, or build it himself, than men who would not put their hearts into the *main work*. 'A medical man, too, must *please* have his heart with us. I would rather trust God's Providence than be hampered with a worldly medical man.'[1] He had been afraid of a river-steamer directly under the control of the mission, and his experiences on the *Pioneer* and on the *Lyra*, had helped to confirm his reluctance. 'I thought of fevers on board, and, far worse, of quarrelling among its crew, and of conduct unbecoming our Christian name, and dishonouring to God, and undermining our mission work among the natives.'

But now he changed his mind. There must be good reason why they were marooned at Malo. The mission, perhaps, was being led to begin work up and down the river, and for this they must have a steamer. 'Why not have mission work on this river, under the management of a priest, and perhaps a deacon, always on board? Why should there not be several, aye, from five to ten villages, on the banks, visited regularly, in which preaching, schooling, marketing, and general civilizing influences might go on? The trip to the sea, once or twice in the year, would make little interruption in this, which would be the main work of the vessel; and if there were this constant passing up and down, at regular or irregular intervals, only not too long, there would be much greater difficulty than at present in transmitting slaves from the east to the west bank . . . All my objections vanish. There would be healthful occupation for the crew, and such employment for their minds as would, I

[1] SPG, MSS. D.24, Mackenzie to Bullock, 29.1.61, from *H.M.S. Lyra*.

hope, give the ship rather a good than a bad influence on their characters, while the whole would be under the command of a clergyman, who would consider that his parish included his fellow-voyagers, as well as the natives on the banks.'

In the bare dank hut which the chief had given them, Mackenzie drafted a letter, to the boat clubs of the Universities of Oxford and Cambridge, appealing for contributions to a steam launch for the mission.

It is probable that the same sense of being brought under providence to Malo led him to stay there—against every consideration of worldly prudence. He might have gone down the river to follow the *Pioneer*; he might have gone back to Chibisa's. But in part they were both so tired that they could hardly bring themselves to face the necessary exertion; and in part, Mackenzie felt that they should waste no opportunity but should use the time of waiting in coming to know and befriend Chikanzi and his people. He had always believed in acting as he thought right and letting the prudence take care of itself.

Mingled with this faith in the future, moments of black depression overcame him, the symptoms of bodily exhaustion. There never would be a steamer. They would never open a line of communication. Livingstone had abandoned them. The mission would never receive adequate stores. His sisters would never come—was it after all no place for women?—he longed for his sisters to come, and once told Burrup that he 'thought it would break his heart if they did not come.'[1] Several times a day he walked to the southward point of the island hoping to descry the *Pioneer* or distantly to hear her familiar chug-chug upon the breeze; but he saw nothing on the river but the rose-coloured bee-eater, or the guinea-fowl, or the crocodiles basking.

Within a few days, Mackenzie and Burrup were both suffering from worse diarrhoea, and then fever came upon the top of it. Till then they had been learning the Greek of daily texts from Romans—'O wretched man that I am! Who shall deliver me from the body of this death? I thank God through Jesus Christ our Lord. So then with the mind I myself serve the law of God; but with the flesh the law of sin . . . I am persuaded that neither death, nor life, nor angels, nor principalities, nor

[1] R 263.

powers, nor things present, nor things to come, nor height, nor depth, nor any other creature, shall be able to separate us from the love of God, which is in Christ Jesus our Lord.' With fever and dysentery, they could not continue even to converse, for Mackenzie's mind began to wander, now apparently breaking under the burdens he was bearing, now under a hallucination that he and sisters and stores were safe, back at Magomero. The three Makololo looked after the two Englishmen with a rough but kindly attentiveness. On 24 January Mackenzie bled profusely at the nose and mouth, his breathing became stertorous, and thenceforward he lost coherence and perhaps consciousness.

On 31 January, the chief Chikanzi told Burrup that Mackenzie must be moved from the hut. Upon any hut in which a man died, especially if he were a stranger, rested a taboo, and the Manganja would have to desert such a hut perhaps for three years. In spite of Burrup's protests, Mackenzie was moved to another hut, less valuable. The movement caused fresh bleeding at the nose and mouth. And there, about five o'clock the same afternoon, he died without regaining consciousness.

Chikanzi and the Makololo wanted the body buried at once. Burrup and the Makololo borrowed a hoe from the chief, wrapped the body in cloth, carried it to the canoe, and paddled across the river to the mainland. They cleared some bushes beneath a large mimosa tree, and with the darkness falling, dug a grave among the long reeds. Burrup had his prayer book with him, but he could not see to read the Burial Service, so he said what he could remember. They did not mark the grave.

Burrup perhaps ought to have gone down the river, in the hope of finding Livingstone or Portuguese help. But he was almost out of cloth, and would soon have nothing to pay for food. He was physically dependent upon the three Makololo who wanted to go upstream to Chibisa's. Magomero, much nearer, was where he knew there were friends. Above all, perhaps, he and Mackenzie had borrowed the only canoe at Chibisa's, and had promised that they would return it within a few days. Yet the river was swollen and the current strong, and to reach Chibisa's would be no light undertaking. The Makololo said that they could not push the canoe upstream and that they must all walk. Burrup still had the vigour to insist that they must paddle him in the canoe. He wrote a letter to Livingstone and left it with the chief. On 2 February, two days after Mackenzie's death, they set out in the canoe and struggled upstream for three days. Then the Makololo said that they could paddle no longer, and landed on the bank. Burrup said he would not leave the canoe. The Makololo said good-bye, and were about to abandon him and the canoe. Burrup perforce followed them. The three days' walk along the bank to Chibisa's—with dysentery, fever, high temperature, and utter exhaustion—was probably the finest physical feat of endurance in Burrup's life. He stumbled along, from time to time falling headlong, but did not collapse altogether until he reached Chibisa's. When he limped or tottered into the village, his belly had swollen to an alarming size.

Seeing he could walk no further, the Makololo and Chibisa's men made a rough stretcher of branches. One of the Makololo lent him some cloth to buy food. He was carried all the way to Magomero, and reached it on 14 February, now perhaps half his proper weight. Dickinson at first thought he had a chance. But soon the diarrhoea came again, and weakness with it. On the morning of 22 February, he was up by six o'clock, walked across the village, and bullied Johnson loudly out of bed to get him coffee. There was no coffee, Johnson made tea. Burrup drank several cups. Waller went over to the kitchen and was having two eggs boiled when Procter came in to say that Burrup was wandering in his mind. Offered the two boiled eggs, Burrup ate them in an almost unconscious state, and immediately fell back upon his bed in a disturbed coma. His body continued heaving until a quarter to eleven, but he never recovered consciousness.[1]

Rowley, conducting the funeral, was moved beyond his wont. He had known Burrup hardly more than a month,[2] and for the main part of that month he had been ill. Burrup was the only missionary besides himself to possess a distant wife hoping for

[1] R 270; Procter in *Guardian*, 1862, p. 638; W 22.2.62; G 416.

[2] Burrup: arr. Magomero 19 November; left for Manasomba's 23 December; arrived Magomero 2 January; left for Ruo 3 January; arrived sick at Magomero 14 February; died 22 February. Rowley was ill with dysentery from 5 December and was still unfit to travel on 3 January. They associated as reasonably fit men for about sixteen days.

reunion with him. As he read the Burial Service, he could not help thinking of the gay young girl now believed to be sailing up the Zambezi, and his eyes filled with tears. 'God grant,' wrote Waller ungrammatically, hearing how Mackenzie had been obsessed with worry over the women, 'God grant that they, poor creatures, may have been deterred carrying out the most unfortunate scheme which, conceived in the love of a brother and sister, could not, nay would not, see it to be inadvisable.'

* * * * *

On 28 February, two English boats—neither of which was the *Pioneer*—rounded the bend of the Shire and reached the island at the mouth of the Ruo. They were manned by blue-jackets of the Royal Navy. The captain sent ashore to ask whether the villagers had seen anything of Bishop Mackenzie. The villagers answered that they had seen nothing, heard nothing, knew nothing. They did not mention that they had been given a letter.

IV

THE RELIEF EXPEDITION

Anne Mackenzie was decidedly unmarried. She was advancing in years, had helped to bring up her brother, had kept house for him in Natal, and had grown into a passionate affection and admiration towards him. A friend compared her, at this earlier time of her life, to a vine which clings as it grows. She was precise, articulate, and self-disciplined. She disliked the idea of sailing up the Zambezi: her imagination filled her with forebodings, vivid spectres of mosquitoes and swamps and crocodiles and savages. But if he needed her, she must go. She believed that he needed her, not only as a feminine missionary and experienced teacher of girls, but as a personal stay and support. She knew that she possessed far more knowledge of the world than he, and believed that he could carry other-worldliness to a point where it became dreaminess. Seeing that he had no comprehension whatsoever of deceit and cunning, she felt herself equipped to guide his simple integrity through the subtleties of scheming and crafty men. She recognized his mathematical ability to be eminent, but perceived the aura of remoteness and donnishness which sometimes girdles the head of the pure mathematician living in his realm of symbolic logic, and she was aware that her own ability was directed to more practical ends. Though he was the fit and vigorous and active man, while she spent hours of her day enfeebled upon a sofa or in bed with a blinding headache, she thought that he was the true contemplative and she must from her sofa be a Martha to his Mary. Her opinion of men as managers was low. She knew herself as decisive, and her brother as sometimes indecisive. She thought the male sex to be lavish, extravagant, and careless in household matters. She was convinced that the camp at Magomero must be in dire need of the orderliness and the economy which a woman could provide.

Just at the time when Mackenzie had resolved to leave his

college comforts and undertake missionary work in Natal, she was ordered by her doctor to a warmer climate. She had therefore come to look after her brother, thinking 'he would require a little keeping in order, lest he should do foolish things.'[1] She had disliked his resolve to go, and had not expected to enjoy her part in his work. She shared the view of many in the colonies, and some at home, that to be a missionary was not to be quite a gentleman.

Natal had done her good. The self-pitying, formidable, spinsterish invalid discovered that there were few sofas in Natal for her to suffer upon, that she was needed in more useful and practical ways than in mothering her brother. Her careful housekeeping pride rose in disgust and rebelled against the teacups that were all cracked, and yet she must endure. She disliked the manners of colonials, she was repelled by insects, she found in herself a physical shrinking from black people, and yet she must endure.[2] She turned to teaching, and under the stimulus of a warm climate and better health, active work for her body and mind, and the discipline of circumstances that killed fastidiousness or an imagined sensitivity, her character began to mature and soften. Those who knew her during the years in South Africa could see how she ripened, how she was rising above the infirm, self-centred hypochondriac lying back to need attention. By the time she came to sail for the Zambezi, she was a more humane lady, a gentle person—but still a critic, still indomitable. Livingstone's engineer once described her type as 'thin and delicate, but awfully tough'. It was characteristic of her that she relished the description.[3]

To the Zambezi, she had decided, she would take Jessie Lennox, her housekeeper in Natal. She would, of course, take her maid. As she was seldom able to walk any distance, she would also take her donkey. The donkey's name was Katie.

Staying with Bishop Gray at Cape Town, she met Mrs Burrup and to her credit liked her unfeignedly. The marriage, within two days of sailing upon the expedition, touched a romantic chord in Miss Mackenzie, and she found Mrs Burrup

[1] Awdry, p. 35. [2] Awdry, pp. 63, 65, 106.
[3] A. Mackenzie to Mrs H. Goodwin, Natal, 10.12.61, UMCA.

to be a lively, friendly, and attractive little creature, a charming addition to the party. She wrote (lying in bed with bronchitis, a blister on her chest, and a decanter of port wine on the bedside table) that Mrs Burrup was 'one of the blythest and brightest beings I have seen',[1] and admired her because she thought nothing of walking twelve miles.

In September 1861, the expected letter arrived from Central Africa. Her brother wanted her 'immediately', said it was safe to go, and that Dr Livingstone would meet her party at the Kongone mouth. Miss Mackenzie would have preferred her brother to come down the Zambezi himself and fetch them up, but she was willing to recognize that Dr Livingstone would do instead.

The party was beginning to assemble. Its membership was not quite what was expected. Her sister, Alice Mackenzie, who was due to be picked up at Durban, became engaged to be married just when they were arranging the voyage, and dropped out. The little maid whom Miss Mackenzie had brought out from Scotland heard that the mosquitoes on the Zambezi were the size of elephants and would not come. It was suspected that she, likewise, was helped by a young man in the vicinity to make up her mind. Miss Mackenzie replaced her with a maid named Sarah. A clergyman expected from England failed to come. But there was a fifth lady whom they must take. In addition to Miss Mackenzie, Mrs Burrup, Jessie Lennox the housekeeper, and Sarah the maid, Mrs Livingstone would be travelling with them. Dr Livingstone had summoned her.

Mary Livingstone, herself the daughter of the great missionary, Robert Moffat, had been married for sixteen years, and had already borne six children to her husband. She had been described by David on their engagement as 'not romantic but a matter-of-fact lady, a little, thick, black-haired girl, sturdy, and all that I want.'[2] In her husband's various and lengthy absences she had suffered severe distress, financial as well as personal. At last his gruff and unsentimental, but utterly genuine, affection was bringing her to be with him on the river-steamer. Her hardships had left their mark on her. Like Miss Mackenzie, she was

[1] A. Mackenzie to Mrs H. Goodwin, 19.9.61, UMCA.

[2] George Seaver, *David Livingstone*, p. 86.

a woman of ill-health, and ill-health in part brought on by emotional and psychological circumstances. She had become moody and temperamental, and her separations had left her with a sense of neglect, a faint resentment, a grievance which she directed, not at her husband, but at the work which he had undertaken. It was a matter of more than surprise, it was a shock of pain to those who came to know her intimately enough to discover it, that this daughter of a Moffat, and wife of a Livingstone, in spite of moments or fits of enthusiasm, cared not for missionary work. Sometimes she seemed to resent it. Mrs Burrup was travelling to join her husband and share in his work. Miss Mackenzie was travelling to look after her brother, and had lately learnt how to share in his work. Mrs Livingstone was travelling to join her husband, and in his work she was showing no interest at all. Bishop Mackenzie, knowing that she was on her way, and expecting that her husband's explorations would prevent her from accompanying him, had written to offer her a home with the mission. Mrs Livingstone was not intending to endure separation again. She had come out to join her husband on his river-steamer, and on the river-steamer she would stay.

These five women needed escort, and the clergyman from England had failed them. His place was taken by a young Anglican priest, Edward Hawkins. Hawkins was the son of a famous father, the Provost of Oriel College, Oxford, and the godson of the more famous Dr. Pusey. He was another whom the doctor had sent out to the Cape for the sake of his health. He ought not to have volunteered for the Zambezi Mission, and was well aware that he ought not. His parents were alarmed and horrified when they heard the news. He volunteered, in part, because he was vexed or ashamed to discover, when Mackenzie's party arrived at Cape Town, that no Oxford man had as yet joined what was nominally an Oxford and Cambridge Mission. Something also there was of youthful enthusiasm for self-sacrifice which went beyond the limits of sane reasoning. He believed that it was more probable than not that he would fail to survive the Zambezi, and without wanting to commit suicide, without even suffering from a melancholic temperament, he was somehow glad that it was so. He was proving himself to himself. 'I seem now,' he wrote to his eminent father, 'to have attained what has really been my wish for many years, and have satisfied myself that I have the power of self-sacrifice, and some other qualifications which my profession needs. I am hoping only to do my duty, not any great thing . . .[1]

One minor property or ailment Hawkins possessed, an ailment which in the event was not to be unimportant. Nature had bestowed upon him, or habit had developed in him, a repellent and noxious variety of parsonical voice.

As the only priest going with this party, he must be in charge of it. He did not relish the prospect. Like the committee at home, he did not think the women ought to go. 'You see,' he wrote to his father,[2] 'I cannot refuse to take charge of the party, but I wish I were going alone. I do not half like being responsible for so many women . . .' He found the expedition laborious to organise. They were responsible for transporting the supplies for the second year of the mission, and he found a mountain of stores and materials. What this mountain contained, Hawkins never knew in detail. The goods were ill-packed, and sent without lists or proper markings. They included a large 'church-tent', four mules, and two farm-carts, to be divided between Livingstone and the mission, and Katie the donkey; various stores ranging from essential articles like fifty boxes of flour, four casks of wine, biscuits, salt-meat, and brandy, to less essential articles like photographing apparatus. Messrs Bartlett and Sons of Redditch had presented the mission with 50,000 fish-hooks.

The larger items in this list, like the church-tent and the photographing apparatus, had in the event to be left behind. For the transport proved to be the brig, *Hetty Ellen*, which was conveying Livingstone's engineer, Rae, and the pieces of the new river-steamer, the *Lady Nyassa*, to the Kongone. Livingstone had ordered the *Lady Nyassa*, and partly paid for it from the royalties on his book, so that he might transport it by land past the Murchison Cataracts and sail it on Lake Nyasa.

Hawkins' misgivings were not diminished when he found that Mary Livingstone wanted to bring with her to the Zambezi a Scottish friend, by name James Stewart.

[1] E. Hawkins, *Filio Desideratissimo*, 1862, p. 41.
[2] E. Hawkins, *Filio Desideratissimo*, 1862, p. 39.

Stewart was a young Scottish minister, and also a medical student, from the Free Kirk. When Livingstone had travelled and lectured in Scotland, Stewart had responded with the deepest ardour of the heart to the appeal of Africa, of commerce and of Christianity. He became for a time far more than an admirer, almost a worshipper, of Livingstone. He burned with zeal to be the instrument of Livingstone's aims, to kill the slave-trade by opening Africa at once to the Gospel and to legitimate trade. He tried to persuade the leaders of the Free Kirk to found an industrial mission in East Africa under Livingstone's auspices. The leaders of the Free Kirk were too prudent to commit themselves to founding a mission on unknown territory in the middle of Africa; they refused him their official backing. Stewart, single-handed, persisted in his arguments. If he could not elicit official support, he would collect unofficial. If it was rash to found an industrial mission, would they not send him out to the Zambezi upon a reconnaissance, to see for himself whether a Free Kirk mission would be possible or acceptable? And so, at length, a committee, unofficial indeed but headed by Dr Candlish, the most eminent minister of the Free Kirk, found him money and sent him off to South Africa with a letter of introduction to Livingstone. He had sailed from Southampton upon the same ship as Mary Livingstone.

On 12 September 1861 Mary Livingstone and Stewart went to stay for two days with the Bishop of Cape Town. In his house they met Miss Mackenzie and discussed the plans for reaching the Zambezi. Stewart's ecclesiastical outlook, at this time, was narrow. When he attended prayers in the Bishop's chapel, he suffered qualms that he was bowing down in the House of Rimmon. He distrusted episcopalians in general and high episcopalians with emphasis, and was agreeably surprised to find how sincere the Bishop's voice sounded when he conducted the service. Like everyone else who met Bishop Gray, Stewart was impressed by the foursquare stature of the man, his frankness and vigour and directness, and was heartened and perhaps flattered by the serene and courteous hospitality which was bestowed upon him. But even while he recognized Gray's merits and kindness, he suffered an internal twinge of guilt that he might be 'worshipping a lord', or becoming a time-server to a prelate.[1] And this inner fear, this readiness to suspect the worst, preyed for a time upon Stewart's mind. His inside was a tangle of jumpiness and resentments.

After dinner on the evening of the 12th, when the ladies had retired to the drawing-room, and the men had moved up to the other end of the table, the Bishop began to ask him about his plans. Stewart hedged. He knew that he disapproved of Bishop Mackenzie, partly because he was a Scottish episcopalian, partly because his mission had the reputation of being a high church mission, and partly because the Universities Mission had gained that assistance and countenance from Dr Livingstone which, Stewart felt, his own presbyterian plans had a better right to expect. He could not help suspecting a touch of 'wiliness' in the Bishop. He thought that he was being pumped, probably for ecclesiastical purposes of a wrongful kind. 'If I am not uncharitable, I saw his game: and I shewed him that I saw it, and when he made one or two attacks and found the attempts only too unsuccessful, I came out of my position of defence, and said what I thought might be said with safety.' The thought of a 'rivalry' between the two missions upon the same ground was at the back of both their minds. 'I hope the country is vast enough for all,' said Stewart. Gray replied, 'I should be very glad to see the different bodies moving on in a phalanx through that country.'

Stewart was glad to hear the Bishop thus welcome his own plans with charity. And yet, even while he felt pleasure at the words, he could not resist a secret doubt whether the Bishop's gladness was wholly genuine.

He was wrong in his doubt. A day or two afterwards the Bishop discussed it with Miss Mackenzie. She expressed her fears of rivalry. The Bishop pooh-poohed her. 'Africa is big enough for both missions, and in such a fight, whether the country is to be Satan's Kingdom or Christ's Kingdom, every aid is to be welcomed.' Miss Mackenzie, though she had liked Stewart when she met him at dinner, was not quite convinced. She approved of his person, she distrusted his purposes. 'I do hope,' she wrote home[2] 'he will keep his mission a long way

[1] SJ 12–13.9.61.
[2] A. Mackenzie to Mrs Goodwin, Bishopscourt, 19.9.61, UMCA.

from ours.' She was inclined to regard him as an intruder into occupied ground.

But now a new difficulty appeared. Rae, Livingstone's engineer, had chartered the brig *Hetty Ellen* from Glasgow and had brought out the pieces of the river-steamer *Lady Nyassa* upon her. He announced that he thought he should not take Stewart on the *Hetty Ellen*: he thought that Dr Livingstone would not approve. He had met Stewart in Glasgow six months before, and was well aware that Stewart possessed no official status, that in spite of his backers he was something of a free lance. He suspected him of being bogus, a trader disguised as a missionary. What would Dr Livingstone say if *H.M.S. Pioneer* was cluttered with speculators?

On 30 October, when this difficulty came to a head, Stewart went to see Mrs Livingstone, and found the Bishop there. His mind leaped to the worst conclusion: 'His visit was doubtless to make the most of the difficulty between Rae and myself. He would gladly offer me a free passage back to England: and very benevolently suggested that if Livingstone could do nothing for me, I should return on the *Hetty Ellen*!' Stewart was satirical at this kindness. He did not believe it to be kindness. He believed that the Bishop was using the opportunity to be rid of this awkward and potential rival. But Mrs Livingstone here broke in. She told the Bishop that if Stewart did not go on the ship she would not stir from Cape Town herself. Stewart was gratified; but he had a sense of being a lone fighter in a hostile world, an upright man surrounded by plotters trying to thwart him in his chosen and providential course. He was not a man to yield. 'I must go on though fifty bishops were blocking up the path and as many Raes were doing their best to leave me in the lurch.'[1] He resolved to treat all men as rogues until they were proved honest.

On 13 November, they all sailed on *H.M.S. Waldensian* for Natal, where the more uncomfortable and crowded *Hetty Ellen* would pick them up. And now Hawkins and Stewart were forced to live together for the first time. Hawkins, with the vagueness of a mid-Victorian Anglican about the differences among Nonconformist denominations, had at first referred to

[1] SJ 30.10.61.

Stewart, inaccurately, as 'a Baptist minister whom Mrs Livingstone insisted on taking with her.' They were both narrow and rigid men. Hawkins had received from Rae an unfavourable view of Stewart, thought that he had no right to be there, and was repelled by the barriers of suspicion which he erected. Stewart imagined that Hawkins' 'drawl and whine' when conducting services was a piece of high churchism, not a natural affliction. He hated it that Hawkins should daily read to Miss Mackenzie and Mrs Burrup a portion of Montalembert's *Monks of the West*—'a defence of monachism out and out' and 'a sign most ominous' of the way the wind was blowing.[1] He believed that Hawkins thought himself the only Reverend on the ship. He was right. That was what Hawkins thought.

On 16 November, the captain asked Stewart to say grace at dinner. Hawkins said grace quickly ('mumbled an irreverent sentence with his eyes wide open', Stewart called it). The next day, Hawkins began reading morning prayers on the poop, though in a miserable condition from incipient sea-sickness, but had not gone far when he was forced to desist and flee, thrusting the book into Stewart's hands as he fled. For most of the voyage two different services were held at different times of the day.

Stewart's hostility towards the Universities Mission was hardening. He had begun with prejudices: under Gray's benignity he had consented to think of Africa as a vast country with plenty of room for two missions. But was it true? Was there not only one Dr Livingstone whose approval and assistance must be gained if a mission was to be established successfully? Was there not only one line of communication, up the Zambezi, or perhaps the Rovuma? He was beginning to think of his own (still hypothetical) mission as the rival, not the ally, of the Universities Mission. If Hawkins was a representative, there could hardly be a happy alliance between the two. And on the *Waldensian* he met a colonist from Natal, who disliked missionaries as a class and who filled Stewart with contemptuous stories of Mackenzie's work in Natal. Mackenzie was a vacillator; he blew now hot now cold; he had not strength of character. These stories were not unwelcome to Stewart. Before he left Scotland he had made a public speech in which he asserted

[1] SJ 16.11.61.

that Bishop Mackenzie was not the man for the work. He thought him 'pompous' (he supposed that if a man was a bishop he must be pompous), and had declared that he cared not if Bishop Mackenzie's band were ten times as large as it was, it was a useless one. As time went on he thought, not in terms of an alliance, nor even of a rivalry, but of a fight. 'Our high and mighty Puseyite friends . . . expect no doubt, at the last great pitched battle, to come off victorious. This will be fought on the banks of the Zambezi.'[1]

The more hostile or reserved that Stewart became, the more he antagonized the others. By the time the *Waldensian* reached Natal, Hawkins had entirely accepted Rae's opinion about Stewart. It was very desirable that this cantankerous fellow, as Hawkins now supposed him to be, should be restrained from rushing up the Zambezi, offending Livingstone and his company, and creating sectarian strife and ill-feeling.

On the afternoon of 14 December, Stewart went on board the brig *Hetty Ellen* as she lay in Durban harbour, and found the decks wet with scrubbing. The captain, a little Welshman named Davis, astonished him by saying that he would have difficulty in taking him to the Zambezi—indeed that he could not do so 'unless with the sanction of the other party.' 'The said party were composed of Rae and Hawkins, the latter being chief in the intrigue. Both yesterday and today they had been on board and did their utmost to get him to leave me behind. I asked what charge they could bring against me. He gave no answer to this. He regretted that matters should be so: but did not wish to offend those who had chartered the vessel, etc . . . Mr Hawkins insisted that I was not of their party, that I had no right to go there, etc. I told Davis by whom I was commissioned; that I was a minister of the Free Church; what my object was; and to Dr Livingstone I would go though I should walk all the way. I feel that I rather put him out by the easy nonchalant air with which I received his information . . . These people are certainly moving heaven and earth to prevent me getting into that country. If I live I may yet become a sharp thorn in the sides of all of them . . .'[2]

He resolved to have nothing more to do with them. Yet he

[1] SJ 21.12.61, p. 153. [2] SJ 14.12.61, p. 139.

must get taken on the *Hetty Ellen*. Two days later he again went on board, and finding Captain Davis 'more than usually snappish', he went ashore and talked with Rae. Rae looked him full in the face and said,

'Well, Mr Stewart, you are not going into the country as a *trader*? Tell me that!'

Stewart boiled internally but was silent under the impeachment. Rae said, 'I was warned against you at the Cape on the ground that you were going into that country in the pretended character of a missionary but really as a trader, and that you had large quantities of beads.'

Stewart said, 'If you wish to see how large a quantity of beads I have, come over to this warehouse.'

In silence they walked over to the warehouse. From the bottom of a packing-case, Stewart fished up a small paper-pasteboard box about four inches square. He tore it open and displayed eleven small necklaces of red and blue beads. He threw down the box and said, 'These are the enormous quantities of beads about which Chevalier du Prat [the Portuguese consul at Cape Town] and yourself have held such grave and solemn and anxious deliberations. These are the goods with which I intend to monopolize the trade of the Portuguese on the Zambezi.'[1]

He walked home by the beach, 'weak, weary, dispirited, wet with rain and perspiration.' In the afternoon he went, as so often, to call upon Mary Livingstone. He found that Rae, shortly before, had visited her. Mrs Livingstone had told Rae that she was determined not to leave Durban without Stewart; and Rae, presumably to cover himself against Livingstone's future rebuke, asked for a written statement that Stewart travelled to the Zambezi under her authority. And so, on Christmas Eve, 1861, while Mackenzie marched through the pouring rain towards Manasomba's village, Stewart embarked with the others in the *Hetty Ellen* and sailed for the Zambezi.

The passage on the *Hetty Ellen* was not comfortable. 'A dirty little brig' she was called by a naval officer who saw her. There was only one cabin, which the ladies were given for their sleeping and dressing; nothing to eat but salt rations; only one plate

[1] SJ 16.12.61.

and one mug between each two or three people. The men slept in the hold on planks stretched across the luggage, with water dripping down on them through the seams, while the forage for the mules and for Katie bred a multitude of flies and mosquitoes.[1]

The double services continued. On the social plane, Hawkins and Miss Mackenzie, now that they had Stewart with them for better or for worse, attempted to make the best of him by jogging him out of his corner. Stewart recognized the friendliness, but would not bring himself to accept it. 'OCM [the Oxford and Cambridge Mission] have been extremely kind for the last two days but I cannot be too cautious. I deserve to regard myself as a fool if I trust to them again.'[2] All the fear, not only of another denomination but of Rae who pretended to be afraid of exceeding Livingstone's orders, of the Portuguese consul who wanted to keep commercial travellers out of the Zambezi, was focused upon the Universities Mission. And when his sullen behaviour elicited a frigid response he assumed that the frigidity issued from sectarian, Puseyite prejudice. Hawkins may be pardoned for not recognizing that this moody, difficult, introspective, solitary, morose young man was going to turn himself, or be turned, into one of the great servants of Africa.

* * * * *

On 8 January 1862 the *Hetty Ellen* arrived off the West Luabo mouth of the Zambezi. They fired guns and rockets, and several optimists believed they could descry a small boat putting out to meet them. But no sign of Dr Livingstone could be seen, no answering gun or rocket was fired from the shore. It was plain that the ladies could not ascend the Zambezi unless someone would take them who was competent to take them. It was possible that Dr Livingstone had already reached West Luabo, and finding no wife, disappeared again into the vastnesses of Central Africa. Hawkins, who still thought the idea of two delicate and middle-aged ladies sailing up the Zambezi to be, under present conditions, wrong and absurd, wanted the *Hetty Ellen* to put back to Durban. But it seemed to the others (except

[1] Cf. the description by Hawkins in *Cape Monthly Magazine*, 1862, p. 264.
[2] SJ 1.1.62.

Stewart, who was not consulted) better to sail northward to Mozambique in quest of news and perhaps assistance. Rae, with the pieces of *Lady Nyassa* on board, could not on any account go back without unloading them at a convenient place.

Stewart disliked the look of the Zambezi mouths as heartily as Rowley eleven months before. 'My impressions of the coast were of the worst kind. I cannot understand how Livingstone could have said so much in favour of a river and coast that promises so little.' The little Welsh captain agreed when he came down into the hold, and said he never saw such a hole of a place and would never come back for any money whatsoever. Stewart, brooding over his innate pessimism, leapt to the conviction that the Zambezi was no gateway at all to Central Africa, and that his journey had probably been wasted. 'It would almost appear as if I were on as real a wild goose chase as ever mortal started on.'[1]

On 21 January, they arrived off Mozambique, and a black pilot came aboard. In the outer harbour they saw a warship which from her rig seemed Portuguese, and the watchers at the rail of the *Hetty Ellen* were unanimous in condemning her for ugliness and build. A boat from the warship was seen to be putting off, and soon an English midshipman, rather nervous, came on board to examine the papers of *Hetty Ellen*. The warship was *H.M.S. Gorgon* of the Royal Navy, engaged in the slave patrol along the East African Coast; and her captain, by name Wilson, had thought he should investigate this brig, of lines unusual in those waters. Wilson, hearing that Mrs Livingstone and Miss Mackenzie were on board, rowed over between nine and ten a.m. to meet them and discuss their plans.

Wilson was a naval officer with a distinguished career at sea in front of him. The vacillations and uncertainties and arguments on the *Hetty Ellen*, where between Rae and Davis and Hawkins no one could truly be said to be in command, were now over. Commander Wilson imparted a decisiveness, hitherto lacking, into the conduct of the expedition. He would tow the *Hetty Ellen* back down the coast and if Livingstone could not be found he would himself provide a naval escort for the ladies from the crew of the *Gorgon*. He invited the ladies to sail in the

[1] SJ 8.1.62, p. 177 ff.

comforts of the *Gorgon*'s cabins, and Miss Mackenzie and Mrs Burrup accepted the kindness. Mrs Livingstone declined and preferred to remain alone amid the rolls and smells and discomforts of the *Hetty Ellen*.

The naval officers, delighted at the occasion of English society, set themselves to please. But like nearly everyone else, they shrank from sending the ladies up the Zambezi. Indeed Stewart, who at first did everything possible to avoid being introduced to Commander Wilson, but was captivated by his address and vigour, understood him to say privately that in his view the launching of this mission into the middle of Africa had been 'rash, premature, and wasteful of means'. He and his officers thought well of Stewart and the Free Kirk, because they planned a preliminary enquiry before they decided whether to send a mission or not. The paymaster of the *Gorgon* grumbled against the plan to which he was now an unwilling abettor—'not content to push a part of their people blindfold and almost purposeless into the wilds of South Africa, but adds to their distressing position by allowing a lot of helpless females, in their blind devotion, to accompany them.'[1] If Rae succeeds in what he has undertaken, thought the paymaster, if he succeeds in getting the ladies and the *Lady Nyassa* to their destinations, 'he will deserve a monument in the Institute of Civil Engineers; but I am afraid the obstacles will even overcome his energy, and that pieces of the steamer will be left here and there—small memorials, monuments of a great but wild endeavour . . . I pity the engineer, I pity the ladies.' He thought that the *Gorgon* was starting them off upon a 'death-march', and was indignant with the unknown men who had placed the ladies in such a position that their devotion compelled them to undertake it. They were deluded; and their husbands or brothers must be showing 'ignorance or want of proper feeling' in tempting them into this 'madness of a journey'. Every evening the officers played *Home, Sweet Home*, on the musical box in the mess, in the hope of persuading the ladies to turn back.

The naval officers discovered with amusement, and perhaps contempt, the 'schism' between the high church missionaries and the low church missionaries. 'I have had demonstrated to

[1] SJ 27.1.62, p. 207; Devereux, p. 164.

me by experience,' meditated the paymaster, 'that the smaller the society, the greater bickerings and splits there are.'[1]

Here are two different descriptions of a Sunday service held aboard the *Gorgon.*

Hawkins: 'I managed to get on board the *Gorgon*, in spite of a very heavy swell, which made getting in and out of the boats a work of difficulty. We had a very nice service on board: the men were very attentive, and there is something very pleasant in the scrupulous nicety and cleanliness of a man-of-war in its Sunday dress.'

Stewart: 'Hawkins appeared all glorious in white surplice and performed the service. The crew were all mustered. He preached a short sermon on the first few verses of Matthew 8, the narrative of the leper. The sermon was very much superior to what I expected, but he missed the important point in the subject so far as pressing home was concerned, or so far as it had any practical bearing on those present . . . But the drawling tone of his voice and his want of simplicity prejudiced the bulk of his audience against him. A few frank manly words would have done far more than all that long and wearisome series of endless repetition.'[2]

At Quilimane, whither the *Gorgon* towed *Hetty Ellen*, they heard news and rumours, news of Dr Livingstone and rumours of the mission. Only six days before, on 24 January, Colonel Nuñes had met Livingstone at the confluence of the Zambezi and the Shire, travelling downstream, and therefore he had possibly reached the Kongone. The rumours said that there had been fighting between the missionaries and the tribesmen; that Bishop Mackenzie and Dr Livingstone had begun to quarrel; that Mr Burrup was dead of fever. Though they hesitated to believe these reports, they could not help seeing them as clouds black with impending disaster. Even Stewart was disturbed and distressed for Mrs Burrup's sake. He was not surprised to hear that the Bishop and Livingstone had begun to fall out, he had prophesied that they would be unable to work together, and he could not quite avert a twinge of satisfaction. 'As to the fighting, that does not matter much. There will be a

[1] Devereux, pp. 166–7.

[2] Hawkins to G, 27.1.62; *Cape Monthly Advertiser*, 1862, p. 266; SJ 26.1.62, p. 206.

good deal of that sort of thing, and the sooner it is done, if it is well done, the better. The devil's spawn of slave-dealers will not allow such work as christianizing to go on quietly without having recourse to their own weapons.'[1]

They met Livingstone and his men in the *Pioneer* at the Luabo mouth of the Zambezi, on 1 February, upon a smooth and glassy sea. Livingstone greeted his wife with quiet affection and pored over her photographs of his children. Stewart looked at him with admiration, indeed with reverence, and was touched to the roots of his being when Livingstone said that he was glad to see him. But Livingstone was less cordial to Miss Mackenzie. In an inarticulate way he was vexed with the mission because it still needed his help to survive and he had perceived that he could not give that help. He was now vexed with Mackenzie for fighting the Ajawa. Though he had written his letter apparently approving of the fighting, he had heard fuller information when he met Mackenzie at Chibisa's and had ventured on a 'friendly disapproval'; and as the ship lay patiently on a sandbank in the Shire a few days later, he had written a letter to Lord John Russell (in which he told him that the expedition to Lake Nyasa had opened a cotton field 400 miles in length), reporting the fighting, carefully dissociating himself from the Bishop's policy, and expressing his regret for his part in the First Ajawa war. He had begun to think the missionaries rash and inexperienced. He said to Miss Mackenzie that he was aghast at the way they disregarded his warnings about the climate, and risked fever by exposing themselves to it. Altogether, Miss Mackenzie thought him 'rather abrupt and ungracious'.[2]

* * * * *

Commander Wilson was endowed with more initiative and resolution than any of the other whites now aboard the three vessels lying at the Zambezi mouth. Since British subjects were rumoured to be in danger among the mountains, and since it seemed to him more than doubtful whether the ladies would safely arrive at their destination, he determined to lead an armed band to the rescue. Even if no one required in the

[1] SJ 30.1.62. [2] Awdry, p. 235.

event to be rescued, the ladies would have safe escort and the show of British force among the mountains would inevitably help the mission in its difficulties with hostile tribesmen. While Rae and the others were unloading the pieces of the *Lady Nyassa* and the piles of mission stores from the hold of *Hetty Ellen* to the beach, Wilson was assembling and equipping fifty armed seamen. There was a rumour that the Bishop had been unable to fetch his sister because he was building stockades to fortify his station, another rumour that he was already besieged inside the stockade, perhaps, said lively imagination, by as many as a hundred fierce and well-armed Arabs. The naval officers were agog to go with Wilson on such a gallant campaign.

Hawkins was left in a tent on the island at the Kongone, near the guard-house of Mesquita and his dismal squad, to look after the huge pile of mission goods unloaded from the *Hetty Ellen* and impossible for the *Pioneer* to transport. One of the naval officers, Devereux, was surprised that Hawkins seemed to take his lot so philosophically—'luckily he has no idea of the hardships in store.' He was less surprised when he found Hawkins lying in his tent, a cask of Cape Pontac and a second cask of English beer to hand, reading the proofs of Bishop Colenso's new work on the Old Testament. Devereux was also surprised at the chaos of mission goods scattered over the beach—clothes, furniture, food, agricultural implements, cooking utensils, knick-knacks of every kind, necessities and luxuries jumbled together half-buried in sand, like goods without an owner. It distressed his orderly soul to think that a large proportion of them would be lost, 'or, at least, suffer deterioration from the want of means of conveyance, merely in consequence of not having a business-like man as manager at the outset. There seems to have been an utter want of geographical knowledge.' Devereux was not aware that the organizers in London saw a picture of the Zambezi different from the scene which met his gaze as he sauntered amidst an anarchy of packing-cases, marvelling at the incongruity between polished wardrobes and the misty swamp of mangrove and slime which surrounded him.[1] Some of the packing-cases were broken open. Both Livingstone and the crew of the *Gorgon* were short of food, and

[1] Devereux, pp. 172, 182, 186.

their quartermasters looked with interested eyes at the disordered plenty upon the beach. Dr Meller reported that Magomero was well-supplied for food, and that the Bishop, finding himself able to buy as many goats as he wished, had asked him to dispose of the preserved meat and biscuit. Confronted by this need and this report, the good-natured Miss Mackenzie, with a complaisant Hawkins, took it upon herself to distribute, with no parsimonious hand, from the mountain of untransportable stores. A bottle of port mysteriously vanished during a picnic; they suspected the Portuguese garrison—or perhaps sailors from the *Gorgon*, who bought bad liquor from Mesquita and ran wild.

Again the *Pioneer* was grossly overloaded, this time with the pieces of the *Lady Nyassa*'s hulk and such stores for the mission as Dr Livingstone felt able to carry. Livingstone was confident that the *Pioneer* would be able to carry the *Lady Nyassa* all the way to the Murchison Cataracts and there unload. The naval officers, on the contrary, prophesied gloomily that they would not be able to start. The *Pioneer* was crammed with people and stores and machinery, was going to tow a pair of boats from the *Gorgon* laden with more stores and the *Lady Nyassa*'s boilers, and was carrying the weight so ill-distributed that there was a pronounced list, with one paddle-wheel low in the water and the other high. Miss Mackenzie was distressed when Livingstone said that he had no room for Katie the donkey; so distressed that she persuaded Commander Wilson to intercede for her, and thereby secured the personal favour that Katie should be allowed to embark upon the *Pioneer*, as well as two mules and a farm-cart. The stem of the *Lady Nyassa* was stood upright upon the deck, and when decorated with curtains made a little hut or cabin for the ladies; but since almost every inch of floor was covered in luggage, they neither expected nor found comfort. The enthusiasm of the naval officers for the campaign began noticeably to wane when they discovered the conditions aboard the *Pioneer*, and at least one meditated asking Wilson's permission to return to the *Gorgon*. Mary Livingstone occupied the little cabin below decks with her husband. The port-holes being impossible to open because the ship was so low in the water, the only ventilation for the cabin was a hole in the deck.

Charles Livingstone decided that she should never have come to this 'execrable' accommodation. 'These hot nights the unfortunate couple are nearly melted, have now to open the door leading to our den. Dearly though I love my own wife, I should regret to see her in this hospital ship.' Even Anne Mackenzie, indomitable invalid though she was, had wavered for a moment into doubting whether this was a suitable expedition for women.[1] Mary Livingstone was more placid. She had come to join her husband and she was content to have found him. One of the men thought her 'a queer piece of furniture', but her comfortable, dumpy figure somehow slipped more quickly than the others into being a part of the expedition; and the cabin below decks, cramped and stuffy though it was, began to look habitable and inviting.

Till they had almost reached Shupanga, the journey was uneventful. They sailed up through the mangroves and the open savannahs, watching the hippopotamuses and the pelicans and the wild geese; they stuck once upon a sandbank; Sarah the maid became an object of adoration to a visiting African chief; a Portuguese bulldog on board fell through the glass skylight of the saloon during dinner and landed with his front paws in a glass of wine and a dish of mashed pumpkin, his hinder paws in the plates of Mrs Burrup and Mrs Livingstone. Progress was slow, too slow for the impatient ladies. Sometimes the list raised one of the paddle-wheels out of the water altogether, and drove the other so deep that it could scarcely turn in the water. Three days after the start the feed-pipe of the boilers burst, spraying scalding water in all directions, and had to be repaired at leisure. Four days after the start, on 13 February, they ran out of coal, and with this load the engines consumed the wood faster than they could cut it.

On 17 February Wilson determined that he would leave the *Pioneer* and push ahead with the ladies in the gig of the *Gorgon*. Even his own officers disliked the plan. Miss Mackenzie was already suffering from a bout of fever; and though Wilson was taking the *Gorgon*'s doctor, Ramsay, some of them doubted whether she would survive a journey of 200 miles up the Shire

[1] Charles Livingstone to his wife, Shupanga, 28.2.62 RL; Anne Mackenzie to Strong, 2.2.62, UMCA.

in an open boat. Devereux, the *Gorgon's* assistant paymaster, who was something of an amateur among naval officers, even criticized his own captain to Stewart, saying that Wilson was 'letting go the substance for the shadow', and 'leaving Dr Livingstone in the lurch'.[1] He thought that Wilson's proper duty was to safeguard and aid Livingstone's expedition, and not to gratify, from motives of gallantry, 'the impatience of two women who wish to shorten by one or two weeks the journey of a year.' He was responsible for loading the gig. 'I had to steel myself against their insinuating and earnest requests to arrange to "get this in"; then, when I thought all had been put away, when the box was already full, and I had encroached on Captain Wilson's share, found there was yet another "wee little thing", and then "only this one, *please* do", and finally, "now, dear Mr Devereux, can you manage to get this very last article in, I shall want it *so much*. I would rather have it in than all the other things if you could only just contrive . . ." At last I was obliged to close the box and rush away, as if running from a swarm of bees. In the morning, Captain Wilson told the ladies that he intended to drink, at least, a pint of the sourest vinegar to render him savage and proof against all entreaties.'

At five p.m., on 1 February, after a farewell dinner, the gig left for the Shire, carrying Miss Mackenzie, Mrs Burrup, Wilson, Ramsay, and eleven blue-jackets. They took with them the whaler of the *Gorgon* in charge of Lieutenant Sewell and with Kirk aboard as a guide. At Shupanga, Miss Mackenzie gained credit among the sailors by exchanging a few words in Zulu with some Kaffirs carrying assegais and knobkerries, and Mrs Burrup gained credit with the Kaffirs by letting down her hair suddenly so that the ends almost touched the ground. Once they lost their way in a channel near the mouth of the Shire; after a few days, through exposure during the day and mosquito-bites during the night, Miss Mackenzie became seriously ill; and when they arrived at the mouth of the Ruo, on 28 February, to keep the meeting arranged for New Year's Day, she was lying prostrate in the bottom of the gig and Sewell, at least, feared for her life.

At the village they enquired for news of the mission. They

[1] Devereux, pp. 211–4; SJW 13.

were disheartened when the villagers said they knew nothing and had never heard of any mission. Sewell being sent back with the whaler, Kirk transferred himself to the gig, and the gig pushed upward to Chibisa's. Kirk, who had enjoyed the masculine jollity of Sewell and the whaler, found the gig less comfortable. The whole stern was occupied by the prostrate figure of Miss Mackenzie, of whose presence Kirk disapproved in any case, thinking her infatuated to have come; if she wanted to move at all, she had to ask for assistance with her pillows. When they landed at night, they had first to construct a shelter for her and then carry her to it. She was in a melancholy mood, and talked of death with her jaws hanging down, asking whether people died on boats. Mrs Burrup on the contrary was full of life, 'talked nautical and jumped about'.[1]

They came in alongside the cliffs of Chibisa's in the darkness of 4 March. As they looked for a landing place, they saw a silhouette standing on the height, and hailed the man. He answered in a mixed dialect which Kirk recognized as that of the Makololo. It was Charlie, one of the three who had lived at the mouth of the Ruo with Mackenzie and Burrup. He came down to the boat and Kirk began to ask for news. When he enquired after the Bishop, 'to my horror I got the answer (in his native language), "He is dead."' Kirk shut the conversation instantly; but Miss Mackenzie, whether from the tone of voice, or because the Makololo dialect resembled the Zulu, began to suspect that something was wrong. Wilson and Kirk and Mrs Burrup climbed the cliffs to the village where the other Makololo gave them letters from Procter and others at Magomero to Livingstone. Kirk opened the letters, and so learnt everything, with the single exception of Burrup's death. None of them felt that he could tell Miss Mackenzie. They thought of the doctor, summoned him from the boat, and entrusted him with the grievous duty.

She was not one to allow the outside world to intrude upon her grief; the death of a beloved, the collapse of her *raison d'être* in Africa, perhaps of her *raison d'être* in life. Kirk, who half-resented her presence, found himself suddenly filled with admiration of her courage. The page of her diary was blotted

[1] K 27.2.62.

with tears, and the hand which wrote was quivering, but the words were restrained. 'Charlie said, "The Bishop was their father, now they had none; when they were sick, he nursed and looked after them; when they were cold, he gave them clothing. The others might be good, but they did not know them. The Bishop was their father and their friend, and he was gone from them . . ." My tie personally to the mission is ended. Of my loss I won't speak here.'[1] She could not walk again for more than three months. It appears that the one thought which kept welling up from her heart was this—'If only I could have been with him . . .'

The letters from Procter which Kirk had opened described a state of famine and suffering at Magomero. At noon, next morning, 5 March, two of the blue-jackets carried Miss Mackenzie up the steep pathway to the village and established her and Mrs Burrup in a hut under the care of Dr Ramsay. Then Wilson and Kirk set off, with a train of porters, a few Makololo, and five or six blue-jackets, to bring relief and supplies to Magomero and to bring Burrup down to Chibisa's. At Soché's, both Kirk and Wilson were suffering from throbbing heads and high temperatures, and they had no medicines with them. Kirk sent a note to Magomero by the Makololo Masaka asking for help and medicine and giving them the news of the ladies.

* * * * *

Mackenzie's death had left the little group of missionaries determined, but leaderless.

Before starting on the campaign against Manasomba, Mackenzie had made a formal will. He had established an order of succession to himself in the event of his death, an order which corresponded with the length of service in the ministry. According to this order Procter, as the priest of longest standing, was left in charge until a new bishop was appointed (if a new bishop was appointed). At the end of Evening Prayer on 14 February, Procter read this document to the others.

Livingstone, when he heard that Procter had become acting head, wondered whether he was fit for leadership. He thought that he would have made a good parish parson in England, but

[1] Awdry, p. 239.

doubted whether he had the personality for the severe and responsible post in which he unexpectedly found himself. He 'has not strength of character,' wrote Livingstone, 'perhaps not the power to bear down difficulties.'[1] Three months later, Livingstone was prepared to take a more favourable view of Procter's powers, but still he had qualms. 'The missionaries . . . want an energetic head. Mr Procter would make an excellent parish parson, but it is probable that he never anticipated being head of a mission. He is a good and sensible man of sufficient firmness, but fighting with the Ajawa put them all in a false position.'[2] Livingstone was not alone in being dubious. Anne Mackenzie, when she later met Rowley, Waller, and Scudamore at Chibisa's, thought that they were like sheep without a shepherd. Charles Livingstone, though he liked Scudamore immensely, thought that none of Mackenzie's subordinates was fit to be head of the mission. Rowley and Waller —Waller more than Rowley—shared something of the same opinion of Procter.

If others doubted about Procter, he certainly doubted about himself. He was an affectionate man, sensitive, and thin-skinned, possessed of a more elegant command of English prose, when he wanted, than any of the others. But among this group of men, whose inner opinions and thoughts are laid so unusually bare by the archives, Procter is the man of least colour, least vivacity. For most of his subsequent career in the Church of England he would drift gently, from curacy to curacy, like a piece of jetsam buffeted by the unpredictable billows of Anglican patronage. He springs to life in a letter from Charles Livingstone: 'Mr. Procter . . . a sleepy sort of fellow, a great eater, and very fond of jam and jelly.'[3] He had a light beard, a young-looking face, with no wrinkles on the forehead; he took snuff, was rather deaf, and played the flute. A tidy, gentle man, uncomplaining and charitable, somewhat passive, more apt to be led than to lead—everyone except Charles Livingstone liked him; Waller at first thought him to be the most congenial spirit of the whole party, and in his hyperbolical

[1] Livingstone to Maclear, 28.3.62, LJW ii. 366.
[2] Livingstone to Maclear, 21.6.62, LJW ii. 369.
[3] Charles Livingstone to Mrs Fitch, 9.1.62, CAA.

manner said, 'He and I are certainly most unanimous in our tenets—could not be more so—pure untrammelled free thought founded on love.'[1] By the end of the mission, Waller and Rowley, though so opposite that they could never be entirely easy in each other's company, had drawn together. Yet we may not leave Procter's character without recording a judgment passed after the tumult and the suffering were over. Kirk said that of all the survivors of Mackenzie, Procter was the man who seemed to have risen best to his position.

It is not easy to succeed a man whom everyone reveres as a martyr. Nor is it easy to succeed a leader whom everyone regards as a saint. When the news of Mackenzie's death reached Magomero, they thanked God spontaneously that he had been the man he was. There are always difficulties about being a locum tenens, about acting as head until the new and true head arrives. And Mackenzie's own conduct of the mission had not made Procter's task easier. Though he had dominated the little group, he had not established his dominance by reason of a powerful personality, or of unusual talents, or of a decisive mind, or by magnifying his episcopal order. He had made himself respected as a leader because his character was as pure as a running stream. They had never before met a man so selfless or with such simplicity of faith, and whether or not they thought his judgement wise, they trusted him absolutely. His leadership had been a moral leadership. In the constitution of the mission, he had behaved as though he had no power at all. He had always treated them as a community wherein the opinion of the youngest must be allowed full weight. He acted as though he were the chairman of a little democracy of intimate friends. And so his authority had rested more upon his person than upon his office. Though Procter was not compelled to sit in the seat of an overriding personality, it was almost more difficult for a lesser man to succeed to an office which had been so minimized as to be almost invisible. Mackenzie would have approved of the Polynesian saying that the voice of the chief should be small.

Procter made his task no easier, soon after Burrup's death, by declaring in conversation that he expected to go home as soon as a new bishop was appointed.

[1] Cf W 24.11.60; Steere to his wife 28.5.63 UMCA.

Only an agreement between those two strong personalities, Waller and Rowley, was needed to oust him, or at least, to diminish his authority. Rowley, who was not so shocked as Waller by the confession that he was ready to go home, saw that Procter's unexpected headship was as trying to him as it was to them, and was prepared to rally and strengthen his hand. But on 3 March, during one of those conversations, round and round, wherein they thrashed out the future of the mission, a fortunate turn brought up the subject of their constitution. Waller saw his opportunity and spoke out. He supposed that he spoke with 'extreme delicacy' to avoid hurting Procter's feelings. But he was under an illusion about his own tact. 'Although,' he said, 'as far as order and custom go, I should be very anxious the poor Bishop's express wish should be carried out as regards his successor, I should never consent to allow Procter's position to be that from which orders are to come on anything like serious matters, should they be contrary to my own convictions in dealing with the welfare of the mission.' He was relieved when Rowley half-supported him, saying, 'The Bishop did but say he *wished* the members of the mission to act under the temporary headship of the senior priest, acting with the advice of the other priests . . . This is but to be taken for what it says, I imagine.'[1]

The mission thereby became an anarchy of friends. Waller silently congratulated himself, 'for the sake of all of us', on the ease with which he had surmounted the obstacle.

In any little group, whatever the constitution or absence of constitution, there will be a measure of leadership according to the strength of the various personalities. Scudamore, though the only other graduate of Cambridge besides Mackenzie, was no leader. Everyone is agreed that he was the most lovable character among the survivors, a man of whimsical mind and pure heart, a big, friendly, smiling ox of a man of poor sight and extreme diffidence, and often forgetful or absent-minded. They always thought of him as 'dear Scudamore', and yet it moved insensibly into 'dear old Scudamore'. And therefore the leadership slowly passed into a debate between Waller and Rowley, who upon many questions were likely to take opposite views.

[1] W 3.3.62.

Waller was a young Victorian knight-errant, a militant Christian, an evangelical of faith and courage. You could imagine him charging on the field of Naseby with Cromwell's cavalry—a deeply religious, loyal, open-hearted man of dash; no Puritan indeed—he relished his port, or his brandy, or his pombi as well as any man, he loved the artists if they were landscape-painters, he had an eye for the beauties in the intricate designs of nature, observing with a numinous sense of wonder the bees' wings and the gay striped colours of the African birds or butterflies; a man with the empire-building simplicity of the Scot, he would question and grumble at his own weakness, but would engage in the highest cause without questioning whether the cause was practicable; a bad politician or diplomat, a hater of compromise, he saw heroes as heroes and villains as villains, he eyed the world in colours of black and white and rarely in grey; a mastiff who would fasten his teeth with unsophisticated purpose and hold till he dropped where he stood; a born camper, in whom the scent of wood-fire and cooking pots evoked ecstasy; who enjoyed rough-and-tumble, and the wearing of old coats, Turkish hats and Highland plaids and deerstalkers; a hairy, tweedy man; a man whose clasp-knife was a friend as well as a tool. It was characteristic of him that he carried his personal possessions, not like everyone else in a portmanteau, but in a fishing-basket.

Rowley, with his shiny bald head, was nearly eight years older than Waller, and he was married (to a wife crippled by a spinal infection), and had that maturity which marriage brings. He was too odd, too angular, too individual to be a fine leader of men; he was the last man you would imagine at the head of a cavalry charge. Where Waller's religion was somehow laic, even though he was later to be ordained, Rowley the deacon had already a touch of the ecclesiastic. He was interested in man as a religious animal, uninterested in the geography or the natural history which were Waller's primary enjoyments. Though they had both come to the Zambezi in the pursuit of a Christian cause, they would have expressed their motives a little differently. Waller would have put as his first aim to destroy the slave-trade, and creating a Christian community was the means. Rowley would have put as his first aim to create a Christian congregation, an African Church, and the destruction of the slave-trade was a necessary means to that end. Rowley possessed a harder head, at times a streak of cynicism, which cut through sentiment and vague idealism and the muddled thinking which sometimes masquerades as piety, with cool and often unpalatable douches of common sense; he could see, too clearly, when Waller's fervour was degenerating into a puppy enthusiasm. Rowley would see an ideal to be desirable but impracticable, he would be more content with the possible, would more readily abandon an aim which he believed to be now impossible to achieve. He knew that men are complicated, that heroes, even though they are heroes, are sometimes constructed with one foot of clay, that villains can often be kindly husbands and fathers. Waller supposed that men were uncomplicated because he was altogether uncomplicated himself. Rowley knew that men are complicated partly because he was himself a little complicated. Though they both loved their Africans they loved them in different ways. Waller loved them first as a cause, as a people and an embodied ideal, he looked upon them somewhat as a selfless and benevolent prince looks upon the citizens for whom he must care, he would not probe their inmost hopes and fears and agonies. Rowley's power of sympathy was more personal. He agonized not so much with the cause as with Jessiwiranga and Wekotani and Chesika; suffering was to be understood as well as fought.

One last difference, which sums them up: Waller, when he was angry, grew hotter and began to shout. When Rowley was angry, his speech became icier and more controlled.

* * * * *

As the debates at Magomero circled upon their mentally exhausting roundabout, the divergence between the two men came into the open. Waller believed that it was their duty to stay where they were, or as near as possible to where they were, until ordered to move. Procter and Scudamore agreed that this was the course which Mackenzie would have wished. Rowley, though not contemptuous, thought this attitude romantic, quixotic. He could not see what good it was to their people if the white men starved or sickened at their post, and with a cool, determined logic he pressed for withdrawal, at least sufficient withdrawal to shorten the lines of communication. He was the stronger in argument because everyone admitted that they could not remain in Magomero. Dr Dickinson had condemned the station on ground of health.

During December and January, they had suffered from famine or near-famine in Magomero. They were short of cloth and of everything else, except a few tins of preserved meat and biscuit which they kept in reserve. The only diet which they had for their people was pumpkins, in which there was little nourishment. The adults knew how to supplement their pumpkins with roots, but the children lived only upon pumpkins and the effect upon their health was altogether deplorable. Ulcers which had seemed to be responding to treatment now began to worsen under the condition of emaciation in which some children found themselves. The whites, though they borrowed cloth off Livingstone and off the Makololo (who had taken it from a slaving party), could not buy enough food nearby since the other villages in the highlands were suffering a worse shortage than Magomero. The whites themselves found the diet of pumpkins, goats' meat, and (after the coming of the crop in February) new corn, trying to the constitution, and they suffered endemically from diarrhoea. Fifty women and children died in the camp at Magomero during those months of insufficient food. With so much dysentery, and so few adults to supervise, it was impossible to provide, or to enforce, adequate sanitary arrangements for the Africans. Unless they were watched and disciplined they would excrete in the corners of their huts, and the rain helped to turn the stream, which was their drinking water, into a kind of sewer. Down in its hollow Magomero seemed to retain all the foulnesses of the air; and as early as 17 December Dickinson had driven them to agree to move to higher ground, 'annoying as it is to have spent so much labour in vain . . .' They could not enter Magomero without feeling that they had been robbed of their vitality, and without finding their physical powers reduced to a low ebb.[1] By April, there was only one survivor of the infants' class in the boys' school. Two or three boys ran away to sell themselves as slaves in exchange for food.

[1] R 233, 254, 285.

Waller's Journal:

24 January 1862. 'The ants fairly took possession of the storehouse today, and no-one could enter without suffering a good deal. These wretches are most curious in their habits. A distinct species they are with large flat heads, with an enormous pair of jaws like pointed pincers. You see them crossing paths in strings of myriads. To tread on them is to find your ankles and boots covered in an instant, each ant immediately sacrifices every other consideration to getting at your shins and legs as soon as he can . . . To get them out of the beard and hair is a task indeed.'

25 January 1862. '. . . Poor Angulembi died in the night, a most merciful release. This morning the body presented one of the most distressing appearances I ever saw. The vast colony of ants that has been parading about for some days had found him out and the head, face, feet, and parts of the body were almost invisible for the festoons of these wretches.'

By 14 February, the new crop was coming in plenty and the danger was over. The gardens of their people could now be harvested, and the whites told them that henceforth they must live off their own produce, unless they were children or sick. The English wheat failed because in ignorance they had sowed it too early, and it was destroyed by the force of the tropical rain; but the barley and oats flourished, and of the Indian corn there was abundance. Though they were now physically capable of moving camp, their plans for a move, perhaps to Mongazi's, on higher ground a day nearer Chibisa's, were brought to an abrupt change by the news of the Bishop's death.

They now felt utterly isolated from human aid. Where Livingstone was they knew not. They were reaching almost their last supplies of cloth, and they saw no means to additional supplies unless someone went down the river. He must canoe or walk to Sena and then seek Portuguese aid to find transport to Quilimane. Livingstone had warned them to have no dealings whatsoever with the Portuguese—his exploration of the Rovuma had been designed with the object of avoiding all such dealings—and they could not help feeling that the action at Mbami's, of releasing slaves owned by Portuguese citizens, would not have endeared them to the Portuguese authorities. 'Honour,' wrote Waller on his birthday, 16 February, 'forbids our going to ask favours of them whose dealings were upset by us.'[1] There seemed however to be no alternative; and they agreed that as a first measure in the emergency one of their number should go to Sena.

By 3 March, everyone except Waller believed that unless communications with the outside world could be restored, or placed for the first time upon a reasonable base, the mission must retire from the Shire and retreat to Quilimane, or even to Natal, or the Cape. Waller, withdrawing step by step from his entreaties that they might all remain, pressed them to leave even one white man in Magomero—'his presence here would at all events be as it were a low smouldering fire which new-comers would at once d.v. resuscitate.' He argued that if they now abandoned the Zambezi, the committee at home would probably be daunted by the deaths and the perils of supply, would refrain from renewing the mission at all, and would transfer them to somewhere safer and more convenient, perhaps, he said contemptuously, 'to a colonial station, with a railway'. He agreed that the committee could not maintain so many white missionaries so far away from the coast. But 'it resolves itself into the question of supplies. It is evident to me that my comrades imagine it to be impossible we can exist without a very large quantity of European eatables, etc. I on the contrary, believe in a healthy situation and native produce, a moderate supply of things from any man-of-war or colonial town being added. I think it cannot be expected of those who came out merely for five years and were given to understand there would be pretty regular half-yearly communications with the civilized world, ladies in the party, and suchlike easy-going matters, I say it can hardly be expected that they should like to stop with such a very altered state of things.'[2]

* * * * *

Their deliberations, and their sense of isolation, were shattered on 8 March, by a letter from Kirk telling them that he and Wilson were sick, without medicines, at Soché's village, and

[1] W 16.2.62; he was twenty-nine that day.

[2] W 3.3.62.

asking for help. Scudamore, Rowley, and Waller set out within an hour, carrying medicine and some of the tins of preserved meat which they had reserved for an emergency.

Kirk, when he opened the letters from Procter and others to Livingstone, had received the 'general' impression that the missionaries were starving, and it was only his conviction of their desperate plight that led him and Wilson to climb the slopes, with sickness upon them, to Mbami's and Soché's. 'The letters from the mission,' confided Kirk to his diary, 'represented their state as one of prostration from disease and famine.' The letter or letters which gave him this impression are not extant; the journals of Waller and Rowley show that all danger of famine had been averted three weeks before. Doubtless Procter had written under the sense of calamities around them, the death of the leader and of Burrup, the plague which had carried off so many women and children, the dysentery of Rowley, the feeling that they would soon be tearing up their shirts for cloth.

Kirk was shocked and irritated (the fever was still on him, and he was afraid for Wilson's life) to discover that they were not starving at all and that his expedition of humanity was useless. 'To our surprise, instead of haggard, starved men they seemed all in tolerable health, Scudamore had lost his wonted life, but Rowley and Waller seemed well and stout . . . We had been accustomed to a scanty diet of beans, goat, and possibly boiled plantain, scanty because sick men can take but little of such food. To our astonished olfactory nerves the missionaries had served up a savoury dish of preserved meats, followed by tea. Lucky dogs, we thought, if this is what you call starving, in fact, on further questioning, they had goats, preserved meats, tea, and coffee in abundance.'[1]

Kirk and Wilson kept their criticism to themselves, and so never discovered, either that the missionaries were thinking in terms of feeding not only themselves but a number of sick and helpless Africans, or that the preserved meats which so astonished them had been carefully kept back for this sort of occasion.

At Mbami's, on 10 March, Wilson and Kirk were well enough to confirm to the missionaries their worst fears about their

[1] K 9.3.62.

communications. The missionaries in their isolation had been hoping against hope that the *Pioneer* would soon be able to reopen their life-line with the sea and keep it regularly open. Wilson and Kirk agreed that the hope was vain. The *Pioneer*, even supposing that Livingstone were to hand it over to them when he had placed the reconstructed *Lady Nyassa* on Lake Nyasa, would be incapable of making regular journeys up and down the Shire; her draught was such that almost all her journeys would be from sandbank to sandbank. If the mission was to survive, it could do so in only two ways: either by possessing a steamer of its own, which would mean a visit to the Cape by a missionary to arrange; or by arranging for regular supplies in canoes, which would mean fraternizing with the Portuguese, with whom Livingstone had strenuously urged them not to fraternize. Waller, who shared Livingstone's attitude to the Portuguese, determined at all costs to avert the second alternative; he would himself go to the Cape to arrange for a steamer. He hurried ahead to Chibisa's to arrange for a canoe.

It was ironic that Kirk thought Waller to be a deserter. He supposed that Waller's hurry to be away to the Zambezi and the Cape was a mere pretext for desertion. He saw traces of the controversy between Waller and Rowley, which were too patent among the weary men. Rowley at first supported the theory that Waller should go to the Cape; and Kirk, remembering the mock-vehemence of the ecclesiastical debates on the *Pioneer*, thought that Rowley really wanted to be rid of Waller because as a high churchman he would be content to be without the low churchman. Kirk argued with Rowley that if he disapproved of Waller's plans for the mission it would be a foolish mistake to allow him to go to the outside world, where his word would be taken as the only evidence available. Rowley took the point. He caught Waller up at Chibisa's and said that he and Scudamore now thought it useless for Waller to go to the Cape, since Wilson knew all the facts and had promised himself to put them before the committee on his arrival.

Waller, unaware that he was now suspected of being a deserter, refused what he took to be a 'kind' suggestion. No one but a man who had been through what they had been through could understand their predicament, and his was the duty, as the organizer of the mission's administration, to lay these matters before the committee. All day on 12 March, he struggled to persuade paddlers to take him down the river. Wilson told him there was no room in the gig. The Makololo refused to paddle him; and he had no idea that Kirk had ordered the Makololo to refuse to paddle him in order to frustrate his plan to 'desert'. The little controversy between Rowley and Waller almost came to an open quarrel. Rowley gave Wilson a letter for the Bishop of Cape Town and the committee, asserting that Waller was acting entirely on his own responsibility and without the approval of his companions in the mission. Kirk thought that Scudamore was the only missionary among the survivors who wanted the mission to continue. He later passed to Livingstone an account of a little scene at Chibisa's: 'Rowley said to Kirk and Wilson in hearing of Miss Mackenzie: "You need not be surprised if some fine day you find us off from this." Scudamore, a real brick, replied, "Never." '[1]

Miss Mackenzie was grateful that Scudamore should have brought down her brother's Bible and Keble and papers. But it is not surprising that even through her tears she should have formed the impression of a mission degenerating into a flock of sheep without a shepherd.

* * * * *

Wilson, ill though he was, hastened to be off down the river. He was short of food and supplies for the blue-jackets in the gig, and he knew that he had already been absent for too long from the *Gorgon*. With the two stricken ladies and Ramsay and Kirk, he rowed away downstream; and Waller, who had at last found some Manganja to take his cloth and succeeded in borrowing a small canoe, followed them a few hours later. Downstream he changed the little canoe for the bigger canoe which Mackenzie and Burrup had overturned and which Burrup had been forced by the Makololo to abandon, tied to the bank.

At the Ruo mouth, Wilson and Kirk landed and went into the village. The chief 'came trembling towards us, not knowing exactly how we would receive him. Being thanked for his kind-

[1] W 12.3.62; K 11.3.62; LJW ii. 366 (Livingstone to Maclear, 28.3.62).

ness he seemed relieved, and a reprimand for keeping him in ignorance of the facts brought out the letter written by Mr Burrup before starting. We got a man to show us the grave. It was on the mainland near a few snags which obstruct the river. It is to the west of a borassus palm and underneath a mimosa tree. The path was so entangled that Miss Mackenzie could not be taken up to it. The earth was raised, and from a thick bamboo, Wilson and I made a rude cross which we stuck at the feet.'[1]

Livingstone was kindness itself when Miss Mackenzie and Mrs Burrup were carried, grey and silent and prostrate, over the side of the *Pioneer* at Shupanga. Anne Mackenzie captured his allegiance by telling him that she meant to spend her strength and give her life to Africa. Mary Livingstone proved to be a solid, strengthening, affectionate body upon whom Mrs Burrup, at least, was ready to lean for comfort, and officers who found her weeping hurried below to fetch Mrs Livingstone to her; and the older woman would take the head of the younger on her bosom and comfort her like a child.

Livingstone perceived the blow to his own hopes. He sat with his head on his hand at the table in the gloomy little cabin on the *Pioneer*, and said, 'This will hurt us all.' But this was an immovable man. 'I shall not swerve a hairbreadth from my work while life is spared'—in some men the affirmation would be a form of self-encouragement, a spur to faith, a piece of romanticism, a sign of weakness. In Livingstone it was prose.[2]

Meanwhile, at Senhor Vianna's near Mazaro, the blue-jackets from the *Gorgon* had run amok. Lieutenant Sewell warned Vianna not to sell them spirits, *agua ardente*, hoggydent as the blue-jackets named it, 'or they would pull his village down and him too'. He sold them spirits, and drunken English sailors ravaged his furniture and beat his person. In the huts they found African women, and wrought their animal will upon them.

[1] K 12.3.62.

[2] Livingstone to Robert Moffat, 25.10.62, LJW ii. 221; Coupland, *Kirk*, pp. 228–9; Stewart in *Sunday Magazine*, November 1874, p. 93.

V
THE RIFT

By violent exhortations to his paddlers, Waller reached Shupanga on 17 March, only three days after Wilson and the gig. Shupanga lay on the south bank of the river, hard by a fair copse of mangroves. About a hundred yards from the beach, and up a gentle slope, in an arc of deep woodland, stood a house of stone, with white-washed walls and a roof of brown tile. The house was dirty, unkempt, unfurnished, the windows had no sashes; but it was a haven for the expedition, with its view across the broad expanse of the river away up to the square-headed massif of Mount Morambala towering into the clouds thirty miles away.

The *Pioneer* had arrived at Shupanga on 23 February. While Wilson pushed ahead up the Shire in the gig, Livingstone was preparing to carry the *Lady Nyassa* to the Murchison Cataracts. Wilson had not believed it to be possible; and before the end of February, even Livingstone recognized that the *Pioneer*, with her perilous list and with the river falling daily, could not sail up the Shire with the *Lady Nyassa* aboard. For ten days they tried their old devices with sandbanks and then abandoned the struggle. And so Livingstone decided to return to Shupanga, unload the pieces of the *Lady Nyassa*, fit them together, and then tow the ship up the Shire. For him it was a sad disappointment and disaster, denying him the ascent to Lake Nyasa until the river rose again early in 1863.

When Waller reached Shupanga in his canoe, he found that Livingstone had taken the ladies down to the Kongone. But he met Rae, left behind to begin the work upon the pieces of the *Lady Nyassa*, and Stewart with him. Stewart's description of the meeting is characteristic:

'As Rae and I were sitting at tea a shout was heard and, on looking out, an Englishman, recognizable enough from the cut of his dress and the gait and air, was walking up the river side.

I thought he was Waller, Rowe called out, "Rowley." To my relief it was the former, much, I must say, better pleased with W. than that queer fish, Rowley. Long talk on many points connected with the mission and other subjects till 10 o'clock. His visit seemed like the visit of a friend at home. I forgot I was in Africa.'[1]

It should be observed that Stewart had never before met either Waller, to be glad to see him, or Rowley, to suppose that he was a queer fish. But he had lived on the *Pioneer* with Charles Livingstone, and had imbibed the gossip of the ship's crew. The conversation on the party, Stewart found, was often disparaging to the missionaries.

For Waller discovered, as he waited with Rae and Stewart at Shupanga, that the attitude of Dr Livingstone towards the mission seemed to have undergone an astonishing revolution. When last Waller had met the Doctor, he had been friendliness itself. Now, according to Stewart and Rae, he had not a good word to say for it. When he heard the news that Mackenzie and Burrup were dead, he had let forth the unsentimental comment that England would send out better men—a comment which he even made in the hearing of the afflicted Miss Mackenzie. It troubled Waller to his depths. He regarded Livingstone as the hero who was leading this crusade for humanity. 'I am disturbed beyond measure to think the Doctor can be so vacillating as to allow his mind to be set against us by sidewinds and uncharitable reports, it seems certain such is really the case.'[2]

What had caused it? What uncharitable reports were these? As he pieced together the evidence—and Rae was a man who talked too much whenever he was given a chance—Waller came to the conclusion that Mary Livingstone was the impetus to the change. 'From what Rae says, I have no doubt a great coolness has arisen towards us and if his surmises are true, Mrs Livingstone has been the cause. She herself having stated at N[atal] that she would upset us indeed, that this process had already begun.' Waller would later learn that Rae liked to make his hearers' blood curdle, and that as he had contributed to the

[1] SJW 17.3.62, p. 35; Waller's description of the same meeting, W 17.3.62.
[2] Waller 28.3.62, MSS. Afr. s. 16/4 (11).

strife between Hawkins and Stewart by spreading rumours about the one to the other, so he was now contributing stimulus to the conversation by spreading 'surmises' about Dr Livingstone to Waller. But Waller, though he did not perceive the quality of exaggeration in Rae's talkativeness, could not doubt that there was substance in the story. Stewart confirmed it; and it is to Stewart's credit, that though on the *Hetty Ellen* he had wanted and hoped for an estrangement between Dr Livingstone and the Anglican missionaries, he showed no desire to gloat or triumph now that an estrangement had come.

'Stewart,' wrote Waller, 'entered into a strange explanation this morning [11 April], relative to a statement in a letter of the Doctor. It was that the missionaries, dead, would be replaced by better men. This, he assures me, means men that he, Stewart, would bring out (?), that the word better was often used as a common expression between them, and in fact that the words did not mean what they said. He was most anxious about this, I had not noticed it nor heard of it before. The same expression had been used before Miss Mackenzie while Stewart was there another time and had evidently attracted notice. It is a most awkward one, and I do not thoroughly understand the matter, although I cannot believe the Doctor would hurt anyone's feelings in such a way.'[1]

Waller only wavered for a few days in his allegiance to Livingstone. So far as he could discover, there were four chief reasons for the coolness.

First, Rowley had sent back from the Kongone, in February, 1861, an article which his wife had published. In this article, written still from offshore, he had advertised the Kongone mouth with its bar as altogether unsuitable for a 'highway for commerce and Christianity', and had thereby implicitly blamed Livingstone for the enthusiasm of *Missionary Travels* which had projected these various bands of Englishmen into the interior of Africa. This news had reached Livingstone when he came downstream at the beginning of 1862. His language about Rowley suddenly became, for Livingstone, severe, and contemptuous ('a sad, blethering fellow')—surprisingly, for Livingstone was not a man to be contemptuous of human beings, even

[1] Waller, MSS. Afr. s. 16/4 (11), Misc. notes.

if they suffered the disadvantage of being whites. Rae, anxious to impress Waller, told him that 'the Doctor was quite pale when talking about it'.

Secondly, Livingstone was now sure that he disapproved of the fight against the Ajawa. He did not see how his own actions had led the missionaries into a situation where fighting seemed the natural and right course. But he remembered that he had told them never to fight except in self-defence; he was afraid of damage to the white name and reputation by what had been done, he had written home to the Foreign Secretary to discover whether his authority as Her Majesty's Consul extended to jurisdiction over an English bishop nearby and engaging in warfare.

Thirdly, Wilson and Kirk had brought back a discouraging picture of the missionaries from their expedition with the ladies to Chibisa's. It was not an unfavourable picture of what had been done at Magomero—on the contrary, if anything, the picture seemed too roseate, a picture of a happy little community, slowly learning manners and morals and self-support under English guidance. But Wilson and Kirk had gained the impression that Waller certainly, and probably Rowley and Procter soon, wanted to desert the mission under its calamities. Wilson and Kirk had given Livingstone the most unfavourable picture of Waller's attempts to come down the river; Livingstone had no use for anyone who was not ready to give his bones to Africa, and his opinion of the English missionaries sank. He thought that if this were true they were hardly worthy of the name of missionaries, and men of a more missionary spirit, doubtless from other denominations than the Anglican, must come out and take their place. These were men who had committed themselves for a paltry five years, while stipends piled up in their banks at home. It was agreeable to this view that he had received appeals for help and supplies from the mission which were almost desperate; yet Wilson and Kirk had returned reporting that they were well off, better off than he was himself. Wilson and his officers, amongst the drunken piles of packing-cases littering the beach at Kongone, and after being forced to order the flogging of four sailors for breaking into the liquor, were convinced that the mission was hasty, improvident, and ill-managed. Waller heard that Wilson had reported the mission to have spent already £70,000.

This was not true. But neither Waller nor anyone else on the Zambezi had any means of contradicting it.

And fourthly, David Livingstone was curiously and sometimes disastrously susceptible to the influence of his brother. Charles Livingstone had determined that he disliked missionaries. When Stewart said that on the *Pioneer* he heard no good word spoken about the mission, it is certain that Charles was the fountain-head of the carping. He did not confine his criticisms to the Anglican missionaries. In his eyes Stewart was as bad. For the first time in the journals we find condemnations of Stewart as strong as those with which on the *Hetty Ellen* Stewart himself had denounced Hawkins. 'What is this Mr Stewart? None of us like him. Is he a humbug, or does he really mean to be a missionary? . . . Her Majesty's exploring ships are no places for missionaries, real or false. We have no room for them. They eat up all the nice things and we can't get them replaced.'[1] By this constant attitude articulate in the brother whom he trusted, Livingstone could not help being influenced.

Waller wrote to Magomero, explaining that Livingstone now condemned their fighting. He could do nothing else until Livingstone returned from the Kongone. He thought it probable that the deaths would work a 'revulsion' in favour of the mission. He felt it almost intolerable that the members of the expedition should have trusted them so little as to refuse the request for a passage down to the Kongone. As he brooded at Shupanga, this was the burden which weighed heavily upon him. It was not a matter of mere personal relations, of a coolness which was unfortunate but could be borne. If Livingstone refused further aid to the mission, the mission was perhaps finished.

As he whiled away the time shooting or reading *Heartsease* ('a poor twaddling novel') he was becoming intimate with Stewart. Waller had none of the scruples of Hawkins. 'I frankly and fully told Stewart all the opinions I held on the country . . . besides stating distinctly my *individual* reasons for giving him all

[1] Charles Livingstone to Fitch, 16.3.62, CAA.

the help I could inasmuch as he came to me with the passport that gained admittance for anyone bearing it to the Christian's presence, I mean the common cause, our dear Lord's Gospel. Coming with this I have withheld nothing that I thought might be of use to him. He thanked me cordially and deplored the escape of words from his lips at Natal before two people.'[1] Stewart was beginning to soften in friendliness towards the Universities Mission. On one occasion, to his own surprise, he found himself reading the service from the Book of Common Prayer for Waller's benefit.

On 10 April, news at last arrived of the *Pioneer* downstream. Waller determined to descend to the Kongone to shepherd the surviving stores of the mission, and incidentally to meet Livingstone and straighten the tangle into which the relations of mission and expedition seemed to have been twined. Two days later, at eight-thirty a.m., his canoe met the *Pioneer* on her way upstream, but motionless because she had stuck upon the inevitable sandbank. To Waller's delight as he climbed aboard, Livingstone showed no trace whatsoever of the alleged hostility to the mission of which he had learnt at Shupanga. 'Dr exceeding kind to me,' he noted. It was true that a few days later he found the Doctor 'much annoyed about Miss Mackenzie and Hawkins' and therefore it was to be presumed that Mary Livingstone had expressed some of the views which she had threatened to express.

But Waller had his own reasons for vexation with Miss Mackenzie and Hawkins. He had discovered from the reports the disaster which had befallen the mission in the loss of the stores at the Kongone. It seemed to him that Miss Mackenzie and Hawkins, who should have been looking after them, had been too generous in supplying the needs of the *Gorgon*; that they had distributed with a lavish imprudence, because they could not conceive the dire needs of the mission. Then the sailors had

[1] W 31.3.62. Stewart's account of the same conversation, SJW, p. 41: 'In the morning I had a long talk with Waller. Got him to go over the queries with me and to give me the benefit of his experience. We talked over the subject of my former verdicts on the O.C.M. I expressed my regrets for anything that had escaped me and told him that I thought I had said enough to convince him what my feelings were on the subject *now*. In fact, in reference to many of those things, the best way is to be imperturbable to the last degree . . .'

broken into the boxes in pursuit of liquor, and Portuguese and African thieves had pecked at the broken boxes like vultures round decaying flesh. 'I find all the wine that is left us is about three-quarters of a barrel of Pontac, thus 5¼ besides a large quantity of beer was got through down at the bar.' Waller wrote indignantly home to the committee in London. The trouble was that if this was supposed to be a free gift by the mission to the expedition—and so it appeared to have been treated by Miss Mackenzie and Hawkins—there was no reason why the Admiralty should refund any of the cost of it. 'Downright robbery,' said the naval officer, Young, who had now officially joined the expedition after having been one of the volunteers from the *Gorgon* for the river journey. Out of fifty boxes of flour landed at the Kongone, no more than eight ever reached Chibisa's; none of the biscuits or salt meat ever arrived. When Wilson's expedition returned with the ladies to the Kongone, they found that the *Gorgon*, with a sick Hawkins aboard, had been forced to put to sea in a storm, and for nearly three weeks there were more than seventy hungry sailors needing food and medicines. Whatever the causes or the extenuating reasons, Waller believed that it was a disaster to the mission second only to the deaths of Mackenzie and Burrup. And Rowley later believed that the decline in the healths of the whites at Chibisa's was due to the absence of an English diet and the forced adherence to native food for which their constitutions were unfitted. 'Pumpkins, cucumber, and new corn are delicious things when you do not have too much of them, but they do not form the best of food for men worn by hard work, exposure, fever, and dysenteric complaints. Our breaking-in to native diet was too severe. It annoyed one to be continually obliged to think of what we could eat, what we could not eat, or whether we could eat at all. I suffered less than most; but it was very painful to see some of my brethren enduring, and sinking, under illnesses which would have been avoided altogether, or from which they would readily have recovered, had they had proper food. I blame no individual in saying what I do . . . but as the loss of these stores entailed much privation, and extraordinary exertions, which aggravated the natural difficulties of our position, and helped to fatal issues, I cannot avoid the responsibility of detailing what we justly regarded as one of our most serious misfortunes.'[1]

* * * * *

On 4 April, the *Gorgon* put off for the Cape, bearing Mrs Burrup, Miss Mackenzie, still unable to walk though now able to be a little more cheerful, a Hawkins afflicted with ulcers all over the body and seriously ill, Jessie Lennox the housekeeper and Sarah the maid. On 14 April, the *Pioneer* reached Shupanga again, and the work of fitting the *Lady Nyassa* together continued apace.

On 25 April, Mary Livingstone fell ill of fever; she was living ashore with the Doctor in a tent, and on the 26th was moved into the quarters of Stewart and Waller at Shupanga house. Stewart thought her face was changing and began to worry. At seven p.m. on 27 April she died, in spite of everything that Kirk could do. Stewart, who still believed that Livingstone was barely well-disposed towards him, was thankful that the Doctor summoned him for the commendatory prayers. 'I had gone down to the ship to get some tea at 6 o'clock, when a message was brought by Rowe that the Doctor wished me to come up. I went at once, but hardly guessing for what. When I went into the room, Dr L. said that the end was evidently drawing near and he had sent for me . . .' They noticed in her dying face how extraordinarily like she became to her father, Moffat. 'The Doctor was weeping like a child. I could not help feeling for him and found my eyes full before I was aware. He asked me to commit her soul to her Maker by prayer. He, Dr Kirk, and I kneeled down and I prayed as best I could . . . In the morning, Charles Livingstone read prayers on board ship. It seemed odd to me that he should have done it. But what happened in the evening set my mind at rest. Out of all the ship's company—

[1] R 286–7; Waller 15.4.62, 22–3.4.62. Waller wrote from Chibisa's (29.5.62, Bishopscourt) to Gray of Cape Town to ask that the naval authorities at Simon's Bay should replace the goods given to the *Gorgon*—'and as the freight paid by the time they got to the Kongone must have well nigh doubled their value this also should be taken into consideration. But it is a delicate matter and the other clause had better not be alluded to as much blame lies with others than the *Gorgon*'s crew. The countenance of the Admiralty is everything to us and must not be jeopardized. No list or notification of any sort has been sent to us of what they took.'

except Dr Kirk, who was attending all day—I alone was sent for to be with the Doctor in this hour of sorrow and trouble. This so far set my mind at rest as to the position I occupied. There [were] C.L., his brother, and Rae, his companion for four years; there was Waller and Young: but no; I, who was supposed by most on board to be *nobody*, came in at the trying hour. It was altogether a day to remember, this long, bright, hot, and clear Sabbath at Shupanga.'[1] Rae having made a coffin during the night, they buried her under the huge baobab tree, sixty feet in circumference, between the house and the village. The grave was dug deep to prevent wild beasts and natives disturbing the body. Behind the two Livingstones in the funeral procession came Waller, Kirk, Stewart, and Young —four men who twelve years later would follow the coffin of the husband up the aisle of Westminster Abbey, each of them thinking of the far-away grave up the little slope from the Zambezi. The Portuguese Bondiera attended the funeral, kneeling by the graveside and crossing himself repeatedly, a sight which Waller found 'piteously strange'. Stewart read the first part of the burial service of the Church of England in the house and the second part at the graveside. Charles Livingstone, prosaic by temperament, was moved by his brother's misery to a gentle sympathy: he came back next day to watch the squirrels and the canaries playing in the baobab tree, and to think of the divine consolation.

Stewart and Waller shared this pity for the bereaved man. But their pity was not only for the bereavement. They pitied a man who seemed to have fallen into a pit whence he could not climb out; a man in command of an expedition, which, it was now clear, must be a failure, and a failure partly from its commander's inability to command. Waller's comment on the day of the funeral was not only expressive of sympathy for the death:

'What a sad, sad day is this, how I pity the poor Doctor all so unorganized now—not a soul but himself and perhaps Charles Livingstone caring—Rae a perfect madman in his complaining —the Gunner so insulting K[irk] he tells me he will leave—the men insubordinate and drunken with some few honourable

[1] SJW 27.4.62, pp. 57–8; CL to Fitch, 2.5.62, CAA.

exceptions—H[ardisty] the engineer going to leave, all is confusion and rottenness at heart and looks black enough—K[irk] should not go—if he does what is to become of the expedition?'

It seemed to the two missionaries, as they waited at Shupanga in the midst of this frustrated party of Englishmen, that the expedition was decaying like the vegetation around them. Stewart, more personal in his diagnoses than Waller, believed that the canker could be found in one member of the expedition —Charles Livingstone. 'That there is an evil genius in a very bodily shape connected with the expedition no one who has any acquaintance with its affairs will doubt, or misunderstand for a moment the allusion. His tongue seems to be against every man and, of course, every man's tongue is against him. What his occupation is would be very difficult to say. This at least he is an adept in, raising disturbances with everyone.'[1]

In fact, the explanation was less simple. There was a fight, for example, between the quartermaster and Hardisty the chief engineer, because the quartermaster seized the engineer by the beard and abused him with foul language. It would have been absurd to hold Charles Livingstone responsible for what a combination of idleness, frustration, and liquor effected in weary, bored, cramped, and unled men.

* * * * *

The journey of Waller down-river for stores and supplies left Rowley's star in the ascendant. Waller believed that the mission must at any cost remain at, or at least near, Magomero once it had adopted that station; he thought that removal was desertion. Rowley believed that Magomero was untenable. The lines of communication were too long, and it was folly to live in a zone of war or no-man's land. He began, with his cool reasoning and quiet persistence, to argue to Procter and Scudamore that the sensible way to shorten the lines of communication was to move seventy miles nearer the mouth of the Zambezi by transferring themselves and their whole protectorate towards Chibisa's on the Shire; and that on the hills near Chibisa's, or on the high bluff overlooking the river, they would find

[1] SJW 5.4.62, p. 48; Waller, MSS., Afr. s. 16/4 (11), Miscellaneous notes.

healthful breezes to expel the fevers caught in the hollow at Magomero.

Within a month, Rowley's arguments had conquered. Circumstances had reinforced them. Magomero was again in the midst of a wave of tribal warfare. The camp was crowded day by day with suppliant chiefs and their bodyguards, trembling refugees, bearers bringing gifts of corn, ambassadors pleading for help against the Ajawa. They now knew that if they helped the Manganja with military aid, they were not driving out robbers and murderers or maintaining justice in the land: they would be the pawns of local intrigue and village warfare. They had perceived that the Ajawa were no more to blame than the Manganja. Therefore, the English had only two courses open to them. They could set up a little English kingdom, based on the few English guns and their white prestige, with all that this would mean in depriving the local chieftains of their rights, and in setting themselves up as magistrates with the power of life and death over all the Africans under their physical power; or they could abandon the region altogether. Of the ethical wrongness of setting themselves up as chieftains, as the rulers of a principality carved out from the lands of others, they were absolutely convinced; it hardly occurred to them as a serious possibility. If the British government were to step in and annex the land, that would in their eyes have been morally different, morally praiseworthy. But that missionaries should turn themselves into secular rulers was impossible for men with the background of the men in the Universities Mission. They admitted to themselves that in a manner they were already little kings. It had to be faced that they were treated by the inhabitants as though they were new and potent chieftains. They had forcibly removed slaves who 'belonged' to other persons and taken them under their own jursidiction. And if it be argued that slaves could not belong to an owner, because slavery was contrary to the law of God, it could be replied that in all the villages round them, and in the nearest European and Christian country, slavery was the custom. It was true that they had not settled without the countenance and approval of chief Chigunda at Magomero. But it could not wholly be said that they were working indirectly though native laws. They had introduced a measure of English law. It had to be faced that the 'English' community was already a kind of theocracy.

Being the men they were, being missionaries and not adventurers, they could not face the conscious pursuit of political power which was the only satisfactory answer, and which in another part of the world, under different circumstances, had led Rajah Brooke to carve out his private principality in Sarawak. And so, when the Ajawa were found to be raiding even near Mbami's, along the path from Magomero to Chibisa's, Rowley won the argument. 'We all clearly saw that if we took up arms again we should be obliged to enter upon a regular campaign; that a single effort would have been worse than useless. Sooner or later, it was evident, the Ajawa must occupy the country; our presence, unless we fought, would only complicate matters, and indeed unless we fought we could not live, for the crops and all the livestock would be destroyed, and we should be left without food.'[1]

On 25 April 1862 the long caravan wound out of Magomero on the road to Chibisa's. Some of the families preferred to remain behind under Chigunda's protection. Of the Bishop's class of boys only one was still alive. 'Scudamore took the lead, I the rear. Taking the route we did, we had to wade through the river. Just as I was about to cross, I heard a child screaming piteously, and immediately afterwards a little girl, about five years of age, rushed down to the river after us, and would have thrown herself in if I had not caught her. She was a poor wizened little thing that I had especially cared for, but whom in the hurry of the morning's work I had forgotten. She begged hard not to be left behind, and we had no intention to leave her, so I took her across the water, and finding she could not keep up with the main body, I had to carry her for the first three or four miles. She was not heavy, but I was weak, and had my gun and knapsack to carry. So when I reached the place where Scudamore had halted in order that all might come up, I was glad to turn her over to the care of an unencumbered woman.'[2] They debated whether to stay on the healthy heights near Mbami's, with their ranging view over the Shire valley, not so far from the future Blantyre. Mbami wanted them to stay, but

[1] R 285. [2] R 290–1.

he appeared to be short of food. They were afraid of inadequate rain for the crops; and so on 30 April they began to build a new village on the right bank of the Shire, just south of Chibisa's, on a treeless bluff eighty feet above the water. The last straggler did not come in until May 6th. Somewhere on the journey Mackenzie's crozier, used by a bearer as a pole to carry heavy goods, was broken.

'As soon as I had fixed upon a site, I summoned the great men of Chibisa's, and fortunately the great man's greatest man was over from Doa, where Chibisa resided. I told him of our intentions, and he expressed his delight to hear that the English were going to live near them. Chibisa would be honoured, all would be honoured; the country was before the English, they might take what they liked, they might build where they liked, and he hoped they would remain for ever.

'Nothing could be more amiable, nothing could exceed the profound bowing and foot stamping and scraping (the latter trick they had learnt from the Portuguese), with which these worthies received the present I gave them on concluding our proceedings. Chechoma the talkative, was there; and as he was second headman, and medicine-man to boot, I had to propitiate him by a present. That done, he sent a herd of men and boys to clear away the bush from the ground upon which we intended to build.'[1]

The new village consisted, at first, of about seventy souls—the children, a few married couples, and a few unmarried women. This number was swollen a little during the fifteen months they were at Chibisa's. From time to time they took a census, and the highest recorded figure was 105. There were no more forcible releases of slaves. The swelling was partly due to fifteen more women who arrived from Magomero in August 1862, and otherwise to refugees from tribal warfare around who came seeking English protection, and sometimes stowed themselves away in the huts unknown to any of the missionaries.

At Chibisa's some progress was at last visible with the language. By the time they had been there six months, Scudamore (who was quicker than anyone else in picking it up) and Waller could both converse, not perhaps fluently, but intellig-

[1] R 295.

ibly, in Manganja. Under Scudamore's supervision, they began reducing the language to writing, a formidable operation because the spoken word seemed to have endless varieties in different mouths. They translated into Manganja the Lord's Prayer, the Creation narrative, and the parables of the Prodigal Son and of the Tares. They were beginning to be able to explain their religious purposes, in the simplest possible form, to strangers who supposed that they were warriors, raiders, or merchants.

Until the drought came, and with it renewed famine, the life of the village community went on with something like stability and happiness. Rowley's health was far better; Scudamore on the other hand suffered severely from the heat; Waller (after his return) thought the valley was a little Sahara, a stifling dust-bowl, and looked longingly upwards at the hills round Mbami's. He had loved the views of high Milanje and distant Shirwa, the rocks and the clefts, the cool streams and the mountain orchids, the greenness of the grass. By comparison he found Chibisa's an oven with a river of lukewarm water running by. The villagers themselves seemed fitter, and began to cultivate their little 'gardens' along the banks of the Shire. Waller's affectionate heart glowed at the happiness of the people. 'The boys, how can we part with them? Such a merry, joyous, splendid set of little fellows, affectionate and as witty and as full of fun, almost more so than English boys . . . pert, merry impudence . . . saucy face. . . . If all the slavesticks in devildom were to be one's funeral pile, the remembrance that the child's laugh rang in one spot in these groaning dark regions through many days while English hearts and hands kept the wolf from their throats would surely ease more than one pang and kill one sorrow for the past.'[1]

Waller was able to make a fine collection of beetles and butterflies, Dickinson of spiders, Rowley was happy with his delicate observation of the specimens of the human race. They would still amuse themselves, though perhaps less than formerly, with theological discussions:

Waller's Journal:

31 August 1862: 'Today we all had a furious argument at breakfast as to real meaning of a day in the account of the

[1] W 4.6.63, 11.1.62.

creation in Genesis. I had to bear the brunt of the whole party, and to my *own* mind more clearly established a belief that the six days were periods of 24 hours than ever I did before. Of course it is the old doubt that goes hand in hand with geology, etc. . . . A good heavy argument is a fine thing in these climates, it exercises the mind.'[1]

They would shoot crocodiles ('we have clearly established now that they are crocodiles here, not alligators') and hippopotamuses, and there was occasionally an elephant shoot. But there was not much spare time.

It may seem surprising that there should have been so little spare time when there were still ten whites (Procter, Scudamore, Rowley, Waller, Dickinson, Adams, Clark, Gamble, Blair—the last came up from Shupanga with supplies in canoes), to administer a village of 105 Africans. It was partly because at any given time it might be expected that two of the whites would be down with fever; Dickinson was delicate and was fully occupied in medical treatment; and partly because though the communications with Shupanga and the Lower Zambezi were far better than they had been while at Magomero, they were still long and arduous, and they had to be kept open if the community was to survive.

Waller, when he went downstream so contrary to the wishes of Kirk and Wilson, had begun the work of organizing supplies by canoe, with Senhor Vianna near Mazaro as the agent and the link between Quilimane and the Shire. When he returned to Chibisa's at the end of May, he had established communication with the Zambezi. It was only a few days downstream in a canoe. But it might take three weeks or a month to come up, and they found canoe-travelling to be torture, cooped up and cramped day after day without exercise under a burning sun, and by night sleeping in mosquito-ridden marshes. Almost always one or more of the whites was away downstream ensuring the dispatch of food, cloth for currency, and other supplies.

Each of them in turn landed at Malo to visit Mackenzie's grave under its mimosa tree amid the undergrowth. In the

[1] Cf. W 26.7.63. 'Read a capital article by Sir David Brewster in *Good Words* on Darwin's ridiculous theory of Natural Selection.'

spring Waller found a wild cucumber growing upon it, and a pair of little birds nesting.

* * * * *

At Chibisa's they were afflicted with a new, and unexpected, thorn in the flesh: the Makololo.

Livingstone had brought the Makololo from the country of Chief Sekeletu on the Upper Zambezi. But partly because he did not need them, and partly because they misbehaved on the *Pioneer*, he left them behind on the Shire, with the implied promise that he would later pick them up to return them to their own country. They had settled at Chibisa's, just down the river from the bluff where the missionaries had encamped.

When they arrived at Chibisa's, they were destitute except for their guns and ammunition. But in the Africa of 1862, he who had guns and ammunition was the lord of his universe. Like a little nest of freebooters, they carved out for themselves a principality along the banks of the Shire. 'We found the Makololo,' wrote Rowley,[1] 'revelling in all the good things that part of the world could produce, masters of the village, monarchs of all they surveyed. They had goats by the score, fowls by the hundred; they ate the finest corn and drank the best of pombi. They and their numerous wives were clothed and decorated without regard to cost. They had sprung all at once from poverty to wealth, from a condition little removed from bondage to that of lords of the creation.' Such was the power of a few guns.

For the missionaries to occupy Chibisa's, therefore, was in a manner to take station next door to an encampment of robber barons. But these barons were unusual. They respected, indeed loved, the English. Livingstone could do anything with them; so could Mackenzie. When Livingstone went down-river and Mackenzie was dead, Scudamore and Waller became the two Englishmen most capable of controlling the Makololo. Moreover, they had acquired the view that they were themselves 'English'. They had been brought into the Shire as Dr Livingstone's servants, they had lived with the English, fought with them, looked after Mackenzie and Burrup in their fatal canoe, lent them cloth; the Ajawa and Manganja thought of them as

[1] R 277.

English. The Makololo thought so too. They no longer felt Chief Sekeletu to be their lord and master. Livingstone had taken his place, they were now part of Livingstone's clan, the tribe of Doto Livisto. They were proud to greet each other with 'Good morning, sir,' whenever they met. They shook hands with each other as often as possible. They delighted in saying 'Thank you' and 'Look here'. They knew the difference between 'port' and 'starboard'. Some of them wore trousers, and one had an old sailor's cap, an emblem regarded up and down the river as proof that the Makololo were warranted in claiming themselves to be the true representatives of the English tribe.

They had learnt enough to know that one characteristic of the Englishmen they had met was abhorrence of slavery. They therefore went out from Chibisa's to hunt the slave-traders and release their captives. They ranged the countryside with their guns, looking for parties to free. They assembled in their village at Chibisa's a numerous company of refugees and any plunder found among the slave parties. They then had to feed the refugees; and so they took the food, sheep and goats and corn, by force from the neighbouring villages of the Manganja. 'The Manganja yielded, and thus arose the bleating of sheep and goats, the cackling of fowls, and the well-stocked houses of corn in the Makololo habitations.' In June, 1862, they had acquired 300 to 400 goats. Of the people they freed, the men became their subjects (not their slaves, though the distinction was far from clear to their neighbours), and the women became, if required, their wives. They were not English enough to practise monogamy. Later, when they had fully established themselves, Ramakukan (who with Moloko possessed the distinction of being pure Makololo in blood, the others being of mixed ancestry), kept an official with a knobkerry to maintain order among his wives.

The missionaries were perplexed. They believed now that they had committed an error in forcibly freeing slaves—and a few hundred yards away fifteen Makololo, claiming to be their servants, were continuing the work with zest. The missionaries believed that the English and Christian name should stand for peace, justice, kindness, civilization. They were moved and touched by the trust which the Africans soon came to place in their fairness and their altruism. But at Chibisa's they found that the English name stank in the nostrils of the surrounding villagers. It stood for freebooters and poultry-stealers. 'We found it was no comfort to the people of some villages near the river to call out, "The English are here, don't fear"; for they did fear, and until they recognized us individually, ran away from us.' The robberies had not been committed without bloodshed. It was difficult to believe every word that Manganja and Ajawa said about the Makololo; but Waller heard a story (and believed it) that some women whom they captured had the poor children dragged off their backs and thrown into the river.[1] In addition, they suffered because their own African people were in a constant state of bickering with the Makololo —accusation and counter-accusation, pilfering on one side or abduction on the other. The missionaries were the only people who could now keep the Makololo in any sort of discipline; Waller shuddered to think what would happen if the mission retired down the river and left the Makololo to rampage through the country. But the state in which the missionaries succeeded in keeping these uncomfortable neighbours could hardly be described as order.

In this predicament the only hope seemed to be Dr Livingstone, still down the river at Shupanga. Rowley, who had lost all faith in Livingstone, thought it 'a very great mistake' on Livingstone's part. He had brought these strangers into the land, and had then left them destitute except for weapons far superior to anything the Africans had ever seen; it seemed almost like inviting them to be bandits. Whether this was true or not, it was clear to the missionaries that Livingstone must quell them or take them away. He was responsible for them: they regarded him as their chief.

The Makololo also perceived that Livingstone might have something to say to them when he arrived. One of the Cape Africans fell into serious trouble for spreading a rumour that Livingstone would cut all the Makololo throats when he came up-river.[2] Waller had to reassure them that he alone had seen Livingstone, and 'he had told me that when he returned to Chibisa's he should be glad to see them all and the past would

[1] R 277; W 3.6.62. [2] W 13.6.62.

be forgiven. This seemed to comfort them.' But they had begun to have a sense of guilt. At first they had expected the whites to approve their activities. They were surprised, and then hurt, and then nervous, to find themselves repudiated by the whites whose disciples they claimed to be. And they no longer wished Livingstone to remove them. To be lords of the Shire valley was more lucrative and more comfortable than to return to the dusty villages of Sekeletu.

On 22 June 1862 Chibisa, who had been driven away with his people from Doa near the Zambezi and had returned to his village, summoned the two Cape men, Johnson and William, to a secret meeting of chieftains in the forest. He wanted gunpowder; and he was determined to get it either from the missionaries or Dr Livingstone. At the meeting in the forest, he lamented the gross injuries which the English had brought upon him and his people. He said, 'I am here, and I cannot go back to Doa, because the English, who say they are my friends, will not help me. I received them as my brothers. They build on my land. I do not ask them to fight for me; I can fight for myself. I only ask them to sell me gunpowder, but, though they have plenty, they will not let me have any. Whose fault is it, then, that I am here? Mine? no, not mine, but that of the English. You say the English are good people?'

The meeting answered, 'Yes, the English have good hearts. They take nothing from us; they pay us well for all they have; they give us cloth for our corn and goats and fowls, and if we go a journey for them they give us cloth for that too. Yes, the English are good people.'

Chibisa was not 'discomposed'. He went on:

'Yes, the English do all that, but what else have they done? You come to me and say—Go away, we do not want you here; your life is not safe here. And I know my life is not safe here, I am in danger of dying. But why? Why is all this? Because the Makololo have been robbing and beating the Manganja. But did I bring the Makololo into the country? No! Who brought them here? Why the English! Then why blame me? Blame the English, for they are the people to blame, not me.'

The meeting was moved by the speech. Its opinion began to veer. One of them said, 'It is quite true the English did bring the

Makololo here, and if they were to give you gunpowder you could go away. They would be our friends then as well as yours.' There was a moody silence while they puffed away at their pipes.

Waller brooded over the report of the meeting. 'These fellows . . . sailing under English colours, have done us incalculable harm, and what is worse continue to do it under our very noses . . .'

Two days later, the missionaries were even debating whether they ought to abandon the mission altogether. If they stayed at Chibisa's they would be regarded by the neighbouring tribes as the heads of the robber band of Makololo. If—as Waller time after time pressed upon the others—they moved back into the nearby hills, they were lengthening a line of communication already too long, and would probably be unable to feed their people. If they went down the river they could move only into Portuguese, indisputably Portuguese, territory, and it seemed to them that this was equal to abandoning the mission. Waller was now afraid that they would never get the rivers open. But were they not under a sacred and honourable obligation to keep where they were until Mackenzie's successor or higher orders reached them? Ought they to leave just at the moment when Scudamore was beginning to be able to speak Manganja? And, above all, could they leave the refugees whom they had collected and who trusted them absolutely, to the combined mercies of the Makololo and the passing slave-raiders?

Waller committed his perturbations to his Journal: 'A life such as this is most distasteful to those who are in Holy Orders'. The absence of safe communication along the rivers 'makes our position very precarious. Seriously, the question of leaving the country is talked of, but I really do not see how it is to be done in any case. To look around and see these poor little children so happy and merry playing about, growing into fine lads and the lads into such fine men, secure and merry as the day is long, working hard and receiving regular pay for which they are very happy—it would break one's heart to leave them. Slaves they would all become . . . Then comes a thought . . . is it not our dear Lord's work, are not these things He must like to see—do not our hearts love these poor things and cling to them because we have done them good and wish to do so still by His means and at His bidding? It is so purely and simply—is there anything of selfishness in it, is it not a holy love for them? It is, it is. Will He not bless it then?'[1]

Their protégés were as aware of it as they were. When Dickinson and Rowley left to go down-river in search of corn, some of the women called out in lamentation, 'Don't leave us; if our English fathers go from us, there is no life in us, we are all dead—don't leave us—do come back.'[2] It seemed to the English missionaries that there was no word of hyperbole in the lament.

In short, by the end of June, 1862, it was clear that they would remain. Whether it was prudent, sensible, or even useful to be where they were, had become irrelevant. They were held there by every tie of conscience, honour, and piety.

In one case the determination came near to being suicidal. By the summer of 1862, it was evident that the home prophets had been right and that Dr Dickinson could not long survive in the present heat, diet, and way of life. He suffered so continuously that everyone could see death facing him if he did not return home by the first opportunity. He had been endemically ill at Magomero; at Chibisa's, the heat made every attack severe. But nothing would persuade him to go until a substitute came. And a substitute could not come for many months because he had to write home to the committee to tell them that a substitute was needed. To the persuasion of his friends he would reply, 'I cannot leave you men without medical assistance. If God spare me I shall be thankful; if it be His will to take me to Himself, let me die in the performance of my duty.'[3]

In the event he survived by a few months the much stronger Scudamore.

Chibisa, failing to persuade the missionaries to give him gunpowder (with which he might arm himself against other Manganja chiefs, the Portuguese, the Ajawa, but chiefly the Makololo), determined to send emissaries with ivory down the river to request gunpowder of Dr Livingstone. The missionaries did not think that the emissaries would get down the river alive unless a white man went with them. And since they had decided to complain to Livingstone of the Makololo behaviour, and to ask him to keep them in order, or remove them to the

[1] R 307-8: W 24.6.62. [2] R 347. [3] R 337, 346-7.

Pioneer and supervise them personally, Scudamore and Job set out in canoes, on 25 June, 1862, with Chibisa's men and the tusks.

The absence of Scudamore, who could influence the Makololo more easily than any other white, did not further peace and harmony. It was discovered that the Cape men were engaged in a long-standing quarrel with the Makololo, and the wrong was by no means all on one side. A woman friend of William complained that a Makololo had hurt her. William went off irritably into the Makololo village and was almost murdered; he came running out with Mobita after him with a thick stick. Mobita, who could run much faster, caught him up; William knocked him down with his fists. They entered the missionary encampment still fighting. Mobita came up to the Englishmen hysterical and sobbing. They washed his much-bruised face; but while their backs were turned for a moment, he snatched a stick from one of the boys and made a rush at William. Waller thought that William would have been killed by the blow if he had not heard Mobita coming. But he jumped about and landed another right and left with his fist in Mobita's face. The Englishmen at last separated the struggling men and sent William back to his hut. Mobita ranted like a madman; and putting a finger on his own bleeding nose, vowed that he would kill the first woman or child from the English village that he came across. Afraid of a brutal murder if they ended the meeting thus, the missionaries told the Makololo to sit down and talk reasonably. For two hours Mobita and his friends sat raving and pleading that they had been brought here by the English, and had been deserted and left starving; and for two hours Waller and Rowley and Procter tried to convince them that Livingstone had not cast them away altogether.[1]

On 5 July, they spent nearly an hour at breakfast time arguing whether to buy a bowl of milk. The milk was from a Makololo goat, belonging to Zomba, and the goat was therefore stolen. They sent for the Makololo and explained to them the laws of England on receiving stolen goods, but they ended by buying the milk.[2] It made them feel less guilty that Zomba was 'about the best of the bunch'.

[1] W 4.7.62. [2] W 5.7.62.

On 2 August, Scudamore walked into the middle of a solemn conclave on the advisability of an immediate move to the hills nearby. He was looking fit and well, and carried with him letters from Dr Livingstone, including one for the Makololo in their own language, and a mail ('God-like gift') from England. They heard that at last the *Lady Nyassa* had been launched at Shupanga. Waller, with that inclination to reverence Livingstone which Rowley found exaggerated, expressed his thankfulness in his journal: '. . . such letters, how we ought to pray he may be spared to humanity. There is something in them that electrifies every nerve and sinew, and makes one long to be under such a leader—who, you feel, must know more in his little finger than we do in our heads. His forethought, his far-seeing vision . . . poor man, it makes us sick to think what would become of this land were he cut off.'[1]

Rowley, as was his way, was less impressed. He had not supposed that a mere letter from Livingstone could turn the Makololo into respectable citizens. But he had to admit that for a time Livingstone's magical power over the African asserted itself. The Makololo did, for a time, behave well, or at least better.

* * * * *

Inside the mission camp, Rowley's critical attitude to Livingstone was reinforced. Scudamore, who never criticized anyone but was well content to take people as he found them, brought back with him from Shupanga the most critical of them all—James Stewart. Stewart had come up-river to see the country, and he was already metamorphosing himself into a highly articulate, and even mordant, assailant of Livingstone's conduct. The missionaries (except Waller) felt that Livingstone had let them down, but they did not often say so. It was not Stewart's nature to keep silent.

Stewart had rejoiced in Livingstone's welcome to him at the Kongone like a worshipper from afar who bows now at the feet of the hero. He had rejoiced again when Livingstone sent him the special summons to the death-bed of his Mary. But even before he came into communication with the missionaries, his

[1] W 2.8.62.

romantic visions of Livingstone had rapidly faded. It was partly the mere conduct of the expedition—the quasi-anarchy and disorganization aboard the ships, the evidence that whatever his other greatnesses (greatnesses of courage and endurance which Stewart was still the first to admit) Livingstone was no commander of white men. Partly it was the un-religious tone of the company aboard the *Pioneer*—the struggle which Stewart found in getting the 'Sabbaths' observed upon the Zambezi.

Stewart's Journal:

23 February 1862: 'I do not feel satisfied with the Sabbaths on board the *Pioneer*. Dr. L. is more faulty on this matter than I supposed. At noon, when we should have had service, he was writing, a dispatch perhaps, or a letter. Rae was doing the same. Charles Livingstone, do. Young, do. Others were reading *Chambers' Journal*, *Dynevor Terrace*, *Monte Cristo* and only one or two their Bibles. I felt wearied, constrained to speak, to take the initiative, but I think it better to wait a little.'

2 March 1862: 'Oh, how I long for something like a Sabbath again . . . but as I cannot do the most ordinary actions, not even preserve my boxes from being destroyed by wet [Charles Livingstone had fiercely attacked him for moving his boxes at the expense of other people], . . . it will not be difficult to understand how I think it better not to take the initiative . . . I am wearied of these godless sabbaths.'

6 March 1862: 'No worship: I spoke to Mrs L. Her answer, There is none now!'

9 March 1862: '. . . worship at night. I am glad of that, but a fragment of the Litany and part of a chapter is like living on half or third allowance of provisions! There is something quite unsatisfying in this form of worship.'

Stewart unexpectedly found himself lonely in his religion. He wanted preaching and 'social worship' and public prayers; he did not allow or perceive that Livingstone had a deep religious sense of man in his solitariness before his Maker, a sense which yet found little need of 'social worship'. He thought that, with the exception of swearing, the atmosphere on the *Pioneer* was as secular as that of the wardroom in any British warship. Moreover he disliked Charles Livingstone; disliked him as a quarrelsome trouble-maker, and thought him a malign influence upon his brother. Worse, Charles Livingstone and Rae spread through the ship rumours so unfavourable to Stewart as to make his predicament mentally uncomfortable and isolated. Rae told the members of the crew that Stewart was no genuine missionary, but an intruder who had come to stake claims to trade on the Zambezi, and was using the title of missionary as a disguise. The other members of the expedition—even Kirk—for a time believed the gossip, and they behaved towards Stewart with a grim chilliness. David Livingstone himself remained the friendliest member of the expedition. But Stewart felt that he had come thousands of miles to join a great venture for humanity. And here he was friendless, suspect, utterly alone; and his soul within him was bitter as the unripe lemon.

Then, at Shupanga, came the news that Mackenzie and Burrup had died at their posts. Whether or no the blood of the martyrs may rightly be called the seed of the church, the deaths helped to change Stewart's attitude towards the Oxford and Cambridge missionaries. He imagined Burrup burying Mackenzie's body through the twilight in the solitary, unconsecrated grave at Malo, and was moved. All bitterness or rivalry against them, the prejudice against Mackenzie's 'pomp', faded quietly out of his mind. Whether they were experienced missionaries or not, whether the venture had been well-planned or not, there was no place now for questioning their determination or their self-sacrifice. 'The high church party have now their heroes. . . . All honour to Mackenzie now.'[1]

Waller, coming downstream in March, 1862, to Shupanga, confirmed him in this new friendliness. He found Waller to be warm-hearted, ready to welcome him as a warrior in the crusade and to give him every help and information in his power. It was probably the first time since Cape Town that Stewart felt himself to be trusted.

When Scudamore came down to Shupanga in July with Chibisa's embassy, Stewart determined to go back with him to see the country. He had come out to prospect the ground for a mission: he must go to the existing mission to see how it fared. On 11 July, he started up the rivers in pursuit of Scudamore's canoe.

[1] SJ 14.3.62, omitted by Wallis.

On the night of 16 July, they camped together on the west bank of the Shire as it curves round the base of Mount Morambala. By the decaying embers of the camp-fire under the midnight moon, with the stillness broken only by the 'swift rush of the silvery river sweeping seaward, and for a few minutes, now and then, by the tramp of some wild beast among the bushes on the opposite bank, or by the constant snort and champing of the hippopotamus among the reeds',[1] Stewart found at last a man to whom he could talk with delight of the things of the spirit.

Scudamore had not endured the mental and spiritual turmoils, the vacillations and uncertainties and agonies, the revivalism and the emotion, through which Rowley and Waller had both come to their faith. Nurtured in a devout home of serene piety, his religion was of that sort, represented at its highest among the descendants of the Oxford Movement by his contemporary, Edward King, where grace looks natural; a quality which seems to be found more readily in the catholic than in the evangelical tradition of piety. Powerful in physique, but gentle and tender as a child in spirit, shrinking from discourtesy or even militancy, a man of a modesty so extreme that in anyone less unaffected it might have seemed absurd, his character might be compared to the light reflected upon rippling waters—transparently incapable of deceit, pretension, inflation, and yet giving the watcher the sense of depth or mystery; partly perhaps because through his innate diffidence he was not articulate, but partly from that aura of mystery which the true man of the spirit carries with him, the stillness which comes from living in another city than this, withdrawn and inviolable.

Sitting round the flickering and failing camp-fire, Stewart felt the power in Scudamore. They conversed far into the night, contrasting the false, the ideal, and the romantic picture of missionary work so prevalent in Britain with the squalor and ignorance and superstition, the rough toil on a 'moral waste' of the reality. They thought of the ideal portrait of a missionary in an English drawing-room—'a dreary being, with mortified flesh and unearthly feelings and aims'—with the real men and

[1] *Sunday Magazine*, April 1875, pp. 477ff. (Stewart).

their share of human weaknesses and faults. They discussed whether this kind of venture, this Zambezi mission, was quixotic folly; whether it was not better to wait for 'civilization', to delay until the railway had come and then evangelize in comfort; whether this kind of venture in faith led to a needless sacrifice of life. They found themselves at one in heart and mind. The Christian man must go where his vocation leads him, and if life was given, it was given to mercy. In Scudamore, wrote Stewart, 'I found a sincere Christian and a true man.'

Two and a half weeks later, on 2 August, William the Cape man in his cocked hat with feathers and his white jacket and glasses, washing his clothes among the grass upon the bank, welcomed them to Chibisa's. Stewart felt himself at once among friends. That evening it delighted his heart to join with them in Anglican Evensong in the little thatched chapel high over the river; and next day he found it odd, and yet gratifying, to be partaking with them of the Holy Communion at an altar made from two boxes covered by a velvet cloth and subscribing to a collection on behalf of the Society for the Propagation of the Gospel.[1]

The metamorphosis was almost complete. He had arrived expecting to separate Dr Livingstone from his unfortunate association with the missionaries. Now he found, not without a sense of incongruity, that the missionaries seemed to be separating him from his fruitless association with Dr Livingstone. Between the two separate services on the *Hetty Ellen*, and the one communion at a makeshift altar at Chibisa's, lay Shupanga and all the pains of the physical and mental navigations on the *Pioneer*.

He did not altogether, and in a flash, lose his suspicions. The nerves had been exposed to view, and they were not soothed without a twinge. There was a moment when he wondered whether Waller's hearty greeting was feigned, and another when he went wrong, as wrong as he ever went in his career, by supposing Scudamore to be guilty of subtlety. But as he came to live with them, the more he came to like them; Scudamore perhaps with the most respect, Waller with the warmest affection, though increasingly he thought Waller's 'adoration' of

[1] SJ 3.8.62, omitted by Wallis.

Livingstone to be ridiculous; but Procter and Rowley and Dickinson too. Perhaps the friendliest picture of Procter in all the sources comes from Stewart's not naturally charitable pen.

Living at Chibisa's, daily growing more intimate in a life with so little privacy, sallying on expeditions with one or other of the party to find a healthier site in the hills, Stewart came to share the opinions of Rowley on what had happened. He now accepted the claim that Livingstone's release of the slaves at Mbami's had led the mission naturally to the military action which Livingstone later seemed to disapprove and repudiate. He soon believed, with them, that Livingstone was fatally responsible for the Makololo, that he had picked them up like a tool and then thrown them away, without any attempt to put them back where they belonged. He nearly quarrelled with Waller over his 'Livingstone-worship'; but it was a moment when they were lying together at night near Malo afraid of a hyena supposed to be snuffing about their heads, and these were conditions under which men understandably quarrel. He had already formed the conviction for himself that Livingstone was 'not fitted for his position'[1] as leader of the expedition, and that he was so regardless of human suffering, whether in himself or others, that he could not lead a team of men of flesh and blood.

But the gravest conviction which Stewart formed—as Rowley before him—was the belief that Livingstone had been guilty, if not of deceit, at least of culpable exaggeration, in his descriptions of the country. Why had Rowley and Procter come out, expecting to find a regular communication with the coast by the *Pioneer* every three months? Why had the Bishop insisted, against so much good advice, in bringing his sister and allowing Mrs Burrup to join her husband? Why had the hard-headed Bishop of Cape Town become a party to the scheme, which Commander Wilson had thought so wild and premature, of planting an English and Christian village in the middle of Central Africa? What had precipitated these little groups of Englishmen into their present and apparently inextricable agony? Missionary endeavour was often enthusiastic, and enthusiasm is not always practical, is sometimes ready to suppose that the faith which moves mountains is a sufficient

[1] SJW 101, 125, 128, 189.

substitute for foresight and careful planning. It was not to be contested that the wave of altruistic passion for Africa which had swept the churches in Britain had contributed to the rashness of the venture. But Rowley, and now Stewart, believed Livingstone was primarily responsible for the rashness. In his *Missionary Travels*, and his subsequent letters printed in England, he had drawn a Utopian picture—a little primitive paradise endowed with a natural harvest of wealth only waiting for the white man to garner; a land of smiling tribes and game, of corn and cotton, of health and rapid communication by noble rivers, a land of serenity and of sanatoria, of natural orchards of orange and lemon trees. The mission had bought a second-hand cotton-gin because it expected to be self-supporting economically within two or three years: they had been told that they might live off their guns; they had been encouraged to think the land safe for ladies. Procter had supposed, from reading Livingstone's letters, that he was coming to 'a sort of African Arcadia'.[1] Livingstone's far-flung eye had seen a vision—a vision which might yet be justified. But he had failed to tell the world of the mountains and seas of toil which lay between his vision and its fulfilment.

Not that he had said anything which could be convicted of being misleading. Nor, as Kirk insisted to Stewart, was it fair to judge Livingstone's picture of Central Africa by the chaos of war and famine which was afflicting the region two or three years later than his descriptions of it. But, though he had not given any detail patently untrue, he failed to state the difficulties and the perils which surrounded what he was describing; partly because his own character of heroic perseverance made him suppose that where he could go, everyone else—missionary, commercial traveller, cotton spinner, planter—could go likewise. 'Let me note,' wrote Stewart on 3 October, 1862, 'the fallacy in Livingstone's method. He meets a difficulty, overcomes it by an amount of perseverance and an expenditure of strength and money which men will put forth once or twice but which it would be ruinous to carry out as a rule. And then he speaks of insurmountable difficulties being surmounted. They have been for the time, but they remain as

[1] SJW 120.

before, obstructions to navigation or any other enterprise that may be attempted.' Wherever he went, Stewart measured areas of cotton-growing, diligently testing Livingstone's claim that he had opened the best cotton-field in the world, the counterpoise to American slavery. 'At present,' wrote Stewart, 'it would be as well to propose some counterpoise to humbug.'[1]

And so Stewart came to believe, like Rowley before him, that Livingstone could even be said to be 'in some respect responsible for the Bishop's death'. 'His accursed lies,' wrote Stewart after an evening's discussion of the question at Chibisa's, 'have caused much toil, trouble, anxiety, and loss of life, as well as money and reputation, and I have been led a dance over half the world to accomplish nothing.'[2]

The climax for Stewart came early in 1863, when he was no longer living at Chibisa's with the friendly missionaries, but far down river at Senhor Vianna's on his way to the outside world and home. Between six and seven a.m., as he was sitting in the shed, two messengers came. They brought a note and two bottles of brandy from Procter. The note, which has been preserved, described how Scudamore was dead. After agonizing suffering from a tumour behind the right ear, he had died in his hut at Chibisa's in the early hours of New Year's Day, on the clearest of starlit nights, with the Southern Cross overhead and all the sounds and smells of Africa around him, the early cockcrow, 'the hippopotamus and the hyena coming back to their day haunts,'[3] and on his lips the words, 'There remaineth a rest'; and he was mourned with an intense grief by his comrades. Stewart, when he heard the news, felt his bitterness reviving. He found the problem of providence and death intolerable to the intellect. Throughout the day he could not rid his mind of Scudamore. It was too tempting to look round for a scapegoat, a human villain who might render the evil intelligible to the mind. That bright, hot, and clear afternoon, he took his copy of Livingstone's *Missionary Travels in South Africa* and walked a little way down the bank. Then he threw the book

[1] SJW 264; cf. 111–12, 120, 173, 211, 263. [2] SJW 125, 189.

[3] W 1.1.63: 'The Makololo seemed very sorry for his loss. He had much influence with them, and I attribute it to his great singleness of heart . . . All could see charity and the harmless disposition in that fine open countenance.'

with all his strength 'into the turbid, muddy, weed-covered Zambezi. . . . The volume was fragrant with odours of and memories of the earnestness with which I studied the book in days gone by. How different it appeared now! It was nothing short of an eyesore, the very sight of its brown covers. I do not think it is as the Rev. R— M—[1] is said to have called it, "a pack of lies", but it would need a great many additions to make it the truth. Thus I disliked the book, and sent it to sink or swim into the vaunted Zambezi. So perish all that is false in myself and others.'

* * * * *

Meanwhile, the disagreement between Rowley and Livingstone was growing into a quarrel.

While Waller was waiting at Shupanga in March, he had written the letter to Magomero transmitting the information of Rae and Stewart that Livingstone was now irritated with the mission, partly because of Rowley's published letter from the Kongone, questioning the value of the Zambezi as a highway, and partly because he thought them to be wrong in fighting the Ajawa. The letter arrived at Magomero, with Charles and the new supply of cloth, on 21 April. For several days Rowley was too busy arranging the trek from Magomero to Chibisa's. But the day after the move was completed, on 7 May, Rowley settled down to write letters; and in them he could not help expressing himself strongly at the news that Livingstone was criticizing them for fighting. He wrote a private letter to a clergyman named Glover, who had given him hospitality at the Cape, telling him that in attacking the Ajawa they had done no more than Livingstone had done. 'I believe he now blames us for our proceedings—proceedings which were but the fulfilment of his programme, the inevitable sequence of his advice and deeds. From the moment he commenced the release of slaves, his course was one of aggression . . . when searching for [slaves] his men entered into every place where they were supposed to be, firing their guns, and making every kind of warlike demonstration.' Rowley described—though not present, he had read Mackenzie's journal with its summary—Livingstone's

[1] Wallis supported Robert Moffat.

last speech to the assembled chiefs at Magomero, how he had told them that if the lesson had not been learnt, he would be up again to 'look after them'.

He warmed to the criticism of Livingstone. Why were they short of stores and suffering from destitution? 'We left . . . nearly two-thirds of the stores . . . on board the *Vega*, the store-ship at Johanna, the *Pioneer* not being able to take them. We suffered much in consequence, but consoled ourselves that we should have fresh supplies in the first month of the year. Livingstone has miserably failed us—but not intentionally—he does not seem to be aware of the exigencies and requirements of his own position, and is I fear getting into inextricable trouble . . .'

The waste of stores at the Kongone he denounced as a proceeding 'most inconsiderate, most heartless'. It was tantalizing to be near the level of destitution and yet hear that stores designed for them, only three hundred miles away, had been wasted extravagantly because they were believed not to need them. He told Glover that the gear for 'civilizing' and 'commerce' was so much waste at present. What use had they for a light cart—'as easy to use in this country as to drive a locomotive up Table Mountain'? They needed the means of livelihood—cloth as currency, flour, sugar, wine, brandy, salt-meat. The talk of commerce was premature. 'The possibilities of the land will not admit of commerce being established—and therefore all expensive material for the purpose of facilitating commerce had better be kept back.

'The highlands are *not* cotton-producing in the sense always understood of them—and if they were it would never pay to bring cotton from thence—the cost of carriage, supposing the article untaxed, would be too great.'

* * * * *

A private letter from a missionary was sometimes printed by its recipient. It was often the only news available, and it was not possible to ask the sender's permission before deciding to print it. Glover bowdlerized the letter. He excised the most formidable sentences which attacked Livingstone, and then sent the remainder to the press.[1]

[1] Full version in Bishopscourt Archives; bowdlerized (e.g.), in *Guardian*, 20.11.62.

In the August and September of 1862, Livingstone filled the interval, during which he could not ascend the Shire, by exploring again the River Rovuma. He found the Rovuma as unsatisfactory for navigation as ever. In November, he arrived at Quilimane in the *Pioneer* on his way back to the Zambezi. He was more depressed by his failure than his wont. An observant Portuguese thought that he entered the town like a cat with his tail between his legs.[1] At Quilimane, he met *H.M.S. Rapid* with dispatches from the Cape and from England, and with further supplies for mission and for expedition. Here he learnt the two charges of Rowley which Glover had allowed to reach the newspapers—first, that the missionaries had attacked the Ajawa, as he understood Rowley to say, 'under his direction'. He refuted the allegations. He was able to show that he had advised the Bishop not to act upon the offensive, and the Bishop's Journal (an extract of which was now public), confirmed that this was what he had said, and that Mackenzie admitted himself to be acting on his own responsibility and against Livingstone's advice. 'It is,' he wrote to Sir Thomas Maclear, 'totally untrue that I ever in any one instance adopted an aggressive policy towards the Ajawa or took slaves from them. I took slaves from Portuguese, but never hunted the Ajawa, nor took the part of Manganja against them . . . I repeat again that slaves were taken from Portuguese people alone—people of Tete, some of whom I knew personally . . . There was no fighting in any case . . .' And as for the second assertion, that the Shire highlands are not cotton-producing, Rowley must be 'unconscious, possibly, that his Bishop bought a cotton-gin from me to show the people around him how much more easily the cleaning process could be effected by it than by the slow process which even Mr Rowley must have seen in every village he entered.'

Livingstone, being a man, resented criticism. And it is certain that in his bald refutations of Rowley he believed himself to be speaking the truth. As the charge appeared in the press, it seemed as though Rowley claimed Livingstone to have been the director or inspirer of all the attacks upon the Ajawa, and disclaimed responsibility for Mackenzie. And this was patently

[1] SJ 10.2.63.

untrue. No one less than Livingstone would have denied a charge which he believed to be true. But the stature of the man came out in his reaction. He wrote to Glover, who had apologized to him for publishing Rowley's letter, 'It will never make me swerve from doing what I can to assist them, nor from wishing them Godspeed from the bottom of my heart.'[1] For this kind of language was not from one who, when offended, found it facile to forgive.

The news of the controversy did not reach Chibisa's until 22 January 1863. Everyone was cross. Waller was indignant with Rowley and his 'unfortunate pen'; he had himself been the only other missionary besides Mackenzie to be present when Livingstone had told the chiefs that if there were more trouble he would come back to 'look after them'. He denied that the words as he heard them could carry any such aggressive meaning as Rowley had understood them to bear.[2]

Rowley set pen to paper again as soon as he heard the news. The day after the mail arrived at Chibisa's, he wrote to the editor of the *Cape Advertiser and Mail*, denying that he had ever declared Livingstone to have *directed* their attacks upon the Ajawa, for which they bore the sole responsibility, but that their attacks upon the Ajawa were 'in principle' no different from Livingstone's earlier attack upon them. 'I have never for one moment endeavoured to avoid the responsibility of our own actions, and entirely exonerate Dr Livingstone from any part in them; but while I say that, I repeat that I think they were the natural sequence of the Doctor's proceedings—proceedings which I heartily approved of at the time, and still think that what he did was nobly done.' He pointed out that Livingstone's speech about 'looking after them again' was to be found 'in substance' in the Bishop's diary—and sent a copy of his letter to Livingstone himself.

[1] Livingstone to Maclear, 20.11.62, Quilimane River.

[2] W 22.1.63: Livingstone's recollection of what he had said agreed with Waller's, not Mackenzie's; cf. Livingstone to Lord John Russell, 15.11.61, LJW ii. 410. The committee at home was urgent to disclaim any attempt to shift the responsibility for what Mackenzie had done. A public controversy between Livingstone and the mission would in any case do more to harm the mission in the public eye than any other single calamity. A representative of the committee wrote in strenuous terms to the press, denying that there was any attempt to shift the responsibility, and showing from Mackenzie's letters that he took it all upon himself.

On the day that Rowley was sending this uncompromising and unapologetic clarification to the press, Livingstone was writing a very different kind of letter.

With the rivers at last high enough, and the two ships ready, he had set out up the Shire on 11 January 1863 with the *Lady Nyassa* in tow. The first sandbank caused the *Lady Nyassa* to ram the *Pioneer*. After further experiment they were forced to lash the two ships side by side. Thereafter, they made surprisingly rapid progress up the Shire. On 23 January, they reached the island of Malo, and Livingstone landed to visit Mackenzie's grave. He manufactured a more substantial cross and erected it. It is somehow symbolic of Livingstone's relations with Mackenzie and the mission, relations always well-meaning but not always effectual, that he should have erected the cross in the wrong place.

Down at Quilimane, he had heard that the missionaries were severely judged at home for fighting the Ajawa. It was his way to stand for the underdog. As he came up the river he brooded over the question, wondering how the comfortable critics at home would have behaved had they the courage to have found themselves in Mackenzie's place. His meditations near the grave completed his conversion, perhaps touched or revived the affection and admiration in him. No longer could he condemn Mackenzie for having fought. When he had returned to the cabin on the *Pioneer* he wrote home this retractation:

'I have just been visiting Mackenzie's grave. At first I thought him wrong in fighting, but don't think so now. He defended his 140 orphan children when there was no human arm besides to invoke. To fight even in self-defence must always be but a sad necessity; but to sit still, and let bloodthirsty slave-hunters tear away those orphans who cleave to us for protection, must be suffering martyrdom for our own folly . . .' He wrote to Waller and others in the same sense.[1]

* * * * *

In November and December 1862 and in January 1863 famine again afflicted the suffering valley and highlands of the Shire. Dying men and women scrabbled for roots, with swollen

[1] Livingstone to Sir Culling Eardley, 23.1.63; originally printed in *Evangelical Christendom* and taken thence into other papers; cf. G 362; Livingstone to Waller, 23.2.63; Blaikie, p. 294; Livingstone to Adam Sedgwick, 16.2.63, CAA.

stomachs and dead eyes and emaciated bones, skeletons were found on the path; from the cliff at Chibisa's, corpses could be seen too often floating down the river. At first the villagers buried the dead in graves, 'then the survivors, being too weak for the exertion of grave-digging, carried the bodies outside the village, and laid them decently under a tree: if a man, his bow, with the string cut, would be placed beside him; if a woman, the fragments of a broken water jar. But as time went on even this attention to the dead seemed impossible—where they died there they remained. You met with the putrefying remains of human beings on the paths, in the villages, everywhere; there was no place where they were not. The River Shire was literally the river of death. Poor hungry wretches would come from the hills, or from the destitute parts of the valley, and attempt to steal what little corn there was growing on the islands and along the banks; no matter that it was not ripe, they took it unripe; but the owners with wolf-like vigilance caught them, and with wolf-like ferocity killed them, and threw their bodies into the river. Mothers also, having no food to give their children, threw them into the river, and jumped in after them. Men did the same with regard to their wives. The crocodiles were gorged with human food.'

One morning, Rowley, high on the cliff, saw what looked like a child's corpse floating down the Shire. 'As I turned aside, sickened at the sight, a little arm was thrown up, and I heard a child's voice beseeching help. The child was alive. We ran down to the river, launched a canoe, and saved the little one. When he recovered from his fright, he told us that his father, who lived at a village about seven miles above us, had thrown him and his mother into the river, and that he had been a long time in the water. Poor child! He could not sink; his stomach was so inflated and distended by scarce and unwholesome feeding, that it kept him up like a bladder. We did our best to keep him alive, but dysentery carried him off; but before he died we baptized him by the name of Moses.'[1]

Amidst the famine around them, the station at Chibisa's did not suffer as once the station at Magomero had suffered. The whites had learnt their lesson: they kept a bigger margin of

[1] R 366–7.

supplies, and they had their people better organized. The village of the English, because it was supplied and rationed by Englishmen, not without frequent, exhausting, and perilous voyages in canoes up and down the river, and the village of the Makololo, because they stole the food of others for their own people, were the only two villages in the land to be fed, and contented. It rejoiced the hearts of the missionaries to see that something, at least, had been achieved. Here was one community which in desperate circumstances was achieving civilized standards of behaviour.

Everyone round (except the Makololo) was starving. Ought they to lower the rations of their own people to starvation level for the sake of finding another mouthful for the beggars who besieged them? It was known that there was corn in the camp. They reduced the level of ration to bare subsistence for their own people, and began to distribute what they could to starving visitors or to neighbouring villages. They would make a public announcement, and then waifs and strays from the countryside would come to receive the few handfuls of corn which was all they could give. Some of the villagers nearby were so emaciated, and their senses so deadened, that they could hardly make the effort to accept what was offered. Waller and Rowley carried a fresh supply of corn to Maduga, a village about a mile away from which they had often found porters. When the inhabitants of Maduga heard why they had come, they came out of their huts. Men who a few months before had carried heavy loads for them now tottered towards them, so emaciated as to be unrecognizable. Some were too weak to stand, and crawled towards them on hands and knees; women dragged themselves to the doors of their huts and exhausted themselves in the effort. Rowley thought that by then he had witnessed so much suffering that his heart was hardened; he had reached the stage where he could see men and women die 'almost with indifference'. But the sight of the long famished children pierced through his heart like a sword, and he was forced to avert his gaze and turn aside.[1]

He reckoned that they were not able to save more than five or six of the people of Maduga.

[1] R 381.

It distressed Waller infinitely, that though their people behaved with better manners and in a more organized way than the people around, there were notable exceptions to the rule. It distressed him that they could not succeed in inculcating the sense of compassion in their people for the starving crowds around. It would have been something if an 'English' African had been ready to share his corn with one of the beggars. On the contrary, if a beggar were driven by his desperation to steal from the 'English' gardens or the 'English' huts, their people exacted the pound of flesh to the utmost compensation. One of their own people, Kandalira, caught a boy stealing a head or two of corn from his garden, tied him up and threw him in the river. In an 'English' village perhaps English law should have run and the English penalty for murder been exacted. But the whites took the view that punishment might only be justly administered according to a custom which the guilty understood; they burnt his hut, expelled him (and his wife and baby) across the river, and said that they would flog him if he came back—and then they had to take surreptitious measures to see that the wife, though now outside their settlement, had enough food to keep herself and her baby from starving. Waller was grieved beyond measure at this kind of incident; he felt it, as Mackenzie would have felt it, a personal stain, he saw himself to be in some manner sharing in the guilt. Rowley took an opposite point of view. It seemed to him astonishing, in view of the temptations to which they were subject, being the only strong men in a tortured world, that they behaved so wonderfully well. Waller could hardly bring himself to write of Kandalira's villainy; Rowley found it regrettable, but to be expected under these impossible conditions, and his sympathy went out even to the black sheep. These men, the 'English' Africans, were for the most part Ajawa, living among a rapidly diminishing host of starving and enfeebled Manganja. It seemed ironical to have begun by giving military assistance to the Manganja against the marauding Ajawa, and to have ended by contributing to the Ajawa conquest of the wretched Manganja. And yet it pleased Rowley infinitely to find their people so honest. It surprised him that they should only once have failed, as a community. They returned in excitement from an expedition with one man, Akumsama, wounded by an arrow. The missionaries sent for them and asked to know what had happened. Matuira, their spokesman, said that they had gone into a village, peacefully and without provocation, to buy food and had been assaulted by the villagers; Akumsama was wounded in the attack. He asked permission that their band might sally forth to punish the village.

From the way in which Matuira told his story, the Englishmen were sure that he and his friends had provoked the attack. They ordered no one to cross the river until further order, upon pain of dismissal from the village, and said that they would themselves climb up into the highlands to examine what had happened.

'A threat to Matuira was like fire to gunpowder. His eyes flashed defiance, and he exclaimed, "If you send one away, all will go. We don't want to wait four or five days before we revenge ourselves, we wish to do it at once, or we shall stink in the noses of the Manganja" . . .'

The missionaries dismissed them angrily; and next day they came back, shamefacedly and without Matuira, to confess that they had been guilty. They had offered the people cloth for food. The villagers said that they could not eat cloth and refused to sell; and then Matuira and his friends tried to wrest the food by force, and so the fighting broke out.

The whites exacted a simple promise that they would not do it again; and the promise was kept.[1]

* * * * *

Meanwhile, the Makololo, in their village a few hundred yards away, were not subject to the restrictions imposed by white missionaries. There was no famine in the Makololo camp; but this was not because, like the whites, they sailed down the river in canoes to fetch supplies. They stole their food from the surrounding villages, and ranged farther and farther in their depredations. At the end of November, Ramaou, whom the missionaries regarded as the worst of the Makololo, attacked a village with a band of his Ajawa subjects, mortally wounded a lad, and frightened some women into seeking escape by jump-

[1] R 364–5.

ing into the river among the crocodiles. Waller, who felt as always a kind of personal responsibility which Rowley never felt, brooded for a time over the possibility that the only answer was 'an exterminating attack' upon the Makololo village by the missionaries; and it hardly seemed feasible to imagine a band of white missionaries headed by three clergymen stealing down upon the Makololo to massacre them. 'God forgive us if it is aught to fear that has prevented us taking up a more active opposition to them, we are not as strong as we were' (Scudamore dying, Stewart gone, Gamble the incompetent carpenter sent down-river in November, for proven robbery and probably worse), 'but this should not matter, many lives would be lost, and the sensation that it would produce at home and abroad would be profound and there is no knowing when the mischief would end . . .'[1] Waller, for all his basic sense and integrity, could sometimes be guilty of foolish imaginings.

It is significant of the strain under which he was labouring, that in the first months of 1863 his loyalty to Livingstone began to waver. He never thought Rowley and Stewart to be right; but the activities of the Makololo had touched him upon so exposed a nerve that he could not help wondering whether thus far, at least, Rowley was right, to accuse Livingstone of causing havoc in the countryside by abandoning the Makololo.

He could not sleep for thinking about it. On 6 February he was having to struggle with despair. 'I think we have tried our utmost. We are not in a condition to work harder, we cannot. We are worn out by this everlasting hoping against hope for the appearance of the Doctor's party, our mails, our friends, our provisions. We are surrounded by all the cares men can well be oppressed with *but one*, the greatest of all, the idea we are forsaken—this is never allowed to come near us.' *All our work the instrument of destruction*—he had to fight his way through the terror in a night of faith. If relief did not come soon, they all knew now that they would not survive the strain. On 24 February, they marked the lowering of morale by agreeing, for the first time in the history of the mission, on a condition for remaining. They resolved that unless the relief supplies arrived by 15 June, they would go down the river. It was evident to

[1] W 1.12.62.

them all that their health was going downhill. In the middle of March, Clark began suffering violent fits of epilepsy, and they despaired of his life. On 17 March, the gentle and delicate Dr Dickinson died suddenly in his hut at five p.m.

Half an hour later Livingstone and Kirk walked into the hut.

* * * * *

It had been seventeen months since they last saw the *Pioneer* at Chibisa's. For the missionaries the time of well-nigh intolerable suspense and isolation was over. The *Pioneer* had again stuck for several weeks in the Elephant Marsh, in the same shallow crossing where it had stuck two years before. Livingstone and Kirk had come ahead, and the *Pioneer*, with the *Lady Nyassa*, arrived at Chibisa's on 30 March, and on 1 April, left again for the cataracts, where they began preparations for transporting the *Lady Nyassa* to the upper Shire. But the cataracts were only three to four hours' walking from Chibisa's, and henceforth communication between the ships and the mission was constant. Rowley and Waller went in turn to 'holiday' upon the ship; the *Pioneer* continued to relieve the mission's needs with a repeated generosity.

Rowley was far from Chibisa's when Livingstone and Kirk had arrived. With Richard Thornton, Livingstone's former geologist who had lately rejoined the expedition and had come up the Shire alone to visit the mission, he had walked overland to Tete to fetch sheep and goats, the precious meat to be shared jointly between the mission and the expedition.[1] After a punishing journey back, Rowley had reached Chibisa's on 30 March, the day when Livingstone at last worked the *Pioneer* and *Lady Nyassa* to Chibisa's. Neither of the Livingstones seems to have shown any coolness to Rowley when they saw him. As his journey with Thornton had secured both mission and expedition from any fear of shortage for months to come, they were glad to see him.

The reunion was not without its controversy; but it was not

[1] Thornton had preceded the *Pioneer* up the river. He arrived at Chibisa's, to the pleasure of the mission, on Sunday, 15 February. He and Rowley set out for Tete on 27 February, and returned exhausted, but with 127 goats and sheep, on 30 March.

Rowley who was responsible. Rowley was content to keep silence over deep disagreement, seeing no remedy. Waller was too honest, too forthcoming, not to tell Livingstone his own opinion about the Makololo.

Soon after Livingstone had reached Chibisa's, he obeyed the missionaries' request and interviewed the Makololo. 'I cannot do justice to the importance of it,' wrote Waller, 'so I will merely say they of course brought up extenuating pleas with all their cunning.' Only one of the Makololo, Mobita, expressed any intention of ever returning to his own country, and Livingstone uttered a forcible threat that if any other complaints were brought before him he would punish to the extreme.[1] The threat contented Waller; but a fortnight later when he was staying on the ship for his health (he had not been sleeping and for several weeks had been covered in boils), he fell into the inevitable argument with Livingstone over the Makololo. It was a purging argument of which they had both been in need.

Though the Makololo had behaved so riotously on the *Pioneer* that he had turned them off the ship, Livingstone still regarded them as his ideal of an African race. They had stood by him through his mighty journey from coast to coast, they had defended him from attack, at the risk of their lives they had saved him in the rapids of the Zambezi, they had shown the same faithfulness and loyalty to Mackenzie and Burrup on their fatal journey, they had helped Mackenzie on the punitive expedition against Manasomba. A few months before, Procter's hut had been burnt in a fire during the night, most of his properties and papers were destroyed, and his guns had exploded; the Makololo, hearing the shots and shouting in the dead of night, had supposed that their friends the English were being attacked and had come running to their aid. They were courageous, rollicking, open people. His faith and his vocation stood by the assertion that the African was no brute but a man, and to the cynic who asked *Which African?* he had pointed to the Makololo. He had told the world that they were honest, respectful, and intelligent. He could not believe the ill of them which the missionaries now told him. He thought that these reports arose mainly from the jealousy of the Cape men, whose conduct

[1] W 18.3.63.

at Chibisa's had become so outrageous that in the end all except Johnson had to be dismissed, and from a feud between Charles or William and the Makololo over mistresses.

In the cabin of the *Pioneer* Waller and Livingstone fell into an argument that was vehement, even fierce. Waller said, 'They have murdered and pillaged all over the country, we know.' Livingstone challenged him to produce any evidence of murders. Waller said that he had seen Mobita fire his gun at a man. Livingstone asked whether he had seen the man die, and Waller had to confess that no one was hurt. Livingstone was irritated because Waller said, 'You wish to make the Makololo out quite innocent.' Waller was more than irritated, he was offended to the quick, when Livingstone asserted roundly that it was Bishop Mackenzie who had taught the Makololo the habits of rustling when he took them on the expedition to Manasomba's.

Waller tried to persuade him to guarantee protection to any African who came up to the ships to give evidence against the Makololo. He said that the difficulty of giving Livingstone adequate evidence was simply that if a Manganja accused one of the Makololo before Livingstone, his expectation of life would be short. Livingstone refused to give any such guarantee. 'Any amount of falsehood,' he thought, 'could easily be foisted up against anyone by such means.' He thought that the missionaries had credulously swallowed every story that they were told by their protégés. 'The people in the huts have pumped in all manner of nonsense into the missionaries' ears, with or without some foundation.'[1] Procter had reported two men as murdered by the Makololo; Livingstone had seen them alive and well.

Waller could receive no satisfaction, and for the first time he found himself thinking that the giant was a smaller man than he had for so long imagined. The coolness between them lasted until after Waller left for Chibisa's, a reinvigorated man, on 14 April. And then, on 21 April, Livingstone sat down to write a charming letter of apology.

'My conscience reproved me for saying something to you which I ought not to have said, but I was too much of an ass to confess it. I ought not to have said that the Makololo began to capture sheep and goats under episcopal sanction. It is possible

[1] LJW ii. 230, 6.4.62; Waller's erased entry of same date; cf. LJW ii. 242–3.

that you may have taken misreports with too much facility, but I ought not to have said that you did or anything else that might give you pain. I am heartily sorry for it, and have grieved over it again and again . . . In my heart and soul I feel kindly to you all, and what came out and anything else you may have disliked you must please take as not according to the general current of my affections.'[1]

Waller thought it a beautiful letter. The giant, after all, was a giant in stature. 'If I thought I saw the small moments of a great man they have vanished and he is greater than ever.'

The rift between Waller and Livingstone was healed, and healed for ever. The deeper rift between Rowley and Livingstone could not be healed, but it was patched. Relations were amicable.

* * * * *

Livingstone was still pressing the missionaries to abandon Chibisa's and go back to the hills. So was Kirk, whenever he was free enough of fever and dysentery to advise anything. Kirk told them that with drought and fever the station was 'quite untenable'.[2] The missionaries thought this advice 'most excellent', and the difficulty was only that it was impossible. 'We cannot help lamenting,' wrote Waller, 'how much easier it is to say go to the hills than to do it.' They had now supplies, it was true, for a long time ahead; but there was a corresponding increase in baggage and impedimenta, they had lost six of their number (Gamble, Scudamore, Dickinson, the three Cape men) and they would lose another (Clark), as soon as they were able to send him down the river. The three leaders were all in their different ways ill, in spite of the various visits to the ships to try to recuperate. To crown all, their people had grown food at Chibisa's, and there was little food to be expected for them in the hills. Nothing would have suited them better than to follow the advice of Livingstone and Kirk and go to the hills, perhaps to Mbami's. Their conviction, that the station at

[1] Livingstone to Waller, 28.4.63 (but Waller's Journal shows the date to be wrong), Waller MSS., vol. III, Miscellaneous.

Waller subsequently blacked out of his Journal the entry for 6 April. The letter of 21 April had more than made amends.

[2] K 19.3.63.

Chibisa's should be irrevocably condemned, was confirmed when young Richard Thornton died at the ships on 22 April. But how to move they could not see. Even at Chibisa's 'but for the near position of the ships our plight would be most sorrowful . . . I am more used up than ever I was since my long illness at Magomero . . . and become as pleasant in temper as that poetical animal (of the Americans), the bobtailed bull in fly-time.'[1]

Nor did the activities of the expedition encourage them. As April wore into May, it became clear even to the most sanguine that Livingstone was not going to succeed in transporting the *Lady Nyassa* beyond the cataracts to the lake. The road which he was starting to build round the cataracts limped brokenly into nothingness. The electrifying news came down from the ships that Dr Meller had ordered Kirk and Charles Livingstone out of the country. The expedition seemed to be disintegrating; and even Livingstone, emaciated and wan as he was, could not hope to achieve much with the few discontented sailors who were now his team. 'It is just a toss-up now,' wrote Waller on 12 May, 'whether the long-laboured for, darling scheme of his heart comes to an end or no, and that principally because he is the only soul on board who wishes well to it and has any interest in its prosperity.' He could hardly bear the thought of the renewed sense of mental isolation and sterility which would fall like a mist upon the mission if the *Pioneer* were forced to retreat down the river, and leave Procter and Rowley and himself to carry unaided the burden of their black peoples.

Then, on the morning of 26 June, the long looked-for help came. An English boat was spied down the Shire, with white faces in the stern sheets. It was the new bishop. A successor to Mackenzie had come at last. The hearts of the three missionaries leapt with expectation. They had held the fortress for eighteen months, against the heaviest odds, at a cost of three white lives. Relief had come, and the martyr-bishop's work could be renewed. Their grim defence could be turned into advance.

[1] W 27.3.63.

VI

THE NEW BISHOP

H.M.S. Gorgon had steamed to the Cape, bearing its sorrowful ladies, an Edward Hawkins whose body, especially at the lips and mouth, was covered with ulcers, and for the world the news of the calamity by the Ruo mouth. At the Cape and in England, the story of Mackenzie's death evoked a wave of shock, sympathy, affection, and pessimism. At the Cape, one or two voices contended that the mission was effectively ended and its abandonment should forthwith be consummated. But the public instinct was the opposite. Many readers wanted to rush with money and men to sustain the survivors.

The picture of the mission at Magomero presented to their readers by the press was roseate. The missionaries had established a firm settlement in a healthy and picturesque locality, they had borne a courageous witness against the slave-trade and had begun its destruction, they were beginning to be able to speak the language, they had created favourable traditions of Sabbath observance, and Livingstone had proved beyond doubt that the Shire highlands could be inhabited and cultivated by Europeans. The mission party, reported one of the Cape papers, was getting on famously; schools and churches were being built, and the missionaries were successfully training the numerous natives round them in 'agriculture and other things'. 'The all-powerful influence of civilization,' reported another, 'is penetrating the native society in all directions.' 'The example of the working Christian has already leavened a large multitude, and prepared the way for effective religious instruction.' Even Gray of Cape Town, preaching in St George's Cathedral on Mackenzie's self-sacrifice, shared the optimism. There was no case for withdrawal. There was every incentive to go in haste and rescue the survivors clinging leaderless to their post, and follow the faithful and tragic example of the young bishop who had died in the path of duty. When the public heard that

Gray was sailing to England by the first mail to find a successor to Mackenzie, there was doubt no longer. The men who possessed all the information were determined to maintain the mission; therefore the mission could be maintained.

There was perhaps an element of prestige, or even 'face', in the motives which led Gray and others to take such immediate and vigorous action to continue the mission. The most heralded mission of the century, from which hung so many hopes, pious and humanitarian, could not be allowed to peter out with a whimper because two men had died. But the motive of prestige was little in comparison with the motive of humanity. Every man of right sentiment hated the slave-trade, believed that the curse of Central Africa could be eradicated only by white settlement and its gifts of Christianity and of trade, and therefore wished the work to go forward. Victories are not won without casualties. What were two English deaths when uncounted hosts of Africans were dying in squalor, in darkness, and in bondage? The men on the spot seemed to expect the mission to continue and to believe it worth continuing. Commander Wilson, interviewed by the committee of the mission at the Cape, gave a report of decisive encouragement. 'I feel confident,' he wrote, 'that the mission, headed by an energetic, active, and determined man, must before long be placed on a firm footing; and will not only be the means of christianizing the heathen, but also of opening the long wished-for cotton trade with Africa, and further of giving the great blow to the slave-trade on this coast.' A letter from Burrup to Gray, which had survived the calamities, showed Burrup's surprise and gratification that the mission had already accomplished such results. Procter's letter, describing the disaster, was printed in the Cape newspapers, and declared that they would carry on Mackenzie's work in accordance with his last wishes until they received a successor or fresh instructions from the Bishop of Cape Town. Above all, the *Gorgon* had brought a message from Livingstone pressing them to reinforce the mission.[1] The experts, the men on the spot, agreed that the mission could continue; and if it could, then patently it should. 'Over the rolling

[1] Wilson's report in Bishopscourt; Burrup to Gray, 18.12.61, Bishopscourt; Livingstone to Strong, 25.3.62, UMCA.

billows,' cried a preacher, 'come their voices inviting us to carry on their work. Let us take up the weapons of war. Let us determine never to lay them down.'

Was not the grave a promise? This pure and godly spirit could not have died uselessly in the Ruo hut. Mackenzie's grave, the Bishop of Oxford told an audience at Doncaster, 'is a pledge to God that having in his person taken possession of that land, God helping us, we will never give it up.'

Within the inner counsel of missionary headquarters in London, there was not unanimity. Several advisers wanted to withdraw the mission from the Zambezi and transfer it elsewhere. But the general committee had cause for perturbation not yet known to the public. When the papers from Magomero were perused, they were found to contain the history of the Ajawa wars. Not for the first time, members of the committee wondered about Mackenzie's prudence. What would the public think if they discovered the Bishop to have led armies against African tribes?

Their first thought was to hush the story, to conceal everything likely to surprise or distress. Henry Rowley was known to have sent his journal home to his crippled and hard-pressed wife in Oxford so that she might supplement her meagre income by publishing parts of it. On 5 July 1862 the new secretary of the mission wrote urgently from London to Mrs Rowley pressing her not to publish the journal yet 'although the committee have no desire to conceal the proceedings of the mission . . . circumstances have occurred . . . which need not with any advantage in all their details be brought before the public . . .' Further reflexion showed the policy of concealment to be wrong and impolitic. The wars must be disclosed.

In mid-July, the Church Congress was meeting in Oxford; and the committee had arranged that the affairs of the mission should be brought prominently forward on the day after the end of the Congress. On Friday, 11 July, three hundred friends of the mission met for a celebration by the Bishop of Oxford at the University church; and after a Litany, a sermon, and the singing of *Jerusalem the golden*, the congregation walked to the Sheldonian Theatre.

Because the committee were feeling nervously defensive they

proceeded to the other extreme. Because they had resolved to conceal nothing and to tell 'everything', they proceeded to act as though the delicate and doubtful parts of the story were most of the story. George Williams, Fellow of King's College, Cambridge, and one of the founders of the mission, rose upon the platform to read his papers—a narrative of the proceedings of the mission drawn almost entirely from Mackenzie's journal and letters; how they resolved that they could not defend their stockade without attacking the Ajawa marauders; how they exacted as a condition of the 'war' that the Manganja should no longer buy or sell slaves; how they gave powder to the twenty of their Manganja allies who possessed guns; how they concealed their 'army' behind a hill while Mackenzie and Waller and Charles parleyed perilously with the enemy, red and white handkerchiefs at the ready; how they burnt two or three hundred huts—a tale, it seemed, of guns and muskets and bows and arrows, of smoking villages, of marches and counter-marches. And because the mission had resolved to disclose 'everything', and because George Williams had so little time, it seemed to the hearers as though the history of the mission, from beginning to end, had been little but a military campaign. It had amused Mackenzie, in his private letters, to describe his punitive activities as though he were striding the plains before the walls of Troy or creeping along the hill to ambush a Hannibal; the language sounded less amusing when read from the platform of the Sheldonian Theatre. When the journal spoke of burning a village, the listeners thought of the pleasant quaint sturdy English homesteads ravaged by fire and sword, and had no knowledge that an Ajawa suffered the mildest of penalties if his makeshift hut were burnt.

In the great audience was one man who had returned from the Zambezi—Edward Hawkins. Invalided back to the Cape by the *Gorgon*, he had travelled to England with Gray of Cape Town in the mail steamer, still with ulcers, still pallid and exhausted, a dying man; and he was staying with his father in the Provost's Lodging at Oriel. He had imbued his father with that view of the mission which a man might see from a tent in an island at the Kongone mouth, a tent surrounded by a littered jumble of packing-cases, the view of a man who knew the Shire only by report, who could picture the conditions of the Ajawa fighting no more vividly than if he had been sitting in the drawing-room at Oriel. The son's collapse in health had given the Provost a distrust of, even resentment against, the conduct of the mission. And now in the Sheldonian, Provost Hawkins was the first to rise and to comment upon the matter which George Williams had so ostentatiously presented to the meeting. He had read the papers in the privacy of his study, and he had not liked them.

He had received, he told the meeting, a 'strong impression' that they had been mistaken to plant a mission in that part of Africa. But of that, in deference to better informed persons like Wilson and the Bishop of Cape Town and Dr Livingstone he would say no more, and he would not urge them to withdraw. But, while claiming not to pass judgement upon men in unknown circumstances, he denounced the 'aggressive warfare' in which these missionaries had engaged. 'I do not say one word against the man; I do not pretend to judge him; but I think that in this or any other meeting held for such a purpose as the present, it ought to be made known that we reprobate the idea of aggressive war as applied to Christian missions, in the strongest manner.'

In the assembly there was a pregnant, embarrassed silence. Captain Burrows, the new Chichele professor, rose to remind the meeting that attack was frequently the only mode of defence, and that the missionaries, given the circumstances of their protectorate over released slaves, could hardly have done anything else. The audience applauded and cheered in its relief.

Yet the effect was killed. Dr Pusey, godfather to Edward Hawkins, rose. If ever there was a man whose words carried weight with his hearers, it was Pusey; partly because he never spoke without measuring what he said with the utmost care, partly because there was known to be no element of self-seeking in his composition, and partly because his person had come to stand for all that was finest and most stable in the church revival of the nineteenth century. In the sanctuary of his heart the Christian life meant self-mortification, martyrdom, making the self last of all: the Christian life was a training in how to suffer. And he found, it is evident, that his deepest springs of gentleness, and his ultimate sense of moral and of priestly duty, were touched by the accounts which George Williams had read —the missionaries had conquered by causing pain, whereas true Christians would have conquered by suffering pain. 'There is no history, perhaps,' he said, 'during many years which has grieved me so much as this, and none which has more impressed upon me what I may call our common human frailty, or how one whom God has disposed so prayerfully should have fallen into so sore a mistake. I think that a mistake is made in the distinction . . . between defensive warfare and aggressive warfare, and that if, as Captain Burrows has pointed out, defensive warfare may be aggressive warfare, we, the clergy, should abstain from any kind of warfare (Applause). It seems to me a frightful thing that the messengers of the Gospel of peace should in any way be connected, even by their presence, with the shedding of human blood . . . There never could have been martyrdom had it been allowable to shed blood . . . The Gospel has always been planted, not by doing, but by suffering.'

He was cheered by that great audience; and other speakers rose to confirm what he had said, and epithet after epithet was flung at the 'mistake'. Gray of Cape Town, in the chair, though he admitted the error, succeeded in diverting the meeting and attempted to weaken the force of Pusey's speech. But nothing could have weakened it. Dr Pusey, the sage and saint of measured speech and inmost charity, had publicly called the conduct of Bishop Mackenzie 'a frightful thing'. The impression upon loyal churchmen in Britain was irreparable.[1]

Whatever the defenders might contend; whatever pleas for tolerance, or restraint, or sympathy were put forward—a wave of condemnation spread through the English church. Even the church papers like the *Guardian* and the *Colonial Church Chronicle* which might have been expected to be friendly to the mission, were as outspoken in their cries of reprobation as the papers like the *Record*, which might have been expected to be unfriendly. Supporters began to tumble out of the subscription lists and the local committees. The Universities of Dublin and (for a time) Durham withdrew from association with the

[1] Report of meeting: *Guardian*, 16.7.62; cf. (e.g.), *Colonial Church Chronicle*, 1862, pp. 285ff.

Universities of Oxford and Cambridge. Eminent laymen like Sir Roderick Murchison, and Admiral Washington the hydrographer of the Royal Navy, eminent churchmen like Dr Goulburn, resigned from the central committee of the mission. Resolution after resolution was passed deprecating the sad error, the lamentable misjudgement, of good men, and asserting that though a new bishop must be sent to replace Mackenzie, he must be a man who would be sure not to follow the same line of conduct, a man who would suffer rather than strike, who would meet slavery and barbarity not with his gun but with the weapons of the spirit.

Not that the laymen always disapproved of Mackenzie's fighting. It is true that a zealot from the north of England wrote to Lord John Russell threatening to prosecute the missionaries for their behaviour. But Murchison and Washington took the contrary view. Indeed the committee of the mission was sharply divided into the clergy, who thought that Mackenzie had acted wrongly, and the laity, who thought that he had acted rightly. But—in either case—support for the mission declined. For if Mackenzie had been wrong, ought we to support a mission founded on such a basis? And if he had been right, was it not manifest that no missionary ought ever to have been placed in such a situation, that Livingstone ought never to have summoned a settlement to the Shire highlands, that the mission was premature and ought to be withdrawn? When Murchison resigned from the committee, he gave the reason that under the conditions now disclosed on the Shire it was impossible for any missionary, however exemplary, to succeed.

This wave of reprobation, and this decline in support, influenced the fate of the little, half-desperate band on the Shire, struggling in the dry heat to hold Chibisa's until relief came. Procter, Scudamore, Rowley, and Waller were looking thirstily down the Shire for a man who would follow in Mackenzie's steps, take up the banner which he had laid down and lead them again in the crusade for Christianity, freedom, and civilization. Gray and the committee in England were looking for a man whose interpretation of the 'crusade' would be altogether different from the ideas of Mackenzie. The public condemnations were sowing the seeds of division and misunderstanding between Mackenzie's survivors and Mackenzie's successor, and that before Mackenzie's successor had yet been chosen.

Gray found it not easy to discover a man suitable and willing to accept the disagreeable, probably dangerous, perhaps frustrating invitation. Mr Boyd declined because he had just accepted 'an important missionary sphere in London'. Mr Warner, though ready to accept, was forbidden by his doctors. A third had been invited and refused before 4 September. The rapidity with which the invitations were issued helps to explain why some of Gray's choices for the colonial episcopate proved to be so calamitous. In the middle of September, a Lincolnshire rector, named William George Tozer, accepted the post; and before the end of the month the appointment had been publicly announced. He was consecrated in Westminster Abbey on 2 February, 1863, and anchored off the Kongone on 8 May.

Tozer, an ugly man with flaming red hair, had been an admirable parish priest at Burgh-cum-Winthorpe; an energetic teacher and builder of schools, a man without brilliance or sparkle, but of integrity, and of business-like habits of mind. The committee sensed uneasily that Mackenzie, whatever the beauty of his otherworldly spirit, had not been business-like. They had endured various trials from various claimants who said that Mackenzie had promised them this or that. They had accepted the verdict of Wilson, who had seen the chaotic mountain of stores leaking over the beach at the Kongone, that the administration of the mission was wasteful, ill-planned, and inefficient. They were suffering from a fear about funds: they knew that already, with stores looted from the hulk of the *Vega* and stores rotting at the mouth of the Zambezi, the mission had been living far above its income, and that soon they would be forced to sell some of their precious capital. The recent publicity had increased their perturbation by markedly diminishing the income from public subscription. They must have no more waste, no more haphazardness. They chose a man accustomed to keep his papers and his accounts in immaculate order, a man who found his way easily into reports and minutes and memoranda, a man as strict and meticulous and systematic with himself as he was with others. He hated blundering, untidiness, anarchy, carelessness, illegality, ill-management. And he had no need to learn for himself that the Zambezi mission had been guilty of all these vices. Everyone who had visited the Kongone seemed to agree in criticizing the mission for these reasons.

Gray and the committee were thus choosing a man who believed, and was told before he was ever consecrated, that he was *not* to be like Bishop Mackenzie. Mackenzie had disregarded Portuguese law, had used force towards the natives, had freed slaves by *coup de main*, had dashed headlong and (some said) unprepared into an unknown and a barbaric country, and had thus precipitated the national and personal calamities along the Shire. Tozer felt himself called to do the opposite of all these. He intended to cultivate good relations with the Portuguese, without whose aid and complaisance the mission must withdraw; to abstain from every act of force even against slave-traders (for, as Dr Pusey had said, it was the work of the Christian to suffer and not to act); to plan every stage with foresight and prudence—and if need be, to face the hard facts and abandon the Zambezi as untenable by English missionaries. As he had toured England for support, he had given his audiences the message which they wanted to hear, the message of peace. He had told them that he thought it wrong to enter a foreign country and inform the inhabitants that they had no right to sell men and women, to interfere with their settled habits, and to compel them to give up the traffic in human flesh whether they liked it or not. The slave-trade, he had said, was repugnant and horrible, the plague-spot of the earth; yet they must not seek to put it down by the point of the sword, they must deal tenderly, not by violent measures, but here a little and there a little, line upon line. He had won loud applause when he had proclaimed that abolition 'must not be done by the force of English rifles, but by the superior force of Christian love and Christian influence.' Time after time he had told his audiences that he would abandon the mission rather than commit an aggressive act. And the Bishop of Lincoln, preaching the sermon at his commissioning, manifestly expected that it would be his duty to abandon it.

In short, Mackenzie and Tozer were selected with different aims in mind. Both, it is true, designed to introduce Christianity and civilization into that part of Africa. But Mackenzie was sent to answer the question, what is a superhuman faith calling Englishmen to do for the African? Tozer was sent to answer the question, what, given this predicament and peril, is the practicable and prudent course for sensible men? Mackenzie had expected the risks to be few, but, finding risks, went straight into them without qualms. Tozer knew the risks to be many and was instructed to avoid them. 'I don't mean to run any risks, either by deputy or *in propria persona*,' he wrote to the secretary of the mission from *H.M.S. Orestes*, then off Quilimane.[1] It was symbolic that whereas Mackenzie went up from the Shire with a rifle in one hand and a crozier in the other, Tozer sailed up the Zambezi beneath an umbrella.

For in England, while Tozer was preparing for his consecration, it was whispered everywhere that the Zambezi was untenable. The English public was now aware that the river was not the open highway which Dr Livingstone had predicted. It was rumoured that Dr Livingstone's own expedition would soon be recalled by Her Majesty's Government, and then how could the mission survive in its lonely isolation beyond the confines of Portuguese territory? Livingstone's recall was not difficult to prophesy; for all the reasons which led Admiral Washington to resign from the committee of the mission were grounds for advising the government to withdraw the expedition. The expedition had failed to open the Zambezi, and was no longer bringing results in proportion to its expense. By the time Tozer left Cape Town, he knew that this was no longer a rumour. For *H.M.S. Orestes*, which was bearing Tozer from the Cape to the Kongone, was also bearing the dispatch from the Foreign Office to Livingstone, recalling him and his expedition.

The Admiralty was convinced that once the expedition withdrew, the mission must also withdraw. The naval officers supposed that without the expedition, the mission ('that academical expedition' as they called it), would be in forlorn condition.[2] Tozer thought that they were possibly right, probably right. But he had been sent to continue the mission if he could do so without further unreasonable risk of life, and therefore he must plan to support his mission without any reliance upon Living-

[1] Tozer to Woodcock, 15.5.63, UMCA; printed *Letters of Bishop Tozer*, p. 6.
[2] Note of 26.1.63 in FO 97/322.

stone. He had expected that the river communications would need to be independent; for the picture of the *Pioneer* which English readers had gathered was of a vessel almost permanently stuck upon sandbanks. But the truly grave blow was to the sea communications. The mission had succeeded in existing because English men-of-war were calling regularly at the Kongone or at Quilimane in support of Livingstone. With the departure of Livingstone, regular communication between the mission and the Cape would become impossible. The nearest useful English base would henceforth be Bombay; and therefore Tozer was already thinking of organizing facilities with the bank at Bombay, whither he could communicate via Zanzibar and the Mauritius. Not surprisingly, he told Captain Gardner while still at sea that, though he intended to make the experiment, he believed he would be forced to evacuate the mission. Captain Gardner thought that he was right. The Bishop thought it a condition of the experiment that *English lives should not be further jeopardized.*

At Quilimane, he heard for the first time that Scudamore and Dickinson had died.

At Quilimane, his right-hand man, Steere, was almost drowned in trying to cross the bar.

* * * * *

Like Mackenzie, Tozer took with him a band of workers, clergy and artisans. There was Mr Alington, a friend from a nearby Lincolnshire parish; Drayton, a student from St Augustine's College, Canterbury; three artisans—Kallaway a carpenter, Tom Sivill a bricklayer, and Richard Harrison; and, above all, a man bigger in mental and spiritual stature than Tozer himself—the still unknown Edward Steere.

Steere was another ugly man, with black whiskers, a huge beard, too long an upper lip, a big severe mouth and beetling brows; a friend of Tozer from another parish in the Lincolnshire countryside. Steere was the first thinker, the first theologian, to appear on the Zambezi, a metaphysician and logician, a lover of argument, an examiner of propositions. Mackenzie had expressed his religion through sermons and through poetry, a religion of the heart. Steere invariably thought in prose. He was a critic of rhetoric, distrusted vaguely idealistic or romantic sentiment, prided himself with justice on possessing a cool, hard head. His highly organized mind kept his emotions on a tight rein. He was a self-contained man; of all the diaries surviving from the Zambezi, Steere's is the least informative about its writer. He confined it to externals, to the weather and the price of goods and the movement or the health of men. He had been married nearly five years; the marriage, though loyal, was never a success in the full sense, and perhaps one of the reasons was his congenital distrust of the affections. His sermons (at this period of his life) failed to move the heart; he had critics who thought that his sermons moved nothing. He rarely spoke; but when he spoke, his words came calmly, his reasoning was judicious, his judgement weighty. Slowly he came to exert power over Tozer's mind. 'Steere,' wrote Tozer to Gray of Cape Town, 'is like two right hands, and ever so many extra brains.' He was blunt, dry, could sometimes be rude or caustic, never used language that was enthusiastic or exaggerated, never suffered from the form of blindness, masquerading as charity, which treats geese as swans, and vitiates every sane verdict on character. His religion, it was said by a friend, was masculine.[1]

Tozer and Steere—a formidable combination, an administrative engine. Tozer himself was under no temptation to be unpractical or quixotic or crusading. But if he had suffered from that temptation, he could not have yielded to it with Steere as his chief of staff. Steere knew that his fault, which accompanied the fear of knight errantry, was over-cautiousness. The too practical man sometimes fails to inspire the great causes which may triumph in spite of every hazard.

The Zambezi tragedy was drawing to its climax. A group of men, for whom every romantic sentiment must be ruthlessly discarded for the sake of a sober attention to the possible, was moving up the rivers to meet another group of men who had staked their all on faith in the ideals of a dead leader, and had

[1] Tozer to Gray, 28.7.63, Bishopscourt; R. M. Heanley, *Memoir of Edward Steere* (1890), p. 8; cf. W. P. Johnson, *My African Reminiscences*, pp. 16ff.; and various comments by Chauncy Maples (e.g. in Waller Papers, vol. III, Miscellaneous).

stayed where they were for the sake of those ideals, practicable or impracticable, possible or impossible. It was as though the mission were a pulsating body wherein head and heart had never moved in perfect harmony; and now the disharmony, the antithesis between the trust and the logic, between superhuman endeavour and ordinary prudence, between faith and reason, was bringing at last its inevitable nemesis.

* * * * *

After sailing up the river with a whaleboat and a big canoe under the guidance of Mesquita, whom their predecessors had so carefully avoided, they reached Mazaro on 10 June. They had already experienced enough of the mosquito, and of the hazards of river communication, to confirm Tozer and Steere in the opinion that Chibisa's was too far from the sea to be a tenable station for a mission.

All reports, and especially those of Livingstone, Kirk, and Waller, had agreed that Chibisa's was unhealthy and impossible. Everyone, from the most headstrong adherent of Bishop Mackenzie to the most cautious adherent of Bishop Tozer, agreed that the mission must move. This verdict was lamentably confirmed by the news that Scudamore and Dickinson had died there. Consequently the mission must either march back into the hills from Chibisa's, perhaps to Mbami's, or must shorten the line of communication and find a site nearer the mouth of the Zambezi. Even if—as Tozer and Steere could not believe—the river communications could be made secure, was it possible to move from Chibisa's into the hills? Waller and the others had been struggling for more than a year to find means of making the move and had failed. Down at Mazaro they knew that Magomero had been proved unhealthy, and thought it impossible to speculate whether Mbami's would be any healthier. From up-country came reports of a land no longer smiling and populated by sheltered, peaceful, flourishing villages, but inhabited by the starved remnants of a people decimated by war and plague. And finally, to live at Chibisa's, or to live near Mbami's, was to live as neighbours to the Makololo. Several of the letters from Chibisa's contained cries of pain or of frustration against the Makololo, told how their presence had caused the English name to stink and had multiplied the mission's difficulties. Tozer and Steere had no intention of beginning their work by settling near the Makololo, whom they had learnt to regard immoderately as 'the greatest robbers and murderers in the country'. And if it was admitted by everyone to be impossible to maintain a mission at Chibisa's, it was mere chimera to suggest that they might maintain a mission sufficiently far *beyond* Chibisa's to be out of the Makololo range.

Therefore they must find a site nearer to the mouth of the Zambezi. This site must be on high ground if it was to be healthy for Europeans. On the river between the Kongone and Chibisa's was only one mountain—the beetling massif of Mount Morambala, just north of the junction between the Shire and the Zambezi. It was believed to be about four thousand feet in height and therefore cool and healthy; it was within easy reach of supplies from Quilimane or the Kongone; Procter and Rowley, when they were moving the mission from Magomero to Chibisa's, had regarded Mount Morambala as the next possible stage in a retreat; and all the available evidence pictured it as the most inviting hill in Portuguese East Africa. Dr Livingstone, in letters published in England during 1860, had described the mountain in terms of almost lyrical praise. Its top was large and well-cultivated, with hills and dales and flowing fountains; orange-trees and lemon-trees grew wild, and pineapples nearly so; at the summit were fine chalybeate springs, and at the base a hot sulphureous fountain; the people were friendly, growing cotton and sugar-cane and maze. 'Had it been English,' Livingstone had written, 'we should have had a sanatorium, and possibly a college, on the mountain.'[1]

At Mazaro, then, they felt almost certain that Mount Morambala must be the site of their experiment. Tozer felt sufficiently confident of the verdict to send Steere and Harrison to Quilimane to make friends with the Portuguese governor (now Major Sicard), and to seek his permission to settle upon the mountain. Thereafter, Steere was to come back to Mazaro

[1] Livingstone to William Monk, Tete, 3.3.59; cf. a letter from Tete of 15.2.59; printed in *Livingstone's Cambridge Lectures* (1860), pp. 352, 357; for Procter's verdict cf. Procter to Gray, 6.5.62, *Guardian* (1862), p. 912.

and canoe up to Mount Morambala to climb it and discover whether its virtues had been accurately described. Meanwhile, Tozer resolved to push onward with Alington in the whaler, see Chibisa's for himself, and meet the harassed men of whom he had heard. From the duty which he had allotted to Steere, it is plain that only strong reasoning would be able to convince him that Chibisa's, Mbami's or any other station would be tenable.

On Tuesday 23 June Tozer and Alington arrived in the whaler at the Ruo mouth. They found a likely-looking villager whom they took to be the chief and persuaded him to show them the grave. They were carried through some rushes to the bank and began 'to make a long sort of burrow through the giant grass and jungle'. Their guide seemed not to know the place, and though they searched for a long time under his vague instructions, they found nothing. They then agreed to separate, and each tried slowly to cut his way through the dense thicket. At last, Tozer found a tall rough cross with the staves of a barrel heaped up round the base. 'There was no sign of the place ever having been tampered with, since the cross was set up. We set to work to clear the ground of the small growth which entirely covered it. I then returned to the boat with the chief for my books. On my return I began the Consecration Service. Afterwards we sang "Nearer my God to Thee", and the words seemed very appropriate and touching.' Tozer tried to sketch the place for Miss Mackenzie, and puzzled how Burrup, weak and ill, could have brought the body through the dense undergrowth.

Though he knew it not, he had consecrated the wrong grave.

* * * * *

Tozer's Journal:

Friday 26 June 1863: 'I was standing with telescope in hand when suddenly I saw a gabled roof ahead. The mission station certainly is coming into view. It looked like a street, with certainly two gabled roofs. It was not long before I saw some movement, and almost immediately the street had its little crowd, gazing with all their eyes at the strange white boat with the English Jack flying from the mast. They stood thus an instant, and then rushed down to the water's side. We tried to make out white faces; and when we thought we were within hail we began to cheer, and they answered, until I was able to rush to the bows and jump on shore and grasp and be grasped all round. "This is Waller," and "This is Rowley," and "This"— and a weak voice from a poor dear sick face said "Procter." Alas! Alas! I needed no one to tell me that he was very, very weak and ill. And then I found which was Blair and which Adams, and "I am the Bishop," I said, which, by the by, was needful, for I had on only my blue sailor's jacket and holland trousers. Giving an arm to my newly found sick friend Procter, we made the ascent of the steep path . . . I made the tour of the place in company with Waller. Soon after we went to the chapel, and had a special service, usual on all fresh arrivals . . . In the afternoon we all visited the two graves of Scudamore and Dickinson.'

For the hard-pressed men on the bluff at Chibisa's the sense of relief was quickly mingled with sorrow. On the very first day they found that the plans were not what they expected. Dr Livingstone was recalled. Waller agonized in his Journal that night. 'The *Pioneer* is to go at once and all her party—why don't the very rocks groan on those beautiful hills—the lamp is flickering and soon enough it will be dark enough, aye, even for the Portuguese slave-trade! Oh, how I dread all this . . .'

The recall of Dr Livingstone was symptomatic of the recall, as Waller and the others saw it, of the mission itself. 'We have had it proposed to drop down to Morambala and settle there, I dread the thought of it. To become the subjects of the Portuguese is loathsome to me and it is interfering in another power's work, that of spreading Christ's kingdom in its own dominions.' This, in the unanimous view of Procter, Rowley, and Waller was the fatal objection to Mount Morambala as a mission station. Chibisa's was not, so far, Portuguese territory. If they settled in Portuguese territory, would they not have to obey the laws of Portugal? And if they obeyed the laws of Portugal, would they not be compelled to accept the institution of slavery? 'A slave-dealer,' said Waller, 'might come and claim every child you have in your school.'

Worst of all was the disapproval of the newcomers. Disapproval perhaps is too strong a word. The missionaries at Chibisa's had heard of the condemnations in England as early as January, 1863, but they had paid little enough attention to them. ('We care very little what people six thousand miles from the spot with a policeman in hail if an organ-grinder doesn't move off to assuage the nuisance say, let them come here for six months.'[1]) Tozer now disclosed to them the full extent of the damage: the withdrawal of support by the Universities of Dublin and Durham, the resignations of leading supporters like Admiral Washington and Dr Goulburn, the marked decline in financial support and public influence at a time when they had perforce lived above their income—and on top of this the news, still to reach England, of the deaths of Dickinson, Scudamore, and Thornton. And yet they might have endured this opprobrium with equanimity and shrugged away even Dr Pusey's condemnation, were it not that Bishop Tozer seemed to share the disapproval of what they had done. That was the hardest to bear—'the silent though not the less deep and utter condemnation of all we did when first we came into the country.'

They had forcibly released slaves: that was the gravamen. They had resisted and transgressed Portuguese law. To Procter, Rowley, and Waller, these actions were still virtuous. To Tozer, slavery was an institution, regrettable, and immoral, but recognized by the British in other places, and not to be overthrown by the *coups de main* of hot-headed zealots. It distressed Waller to see the new Bishop quietly taking slavery for granted. In Tozer's mind it seemed to be no objection to Mount Morambala that they would be living in a country where slavery was a legal institution. Waller said to the Bishop, 'Would you allow the slave-dealer to come to your schoolroom door and abstract a child to put a slave-stick on its neck?'

Tozer replied, 'I must. There's no alternative, it's the law of the land, recognized as such.'

'Would you adopt the position,' said Waller, 'in preference to retiring from the country and thus leaving untried the very equivocal experiment of implanting church missions in another Christian power's territory, a power that encourages such a special abomination as this particular slave-trade is?'

Tozer said that he would.

[1] The reader will discern from the grammar as from the vehemence that the sentence is Waller's, W 22.1.63.

Waller wrung his hands over the argument, the attitude. He had expected relief; and he was being encouraged to a course of action which seemed to him not relief but repudiation. 'I cannot reconcile my own mind to it . . . We renounce at once the original programme of turning the slave-traffic aside by our presence from one part of Africa. Ah! me, well it is the dear Bishop is not here to see this day—it is enough to make him come from his grave to weep on Malo island.'

Tozer was unimpressed. Waller thought it iniquitous to put themselves under Portuguese law. Under what law should they put themselves? Certainly not under that of the Manganja or the Makololo chiefs. Then under British law? Waller seemed to be saying, in effect, that they must establish a little British state beyond the confines of Portuguese territory, that they must annex a territory of Nyasaland to the British Empire, at the very moment when the Foreign Office had ordered out of the country the only British official within hundreds of miles.

For nearly a week the debate proceeded. On Sunday 28 June they held the full service with singing. It was a delight to Procter and Rowley and Waller to sing the service again, for they had felt too weak and too few to maintain it. But in the middle of the service the Bishop startled and shocked them by coupling with the prayer for the Queen a prayer for Louis, King of Portugal. 'As a king and a good king too I believe,' communed Waller uncomfortably, 'no one would withhold his prayers for him—but I cannot couple him in *this* prayer—let it rather be for him that he and his people may enquire and know that the most degrading chapter perhaps of Satan's work on earth's surface is being carried on under his sway . . . Maintenance (of true religion and virtue) indeed—it assumes religion and virtue have some *locus standi* out here.' In another debate shortly afterwards, Tozer argued that St Paul lived as a subject of the Emperor Nero and would not try to abolish slavery. Waller was not moved by the contention. 'Poor fellows all of us, they to bring such calm, peaceful, placid, polite minds into the country, we to fume and twist about under the rap on the knuckles it is . . . Cool, delightful weather . . . all else looks black, blacker, blackest of all . . .'

With Procter and Rowley (in whom the excitement of the

Bishop's arrival had brought back dangerous symptoms), down with fever again, it was left to Waller, overstrained though he was, to carry the burden of argument. Every act of the newcomers now seemed to jar. If they introduced any novelty it looked to Waller like implicit criticism of the existing arrangements. On 29 June, Tozer's tidy mind drove him and Alington into beginning an inventory of all the mission's goods. Waller was contemptuous. 'Inventory making, every little piece of lamp, wick, etc., being carefully stored and if not put down narrowly escaping it.' Apart from overstrain, Waller was suffering from one discomfort of which he was barely aware but which is evident from his papers. He had become accustomed to the charge of the practical side of the mission's work and to a leading part in its decisions. Suddenly he found everything taken out of his hands and the new Bishop making decisions. He could not but resent and criticize. Mackenzie consulted men and seemed to take decisions in accordance with their advice. Tozer consulted men, but his decisions seemed to be his own.

Meanwhile, the argument raged over the move to Mount Morambala. Some of the points scored were merely peripheral, makeweights thrown into the debate for good measure. Mackenzie's men urged that to occupy Morambala would be to commit an irregular act, intruding a mission into a sphere which was the proper field of Portuguese missions under the diocese of Mozambique, and locating it where they would be regarded, in Livingstone's picturesque but misspelt phrase, as 'eggregious schismatics'. The practical Tozer thought it absurd to regard themselves as intruders into the area when there were only three half-caste priests in hundreds of miles of country, and the diocese of Mozambique had been kept vacant for several years. Mackenzie's men argued that to hold land on Morambala was to rent it from Senhor Vianna, an immoral wretch. Tozer agreed that a tenancy from Vianna was undesirable. But these arguments, and others like them, were not what the debate was about, and both sides knew it. The only question which mattered now was this: admitted that it was more difficult, more expensive and more dangerous to establish a mission at Mbami's than at Morambala, was it nevertheless the moral duty of the mission to attempt it? For Mackenzie had been sent to the land of Nyasa and the Shire highlands; and Mackenzie had gathered round himself a band of waifs and strays whose fate, if the mission left, would not be likely to be happy. It was manifestly 'inexpedient' to establish a mission at Mbami's—was there nevertheless a moral obligation to commit the inexpediency?

One argument weighed with Tozer which he could not unfold to Procter and the others, but which he put prominently and uncompromisingly in his letters to the authorities at home. He was disturbed—perhaps the word is not quite strong enough—to find that no one had taught the Africans the Christian religion. Why not? Was this a mission, or was it a few overpressed Englishmen desperately trying to keep a random century of Africans alive?

They told him that Mackenzie had shrunk from teaching until he could teach; that Scudamore was near to starting it, but then he had died, and after that they could do no more than 'fight for life'. Procter surprised Rowley and Waller by suddenly saying that he had taught the people some Bible stories and told them some of the parables. For two years the mission had taken charge of so many Africans, and a few stories and a few parables was the only 'definite' instruction which they had received.

'This extreme caution in communicating religious truth to the people,' wrote Tozer to Wilberforce, the Bishop of Oxford, 'is coupled with another plan, which I believe to be as fundamentally wrong in its own way—I mean, the omission of English as one medium of conversation. The effect of this is, that by the break-up of the present party there will be no clergyman left who can exchange a single idea with any of these people. And to make the matter still more disastrous, those now living at the mission station are Ajawa, understanding Manganja indeed, but speaking among themselves a totally different dialect not yet mastered by any of the English, while the Manganja people have from the recent troubles been swept away altogether; and yet the Manganja language has been selected by the mission, and to some extent systematised, as the medium of intercourse with the natives.'[1]

Was it then necessary to the continuity of the mission to

[1] Tozer to Wilberforce, 23.7.63, Bishopscourt.

remain at Chibisa's or Mbami's? Tozer could hardly see that there was any mission, worthy of the name, that could have any claim to continue. On moving from Chibisa's to Morambala, they would not have to take, or to leave, a single convert, a single catechumen. They were not deserting a Christian community; they were transferring their endeavours from one area, where the struggle had been fruitless, to another area with a better chance of success.

On 4 July, the Bishop and Alington sailed northward to the cataracts to meet and consult Dr Livingstone.

Livingstone regretted, even resented, his recall by the Foreign Office, but did not blame Tozer for being the innocent hand which brought it. Two days before he had heard through Dr Meller and Moloko, the Makololo, of the Bishop's arrival at Chibisa's and of the stir which he had caused. On 3 July, the day before he met Tozer, he noted in his laconic graphic way: 'Bishop a non-resistance man, vegetarian, and inclined to leave the country: prays for their Majesties of Portugal.'[1]

But he greeted Tozer with pleasure and was impressed by his character and his energy. He was not surprised to hear that the Bishop was contemplating withdrawal. It seemed the natural course to contemplate now that he and his expedition were ordered out of the land. He was attracted to the practical ability manifest in Tozer's speech and manner. 'We liked the Bishop very well indeed,' he wrote to Waller.

Tozer asked his advice about the proposed move to Mount Morambala. Livingstone said that he saw no fatal objection to Mbami's in the length of communications and the remoteness, though 'as a general proposition' the long river journey was undesirable for Europeans. Mount Morambala, he was sure, would be healthy to whites and secure from all risk of starvation, and he remembered that he advised the Portuguese to establish a sanatorium there. But he thought the mountain was too near the Portuguese and too uninhabited to be a permanent site for an extended mission. At the end of the conversation,

[1] LJW ii. 241 (notice that Livingstone wrongly thought the date was 5 July). Cf. Livingstone to Waller, 3.7.63 (Waller MSS.): 'Meller tells me the new Bishop is vegetarian—alas for the goats! . . . I am very glad to hear that now you have a head and an energetic one too.'

Tozer summed up the rival arguments in favour of Mbami's or Mount Morambala, and asked whether Livingstone did not agree that to move to Mount Morambala was 'the more prudent course'. It seemed to Tozer that Livingstone assented. The use of the word *prudent*, indeed, made the proposition undeniable.

They parted with mutual respect. After Tozer and Alington had sailed downstream, it occurred to Livingstone that he had failed to warn Tozer of one demerit of Mount Morambala. The mountain, being detached, was clothed with a mantle of cloud round the summit morning and evening. He felt that perhaps he had allowed Tozer to depart with too enthusiastic a recommendation of the mountain as a sanatorium. Waller, on hearing the news, was disappointed. He felt that Livingstone had been too silent, and was surprised and regretful to find that he was not opposing the scheme.[1]

Thus the move to Mount Morambala, provided Steere reported favourably, was decided.

And now a new question arose to divide the Englishmen on the Shire. Should they move all the inhabitants of the 'English village' at Chibisa's to Mount Morambala?

Tozer had told Livingstone that he would take 'the women and children' to the mountain. On the way downstream he reflected that to take the women with him would be to saddle the mission with an awkward and hampering burden. He was moving the mission into unequivocally Portuguese territory. He had been sent with the aim of understanding the Portuguese point of view and avoiding the forcible actions of his predecessor; and he had soon learnt that the Portuguese regarded Livingstone as guilty of 'highway robbery' in releasing the slaves, and therefore regarded the mission as receivers of stolen goods because they had accepted the care of the freed men. He foresaw (as Waller also foresaw) 'endless complications' if they brought down the 'English community' to Mount Morambala. The orphan boys he would take; they would be the first pupils at the missionary college which he hoped to found on the mountain. That same evening, 4 July, he announced to Procter, Rowley, and Waller that he would take with the mission only some of the boys.

[1] LJW ii. 242: Tozer's account of the interview in memorandum written at Chibisa's that night, UMCA; Waller MSS., Afr. s. 16/4 (20).

All three were enraged, and could not conceal it. They said nothing, though with difficulty, to Tozer. Rowley told Waller and Procter that he would go home if Dr Meller would invalid him. Waller told Rowley and Procter that he would not serve as a missionary on Mount Morambala because he saw it to be hopeless. Procter had already been invalided by Dr Meller and ordered down river with the Bishop, but he agreed. These were their children, Mackenzie's children, the souls for whom Mackenzie and Burrup and Scudamore and Dickinson had died, the human jetsam rescued from the slave-trade—and they had been happy in trusting the word of the English. Waller poured his bitterness of spirit into his Journal: 'Setting aside the terrible sorrow to ourselves it would be to leave them . . . we could not do so as Christians, men of honour, or men of truth . . . No sooner shall we leave than a regular scramble will take place for them . . . These poor things had our word pledged to them at the first, they have lived with us trusting implicitly to us, and English truthfulness and honour is now firmly rooted in their minds as the rocks on yonder hills.'[1]

Surprised and moved by the fierce opposition, Tozer, for the first and only time in this episode, vacillated. On the evening of Sunday 5 July, he consented that everyone, 'except those who are really not desirable,' might go with them to Mount Morambala.

On Monday 6 July, leaving Alington at Chibisa's, Tozer sailed off down the Shire to meet Steere and make the final plans for Mount Morambala. Procter, watched with deep affection by Rowley and Waller, embarked with him, an invalid for England. Rowley himself, without soliciting—indeed the contrary—had now been ordered out of the country by Dr Meller; but he would not leave until the Bishop had enforced Meller's order, and began to descend the Shire with Johnson the black cook, on 7 August.

* * * * *

By a lucky chance Tozer met Steere near the foot of Mount Morambala. After an unsuccessful climb on 8 July, they found

[1] W 5.7.63; cf. Rowley's plain speaking to the Bishop in the letter of 4.7.63, Bishopscourt.

a reasonable route up the steep ridge of the mountain two days later. They were pleased with the mountain and felt that they had confirmed what Livingstone had promised. 'The air was keen and fresh, the soil good, and the climate such as can produce orange trees and bananas, side by side with very English-looking peas and beans. Tobacco, sweet potatoes, and Indian corn . . . were all in various stages of cultivation. Our guide showed us the road to a hot spring . . . The character of the land was undulating, partially covered with low brushwood, and in appearance not unlike English scenery, the common fern being found in great abundance, while the slopes of the mountain are for the most part covered with enormous trees.'[1] It took them only a day and a half to return to Mazaro. They would be comfortably in reach of supplies of every kind. The contrast was too great between this reasonable chance of health and security, and the famine-stricken death-stained Makololo-ridden record of Magomero and Chibisa's. On 18 July, Tozer wrote from Mazaro to Waller and Rowley instructing them to make preparations.

The letter contained a harsher blow for Waller than the instructions which he had expected. Tozer had changed his mind about the refugees, or as Waller preferred to think of them, Mackenzie's children. Away from the emotional pressure of angry men, and able to consult Steere's cool mind, Tozer found logic reasserting itself. He could not see what useful purpose would be served by bringing adults to Mount Morambala, and he could see the legal and political complications into which their presence would throw the mission. Mackenzie's men had talked to him at Chibisa's of a 'pledge' which they had given. It seemed to Tozer that the language was rhetoric. Mackenzie had taken some freed slaves and helpless captives under his protection. Was this to bind the mission for all time and under all circumstances? The funds of the mission were intended to be used for the religious purposes of a mission, not for the political purpose of establishing police protection in a bandit-infested region. You feel, he told Waller and Rowley 'in honour bound by the pledges' of Mackenzie's mission. 'But I feel equally bound for myself and those who accompany me to

[1] Tozer to Woodcock, 16.7.63, UMCA.

repudiate such a liability. If such pledges were given, I believe it was beyond your authority to do so and that such an application of funds subscribed for another purpose would not be sanctioned by the committee at home.'[1]

The letter arrived at Chibisa's, escorted by two canoes, on 6 August. Waller received it like a death-sentence. He thought it a denial of what Tozer had promised them when he was at Chibisa's. He hated the word *repudiate* and his letters harp on the word thereafter. 'Is it straightforward to write thus? Is it honour by one's God thus to deal harshly with one's poor forlorn ones? Is it honour to the memory of the dead ones thus to repudiate their deeds, is it sympathy, condolence, or support to those who survive to fence, change, to torture them thus? Both Rowley and myself feel it most bitterly.'[2]

At Chibisa's they argued and argued, and partially won Alington over to their side. But a different complexion was put upon the matter when they discovered that hardly any of their people wished to move to Mount Morambala. With very few exceptions the adults preferred to remain where they were. The exceptions were a few women, old and sick, one a helpless cripple. There were two young mothers with babies but without recognized husbands, and a few young girls. Round these exceptions, the helpless of the helpless, the debate henceforth raged.

On 7 August, Rowley, Waller, and Alington faced the people, and told them that the English must go. Their audience seemed surprisingly, almost disappointingly, resigned to being deserted, though the women were patently afraid of the Makololo. Rowley went back to his hut to make ready his luggage for the voyage downstream. Jessiwiranga followed him with her baby, and 'sitting down on the floor began to cry; not loud and boisterously, after the usual fashion of the natives, but quietly and sadly.' She said, ' "I do not like our English fathers going from us; they said they would never forsake us. It is bad, very bad, to lose them. When they are gone, what will happen? The Chakundas [slave-traders] will come and make slaves of us again, and then what will become of my little babe?" And she hugged her little one as though to shield it.'[3]

[1] Tozer to Waller and Rowley, 18.7.63, Bishopscourt.
[2] W 6.8.63. [3] R 409.

Rowley tried to comfort her, but it was a fruitless effort when he knew that he agreed with every word. As he canoed away down the river, he miserably watched the crowd as they waved to him from the bank.

At the Ruo mouth he visited the hut where Mackenzie had died. He found that no one had yet ventured to occupy it. Then he went to visit the grave. He hacked his way through the giant rushes, the long grass and the bindweed, and only after an exhausting search was able to discover the right cross of bamboo and, some distance away, the cross of board which Livingstone had erected. He came wretchedly to the overgrown mound—a wasted life—wasted because his successor was abandoning everything which he had achieved. The death of Mackenzie had suddenly become so useless, so foolish, so extravagant, a magnificent venture of devotion and self-sacrifice which had ended in nothing but dust and soil vanishing among the bindweed. But, as he stood by the grave, he imagined the presence of Mackenzie's spirit; and then he remembered—pictured—saw more than remembered—his cheerful, patient, trusting hopefulness. For the first time in more than a month Rowley felt his heart lifting out of despair and into hope. He had wanted to see results, he had wanted visible signs that the blood of the martyrs is the seed of the church and now even the faintly visible signs were being wiped off. And yet, he reflected, the wisdom of God has ever been foolishness with men. Kneeling by the grave, he was content at last to make an act of faith that the wisdom of God was wisdom indeed.

It was characteristic of his detachment that he left both crosses where they stood, the wrong one as well as the right.

* * * * *

On the day that Rowley said his prayers by Mackenzie's grave, Waller and Alington at Chibisa's agreed to make an offer to Bishop Tozer. They agreed that they would bear the expense of the female refugees from their own pockets if they were allowed to bring them to Mount Morambala—three women, four girls, three young girls, and two infants. On 11 August, Alington sailed down the river to find the Bishop and propose the plan. He found him at Morambala foot.

Tozer had decided. There was no more reason why he should take charge of these particular women than of any twelve others of the millions of African men and women helpless in the grip of tribal strife and slavery. And he was determined not to mix the sexes on Mount Morambala. He was founding a college. He would have no facilities either for looking after women or for averting the promiscuities which had blotted the records of Magomero and Chibisa's. He refused the request.

He had not the imagination to sense that the little band of refugees was necessary to Waller's faith and integrity. It was the last remnant of a visible sign that Mackenzie had not died in vain.

Meanwhile, Waller was engaged in trying to establish the 'English Ajawa' politically. Being Ajawa they would be easy prey to the Manganja around them, still easier prey to the Makololo a mile away. Waller would never have made an effective diplomat or politician. The advice which he gave his people was perhaps more likely to precipitate strife than assuage it. But, as a counsel of despair, he urged them to send an embassy and ask the protection of the only effective Ajawa chieftain in the neighbourhood—Kapene, whose menacing presence had helped to drive the mission out of Magomero.

On 23 August Kapene, a very tall, thin man with a long face, a short pointed beard, a high round forehead and the coconut-shaped skull of an Ajawa, walked into Chibisa's surrounded by a tough, hard-looking bodyguard. He was friendly and vivacious in manner, and brought Waller the present of a fine sheep. It appeared that he was by no means the fearsome invader whom Waller had expected. Indeed, he came to ask for Waller's help against the Makololo who, he said, had stolen his wife. She was now living with Moloko.

The Makololo, when they heard that Kapene was in Chibisa's, raged with indignation and prepared themselves for war. Waller received a friendly message warning him not to sleep in the village that night. He sent for Mobita, who came with Seseho and two others. They were armed to the teeth with spears and muskets. Seseho had a bayonet, which Waller had never seen before, stuck in his girdle. As they marched down to the village, the women hurriedly left in expectation of the fight.

Kapene's bodyguard took up a defensive stance. Waller parleyed with them away from the huts. He asked Mobita, 'What is the meaning of this warlike array?'

Mobita replied, 'I merely heard drumming at Chibisa's village and went there to see it. As to the gun I want it to shoot birds with.'

Waller had to be content with this peaceable, if barefaced, lie. He pressed upon the Makololo that Kapene was the guest of the English and that English hospitality must be treated as sacred. Next morning, Waller had not got out of bed before he was surrounded by a clamouring crowd of Makololo and their minions, again armed to the teeth. This time they were led by Moloko, who was living with Kapene's wife.

'Where is Kapene?' asked Moloko. 'I want to see him.'

Waller again insisted on the rights of hospitality. He made Moloko and his friends promise that there should be no fighting in his presence. Moloko promised. Waller thereupon sent for Kapene. Kapene soon walked in, and he and Moloko eyed each other impassively. Waller wondered whether they were as impassive inside.

A low argument followed. Then Waller spoke—of Bishop Mackenzie's death, and Magomero, the work of the mission and its tale of death and suffering and war and famine—and urged upon the two warriors peace and unity. Later he sent Kapene up to the cataracts to see Livingstone and thus make the Makololo understand that he was under English protection. Kapene came back from the ships slightly tipsy, but gloomy because a gorgeous piece of scarlet cloth, given him by Livingstone, had been blown by a gust of high wind into the river and consumed by crocodiles. That night Waller made him sleep the other side of the river for fear of the Makololo, and sent him away next morning.

It seemed hardly probable, on the face of it, that Kapene would become the political protector of the 'English Ajawa' against Makololo and Manganja, when Livingstone and Waller had gone down the river.

In the midst of this delicate and tense negotiation, Alington arrived from the foot of Mount Morambala. He brought Tozer's refusal to receive the women and girls.

Waller had first seen one of the children when she was three years old, being carried into camp on Mackenzie's shoulder. He boiled over. '. . . At what an expense of Christian charity, Church of England charity—and the honour of others. As Dr Livingstone says, he shall not have it in his power to disgrace our glorious and generous old English church. Before God it is wicked, in the face of society it will be an abomination, and justly so.'[1]

On 29 August, Waller sent off Adams with two canoes and several boys to Mount Morambala. With the party he sent what he regarded as 'a very civil letter' for Bishop Tozer. '. . . I, as sole survivor of the late Bishop Mackenzie's executive staff on the spot, do not feel the liability that devolved on his survivors is done away with by your resolution . . . I feel obliged to state I cannot abide by your decision, involving as it would a wicked act of desertion towards the fatherless, the widow, the infant, and the sick, and this after the word of Christianity has gone forth it should not be so.' He signed himself, *your obedient faithful servant.* He told Tozer that under Livingstone's guidance he would bring to Mount Morambala such of the people as he thought it unsafe to leave at Chibisa's, and there await Livingstone's coming.

On 5 September, Waller sailed away from Chibisa's, imagining, as he slid downstream, Scudamore and Dickinson rising from their graves on the cliff-top to wave him farewell. He passed by a village where he was almost in danger of being lynched because the villagers knew that the departing English were leaving the Makololo behind. He visited Mackenzie's grave at Malo; and being a man of action, he dismantled the cross which Livingstone had erected and made sure that a new cross, brought out from England by Tozer and placed there a few days before by Adams, was in its proper position at the head of the right grave. Two days later he met Adams hastening upstream with a letter from the Bishop.

To Tozer it appeared an impossible situation. Waller could hardly be a member of the mission and refuse the decisive orders of its head. He told him that if he insisted on acting independently he could no longer regard him as a member of

[1] W 25.8.63.

the mission. It seemed to Tozer that he could hardly reciprocate such friendly advances as Waller's letter contained until he had resigned from the mission and so cleared himself from the imputation of disobedience. 'In the event of your deciding to leave the mission at this crisis, you may rely on my ready help in assisting you to the utmost of my power in carrying out your own private plans for the good of those to whom you are so strongly attached. I cannot conclude without assuring you that in many ways you have my warm sympathy.'

Waller read the letter sitting by the bank of the Shire among the high reeds bending in the breeze, and gazed at the cluster of African girls at the end of the canoe. He looked protectively down at their helplessness and knew without a doubt what he must do. 'I have to decide on either following the steps and the deeds of Bishop Mackenzie's own true heart, or the whims, the hallucinations, the worldly wisdom of his successor.' As the canoe neared Mount Morambala, he wrote his letter of resignation from the mission.

He had a sense of going off into a wilderness. The closer they came to Morambala the more bitterly he resented it. On the bank in the evening he poured the anguish of his spirit into the Journal, for page after page.

He reached the landing-stage at Mount Morambala on 10 September. He stored his gear in the empty well-built Portuguese house, and erected a tent as a home for his little flock of women and girls. On 12 September, he climbed the mountain for an interview with the Bishop and slept the night in the new settlement. To his surprise, and perhaps a little to his distress, he found the Bishop welcoming and courteous. Tozer said that he would do all he could to help Waller while his party was here, and grieved him sorely by insisting on surrendering his hut and himself sleeping with Steere in the storehouse. But he would not discuss the women. The moment Waller attempted to raise the question, Tozer instantly refused to converse upon it.

* * * * *

It is intelligible that Tozer should have refused to discuss a matter where, he knew, Waller held views altogether opposed to his own. Tozer was business-like, methodical; and methodical men prefer to have their affairs transacted in writing, where there is room neither for the personal pressure which may unbalance the cool judgement of reasonable men, nor for the misunderstanding of what has been said. But that refusal, in a windy hut on the summit of Mount Morambala, was unfortunate. For the misunderstanding, and with it the rift, was deepened.

Tozer, it is clear from the archives of Bishopscourt at Cape Town and of the Universities Mission in London, believed that he had offered Waller an alternative to leaving the refugees at Chibisa's. He believed that he had offered to send the women to Natal or Mauritius and to share the expense of their removal from his private purse. This offer had been made, not to Waller in person, but to his emissary, Alington, on the Shire bank. Waller had regarded it with disfavour, partly perhaps because he was surprised at Tozer's view that the mission funds could not bear the expense of the removal, and partly because he was not yet reconciled to leaving Chibisa's. But throughout the subsequent exchanges, Waller had plainly forgotten that the offer had been made, or was unaware that it still stood.

Throughout his journal and his numerous letters, there is no recognition that the Bishop was offering a practicable alternative to leaving the women behind to the clutches of the Makololo or the slave-raiders. The Bishop had decided that the women must not come to Mount Morambala. Waller thought that the Bishop had decided that the women must be left at Chibisa's. And because, on Morambala summit during the evening of 12 September, Tozer refused to discuss the question, these two opposing personalities would remain at cross purposes for the rest of their mortal lives. Waller's arrival at Morambala finally convinced Tozer that Waller was a mere zealot and individualist with whom it was impossible to work. If he was insisting that the women must leave Chibisa's, why did he not sail them straight down to the Kongone in the expectation of evacuating them from the country? Why had he brought them to the only place which could not receive them and which his bishop had prohibited?

For nearly three months, therefore, two different parties

camped upon Mount Morambala: at the summit Bishop Tozer, Dr Steere, and the mission with its boys to instruct; at Halfway House (so-called, though it was nearer to the landing-stage than the summit) Waller with his boy Chinsoro and thirteen women, girls, and infants. Tozer was waiting to see whether this last site in the Zambezi country was workable. Waller was waiting for Dr Livingstone to descend the Shire from Lake Nyasa, and to convey or smuggle the African girls out of the country.

Relations between the two encampments were cool but correct.

VII

EVACUATION

THE Bishop could not help feeling sorry, in part, that Waller had resigned. He recognized, and was generous enough to report to the committee at home, the devotion with which Waller had ministered to the sick since Dickinson's death. But a part of him could not help feeling glad. Perhaps the sense of a 'fresh start' was thereby made easier. Of Bishop Mackenzie's men only the two artisans, Adams and Blair (one of whom, Blair, had only arrived on the Zambezi as Mackenzie died), were now with Tozer on Morambala. Tozer had a passion for system and tidiness. He thought that Waller who, as lay superintendent, had been primarily responsible for what system and tidiness there ought to have been in mission affairs, was unsystematic and untidy, indeed culpably so. It pained him that there was no full account of the expenditure of trust money, subscribed by poor people all over Britain. In October 1862 Waller had bought ten muskets from Senhor Vianna at a cost of nearly forty pounds. *Muskets* stood for precisely that side of the mission's work which Tozer had been selected and instructed to avoid. Those muskets had never been used and under Tozer's regime never would be used. Now they had to be resold at a loss. 'The lay superintendence of business and accounts has been so inefficient, and the waste of mission property so prodigious, that I cannot conceive what Waller has considered as his special work.'[1]

It was true. The accounts were muddled. There were not enough receipts to guarantee that Senhor Vianna or Senhor Nuñes might not charge the mission twice for the same goods. There were discrepancies and blanks. The accounts had not been well-kept—had hardly been kept at all. It was regrettable. And yet Tozer ought to have seen that in men, leaderless men, fighting for their lives and the lives of their people, it may be pardonable not to keep accurate accounts.

[1] Tozer to Gray, 6.10.63, Bishopscourt.

But when Waller, from time to time, ascended the summit to see the mission station as its buildings were completed, he could not help admiring the results of tidiness and orderliness. By comparison with the huts of Mount Morambala, the huts of Magomero and Chibisa's had been shaggy, unkempt. Four thousand feet up, above a mountain-side rent with clefts and gullies, with a view ranging down the yellow and white line of the Zambezi to the delta and the sea on one side, and over the vast expanses of flat river swamp dotted with palm trees and lagoons to the far distant Milanje mountains and the Shire highlands on the other, amid glorious air and strange mountain plants, a neat little village was created. Tozer had taken care to bring adequate and effective tools—long the property of the mission but left behind at Cape Town, and Waller could not conceal his chagrin at seeing them. More important, Kallaway proved to be a first-rate carpenter. Where the huts and church and storehouse and furniture at Magomero and Chibisa's had been built by amateurs, and Gamble, an alleged carpenter, had proved more ham-fisted than anyone, the village on Morambala was constructed under the direction of an expert worker in wood. The church when completed was a work of art and its roof was the best piece of thatching which Waller had seen in Africa; and inside it the altar cloths and ornamented wood were given a fair setting in a sanctuary worthy of them, lit by a wooden corona and with a reredos made from blue barter cloth on which were hung seven pictures. The harmonium left by Mackenzie at the Cape could not be carried to the top of the mountain until it had been dismantled into three pieces at the bottom; but carried it was. Here was another of the illuminating contrasts between Mackenzie and Tozer. The article most difficult to carry up to Magomero had been, not a harmonium, but a second-hand cotton-gin.

The church was thirty-five feet long and eleven feet wide (for it was to house Africans as well as English in its congregation), with a south porch and a round apse at the east end.[1] On Sundays all the English dressed in the best clothes they had

[1] Best descriptions of the community at Morambala in Tozer, 26ff., 38–9; Steere, 66–7; W 14.9.63, 19.10.63, 27.10.63, 15.11.63; Tozer to Finance Committee, 5.10.63, UMCA.

with them; on weekdays they were in flannel shirts and corduroys; Tozer himself wore a light, narrow-brimmed wideawake hat.

After an experience of three weeks, Tozer did not think Dr Livingstone's praise of Mount Morambala to be accurate. 'Dr Livingstone's extravagant description of this mountain . . . unhesitatingly written soon after a short visit of, I believe, an hour or two at the northern end, is but a specimen of all his writing. The top is not "large", nor from its nature can it be "well-cultivated". Lemons certainly grow wild, but "oranges" are unknown. Water is *scarce*, and the inhabitants very few and very poor. The ascent is so difficult, that the idea of making a Portuguese sanatorium here, is a good specimen of the way in which Livingstone leaps to any conclusion he may wish to see adopted. I believe him to be a good man, but to use the phrase of one of our party, a "very dangerous one".'[1] However, the soil was good, and seeds were planted. Though the nights were too cold and damp, the days were cool and breezy. Waller, with his memories of the dust bowl of Chibisa's during the drought, more than half agreed with Tozer and Steere that (if health were the sole criterion) Morambala was preferable to Chibisa's. And Tozer ought not to have been so critical of Livingstone, since he had reached much the same conclusion on his first inspection of the mountain.

Determined to avoid the reserve in communicating religious knowledge so characteristic of Mackenzie's plan, they began at once to instruct the twenty-five African boys brought from Chibisa's. And since the only person who knew enough Manganja to be intelligible was now encamped more than two thousand feet below, the instruction must patently be in English. ('Our communication with them is at present very restricted,' said Tozer.[2]) They began to teach the boys to jump to English commands like *Hands up*, to answer their names with *Here, sir*, to say *Thank you* when handed their food. The boys, however, seemed to be slow in responding; and when the various English dialects on Morambala are considered, their difficulty does not surprise. 'There was Kallaway teaching Devonshire of the broadest kind, Sivill the most undoubted Lincoln-

[1] Tozer to Gray, 6.10.63, Bishopscourt. [2] Tozer, p. 28.

shire, and Adams indulging in low cockney slang, where "grub" stands habitually for "food" and "kid" for "child". The effect was that the boys who heard all this jargon were naturally puzzled, and, with the exception of a few such sentences as "O my eye" and the like, made but a small advance in speaking English.'[1]

From early in November, the boys attended the daily service in church, and by then, for at least six weeks, they had studied, in three classes according to intelligence, for an hour between two p.m. and three p.m. every weekday afternoon. As they became accustomed to it the period of study lengthened, and on 6 November, the Bishop did not release his class until three forty-five p.m.

By 11 November, the Bishop had decided upon evacuation from the Zambezi.

In London he had been pressed to retire by Admiral Washington, who saw all the naval reports which came in from African waters and was therefore more expert in the problem than anyone else at the Admiralty. On the high seas between Cape Town and the Kongone Captain Gardner, now commanding the naval squadron off the East African coast, had given it as his opinion that the only sensible course was retreat. On the summit of Mount Morambala he received a letter from his own former diocesan and adviser, Bishop Jackson of Lincoln, recommending him to withdraw. From the evidence available to him when he left England he was half-convinced that retreat might be necessary; and the news which greeted his arrival, that Scudamore and Dickinson had died, balanced him further towards that opinion. Nevertheless, for the sake of those who had subscribed to the venture of faith at home, and of those whose bodies now rested in the graves by the banks of the Shire and in the highlands, he had determined to make the experiment of continuing. Two conditions must be fulfilled if the experiment was to succeed. Mount Morambala must prove healthy for Europeans to live and work; and it must be found to be a reasonable base for missionary operations among the surrounding tribes.

As early as 31 October, after less than two months on the

[1] Tozer, pp. 28, 104.

mountain, he knew that neither of these conditions was fulfilled.

The mountain, Steere admitted in the early days, was a 'paradise' compared with the Shire valley. But comparative standards are misleading. If the summit was airy and cool in the sunshine, it was damp and misty at night and in the early morning. In its grandeur of isolation in the plains, it attracted and collected the clouds: they sat gloomily upon its undulating top like a wet towel wrapped round a forehead.

It was impossible to keep the damp out of the huts. They began by building the huts each with its entrance to the square or campus, like a little college; they soon had to alter the doorways to the leeward side against the prevailing wind. They left fires burning in the huts through the night, but still they woke up shivering, and found everything round them to be soaked. 'On opening the door for a little light, you find that a thick mist is driving across the top of the mountain, and this lasts sometimes the whole day, but more frequently the sun shines out about noon. The mist is always accompanied with a high wind, and very often with rain. One generally finds that two mornings out of the seven are misty. I think that this is quite the worst feature of our new home.'

At first they had no doctor; for they had expected to find Dr Dickinson. Drayton the student from Canterbury acted, without enthusiasm, as medical adviser. But to their excitement and astonishment a doctor named Waghorn arrived from Quilimane, after a solitary journey, on 9 October. The committee, hearing of Dickinson's resignation, had selected Waghorn to succeed him, and had mercifully dispatched him to Africa before Dickinson's letter withdrawing the resignation had arrived in London.

It seemed to Waller, when he visited them on 27 October, that they were all, more or less, ill. He thought that without more protection from the drenching mist they could not expect health. By 31 October Tozer reported to the Bishop of Cape Town that his men were looking haggard, most observable in Steere, least so in Alington; he saw a lengthening of the face, a falling in of the cheeks. Everyone complained of lethargy. During the second week of November, six out of ten whites were in bed. The water, never plentiful, was now found to be stinking, and they feared that this was causing the little epidemic. When Waller came up again on 10 November, he found the Bishop ill in bed, Steere looking sickly and altered, Adams and Sivill ailing. 'I had a long talk with Alington, and they evidently look on the mission's prospects out here as almost hopeless and are very much disappointed at the apparent unhealthiness of the place.'

Meanwhile, they had been trying to explore the mountain and its surrounding villages. Few inhabitants lived upon the mountain, and they poor and wretched. On 22 October, and again on 31 October, Steere, Alington, and Drayton went down the mountain on the Quilimane side to discover whether the country was suitable for work among the villages. They returned with dismal news. The land was barren, marshy, and uninhabited. Steere said sweepingly that what was not rock was swamp and what was not swamp was rock. They understood that the Central African Mission was situated with twenty-five reluctant African boys at the top of a high mountain, and with negligible opportunity of extending its work. It was like a group of men trying to evangelize the citizens of Yorkshire from an eyrie at the top of Ben Nevis.

The chief depopulator of the village was the brigand, Paul Mariano, or (by his native name) Metakenya. Mariano was a half-caste in the prime of life, with a great belly, heavy jowls, a small mouth, and Indian-looking eyes.[1] His encampment was a few miles from the foot of Mount Morambala. His business was slave-raiding and selling his captives in the markets of Quilimane or Sena. He had long been a thorn to the Portuguese authorities. They disregarded his raids provided that he captured his slaves outside what was patently their dominion. He had once blundered into kidnapping slaves belonging to other Portuguese citizens and had been sentenced at Quilimane to a fine and an imprisonment of three years. While he was in gaol, Livingstone had used the wood of his stockade as fuel for the boilers of his ship. Released to find ivory with which to pay the fine, Mariano had re-established a fastness near the junction of Shire and Zambezi. He owned a house not far from Shupanga, but on the north bank, a large mud building fronted with a broad verandah.

[1] SJW 10–11.

By the late summer of 1863, the Portuguese authorities had ceased to exert any effective control over his band. To the camp fled escaped slaves and malcontents of every description, to live perforce by plunder or by the capture and sale of slaves. There were reported to be 2,000 men with guns whose only means of livelihood was the sale of human bodies which first they must catch. Bands of well-armed men raided the villages, drove off such of the population as could still be found, and sold them in Sena. As the villages nearby were decimated, the bands extended their range northwards up the Shire, and in September, were reported to have destroyed the village at Malo where Mackenzie had died: the jungle round the grave extended its domain. By exchanging Chibisa's for Mount Morambala the mission had not yet found 'settled' territory. It had exchanged the depredations of the friendly Makololo and the potentially friendly Ajawa for the depredations of a band better organized, better armed, and not so subject to the scruples of tribal custom or superstition. Waller wrote about the mission to Livingstone, with a measure of pardonable excess, that 'there may be a dozen starved natives near them, but for this Robinson Crusoe would have been gay to them.'[1]

On 9 November, Tozer summoned a council. Steere, Alington, and Drayton were unanimous in pressing him to remove the mission from the Zambezi as expeditiously as possible; though Alington wanted to be allowed to stay behind to prospect for other openings with a smaller party. They had just received (from Rowley, still waiting miserably at the Kongone for a ship), the report that Livingstone had been murdered on or near Lake Nyasa. Waller and Alington agreed in pooh-poohing the rumour, though Waller's Journal shows him a little more uneasy inside than he allowed to appear. Tozer thought the story not improbable. The report, whether true or not, brought home to them their impending isolation.

Tozer's papers show that even by 31 October he was sure, and that the next week or two, and the various consultations, were merely the refusal to hurry the experiment which had so manifestly failed. He wrote to the home committee on 16 November, and to Gray of Cape Town on 24 November, that

[1] Waller to Livingstone, 3.12.63, CAA.

he had determined to evacuate. 'Practically the mission is now begun afresh, with new members, a new site, and a necessarily altered programme. In leaving now we should be abandoning no work already begun, and the boys, who are our special charge, must accompany us . . . Had the foundations even of the house been laid, it might have been a plain duty to have remained for the uprearing of the spiritual Temple. But, with the exception of these boys, we are really committed to nothing —and I feel a deep responsibility in advising the church to *commence* a mission which she may have perforce in a few years to abandon . . .'[1]

* * * * *

Nearer the foot of the mountain and the Shire landing-stage, Waller had been living in a loneliness which brought upon him an ever-deepening mood of depression.

He was a lusty, companionable, gregarious man, and he did not like living alone. He looked after his little tribe of women and children, went shooting for their food, taught them the Lord's Prayer in Manganja, tried to protect them from robbers —not wholly with success, for on the night of 20 September they lost a lot of chattels to thieves who put their hands under the tent while everyone was asleep. He lectured to them on the Creation and the Fall, but was not confident that they understood either his pidgin Manganja or his theology. They were poor company to a man of Waller's temperament. Though he reverenced Livingstone, he was in this respect utterly unlike his leader. Livingstone would go quietly on his way for months or years hardly feeling a need to see another white man. Waller at times was desperately lonely. He was delighted by the occasional visits of Alington from the summit, the infrequent traffic by members of the mission from the mountain to the landing-stage and back. He tried to console himself by keeping a pet hornbill in a cage. His best moments were when he forgot himself in the hunting of zebra, hartebeeste, waterbuck, or buffalo. Adams came down one evening and gladdened him with, 'Mr Waller, you look more like a Hafrican than ever I saw you.' He found one pretext or another to visit the summit

[1] Tozer to Gray, 31.10.63, Bishopscourt.

—a fruitless discussion with the Bishop, or a botanical expedition. But he felt oddness and bitterness growing inside him. The isolation, he found, had 'very bad effects indeed on my spiritual state. Its outset finds me bitter beyond measure with one who all thought would have been a good and dear friend to me, and the warfare, for such it is, as carried on is fraught with the greatest danger to myself.'[1] He brooded sadly over the past and present. Like many people too much alone, like even Livingstone in his last journeys, he nursed his grievances, magnified them out of sane perspective. He had nothing fresh to read. He meditated on Goulburn's sermons, which he had picked up on a bookstall in Cape Town, he dipped again into Livingstone's *Missionary Travels* and found that the magic still enthralled him.

As he paid his frequent visits to the landing-stage, he began to perceive that he, who had come to Africa to destroy the slave-trade, was now living within a few miles of the chief centre of the traffic in Portuguese East Africa. Once he went down to the bank, expecting to shoot a marabou, and found about thirty people sitting on the shore waiting to be ferried across the river. He knew many of them by sight as inhabitants of nearby villages, and supposed that they were going out to fish or to find nuts, or perhaps were merely moving house. He jumped into the whaler and offered to ferry them across. Most of them accepted the offer. When the ferrying was over and he was walking away, he learnt that these were some of Mariano's men on their way to Sena with women to exchange for corn. They had compelled the villagers to go with them to bring back the loads of corn.[2]

It was bitterness and gall to his spirit that he was living with slavery and could do nothing. One day a man came into his hut and rolled on the ground, throwing dust all over his body. Then he stood up and asked Waller's protection and leave to live there: Mariano's men had stolen his wife and beaten him. Waller had to say that he would not be here long, he could not undertake to protect anyone who must later be deserted. He longed for the old days and the old leadership. '*Tempora mutantur*!' he cried. 'In good old Magomero days we should

[1] W 25.10.63. [2] W 23.10.63.

soon have settled this . . .' He met traders openly engaged in buying slaves in the nearby villages: 'it is useless to attempt to interfere, Portuguese property it is and I have voluntarily come into it.'[1]

On 25 September, a long file of men, headed by Mariano's lieutenant Bondiera and with his secretary Senhor Fernandez in the rear, climbed the mountain as far as Waller's house. They wanted medicine for Mariano who was dangerously ill. With Waller they exchanged presents. Waller gave them all his black tea and a small lancet out of his knife, Bondiera put a little native ring of gold on the protesting Waller's finger. Then they addressed him in a speech of complimentary and absurd rhetoric. Under the influence of Waller's brandy, Senhor Fernandez became communicative. He seemed to imply that Mariano only wanted an Englishman to visit him and hoist the English flag and he would admit this symbolic claim to English suzerainty, whereas he would never respect the Portuguese government.

The romantic proposal touched an answering chord in Waller's soul, even while his head knew it to be ridiculous. He had to admit to himself that his reason for purchasing the ten muskets for Chibisa's, the muskets to which Bishop Tozer had so objected, was his desire to make the English the power in the land, the power to give the Africans the lead. The only future which could ensure the happiness and civilization of this anarchic, famine-stricken, warring valley, he believed, was annexation by the English—the creation of a Nyasaland. In a day-dream of his loneliness, he once imagined himself giving leadership and coherence to Mariano's ruffians, and carving out a little English principality along the Shire. On 30 September he learnt ('with very mixed feelings') that Mariano was dead. 'What a chance for an Englishman to step in and say, I will be your leader and ruler, what reins to hold too.'

A mail brought a letter from his parents begging him to return home. Return he must, though not without his girls. Suppose Rowley's rumour of Livingstone's death were true? He could hardly ask Tozer to evacuate his girls for him. He had written to the Bishop that he was now putting himself under Dr

[1] W 25.11.63, 16.12.63, 22.10.63; cf. 4.11.63, 17.11.63, 19.11.63, 9.1.64.

Livingstone and that he looked to Livingstone to evacuate his people. What if Livingstone never came down the rivers? As Mackenzie had once stood on the southern point of the island of Malo straining for a glimpse or distant sound of the *Pioneer* coming from the south, Waller paced up and down the landing-stage or the high ground above it straining his eyes and ears for a sign of the *Pioneer* coming from the north.

On 5 December, a letter arrived by canoe from Livingstone, written from the cataracts. The Doctor was undoubtedly alive and thus far gave Waller cause for heartfelt relief. But, for one reason or another, the letter discontented him.

Since Livingstone had met and liked Tozer, he had passed through a period when his attitude was critical. In mid-July and August, hearing from Waller how the Bishop was refusing to receive the refugees and how he intended to be friends with the Portuguese, and at last accepting Waller's view that Tozer, in retiring to Morambala, was 'turning tail', Livingstone had written Waller letters sufficiently critical of Tozer to make Waller certain of his support. Waller's letter announcing his resignation from the mission had gone to the cataracts when Livingstone was away in the north on a final journey of exploration on foot round Lake Nyasa. But though he arrived back at the ships on 1 November, he wrote Waller no answer for nearly a month; and the letter was not quite the letter which Waller expected. Resigning from the mission, he had placed himself under Livingstone's protection. And now Livingstone wrote rebuking him for separating himself from the mission. Worse, Livingstone seemed to think the Bishop right in wanting the females separated from the males. He agreed to see the women down the river or settled and 'raising a crop'. But to Waller the letter seemed unsatisfactory and even alarming.[1]

He found himself uncomfortably in danger of being stranded. Tozer did not want to provide for a man who was no longer a member of the mission, and evidently had conscientious scruples about using the mission's money to pay for an evacuation of which he disapproved. Now Livingstone seemed reluctant to take Waller under his command. Tozer was troubled

[1] It was written on 28 November from the cataracts and is in Waller MSS., vol. III.

that Livingstone should thus act. To him it seemed that Livingstone had encouraged Waller to throw off his allegiance to the mission, and was then refusing to face the consequences of the action. With the utmost reluctance he supplied the almost destitute Waller with soap, wine, and tea; and Waller only received enough cloth (as currency) because Alington made him presents.

The temperature, which had simmered down during the two months of waiting, was now rising again. It was brought to the boil by the African boys upon the summit of Mount Morambala.

In spite of feasts, the interest of being taught the ways of the English, and on one festive occasion the present of a clasp-knife to each of them, the boys disliked Mount Morambala. They were far from their homes and their peoples, they were unaccustomed to the cold mists driving across the top of the mountain, they did not readily conform to the discipline of a boarding school. When in early November they heard the rumour that the mission would soon be leaving the Zambezi, the senior boys determined to return home to Chibisa's. Katapola, the oldest there and by African standards an adult (two of his friends had married just before he left Chibisa's), and Wekotani, the boy who had waited at Mackenzie's table in Magomero, announced that they were going back to Chibisa's. Four of the younger boys immediately followed their example.

The desire of the boys to leave Morambala puzzled and distressed Tozer, and still more Alington. More than anyone else at the summit except the cockney, Adams, Alington sympathised with Waller. He believed that to allow Katapola and the others to return to Chibisa's was like sending them back into slavery. He pressed his view forcibly upon the Bishop. He said that to allow them to go would be like opening the door of the canary's cage and letting the bird escape with the knowledge that it would soon perish. Tozer and Steere saw the point, but disagreed. The boys would grow up in the natural condition of the country and were as well equipped for survival as any other boys. And was it possible to keep them against their will? If Katapola was an adult, to keep him would be equivalent to bondage. It would be serious to restrain younger children from returning to their tribes and families if they wished, even though they were incapable of measuring the dangers and disadvantages of the return. If the mission evacuated, the only alternative was to take them out of the country. And to take them could be represented by the Portuguese as the illegal removal of stolen goods, and would force the mission to expend money which it did not possess—Tozer reckoned it at £337 10*s.* per annum—on transporting, maintaining, and educating them. He recognized the force of Alington's argument; but believing that Alington, like Waller, was letting his judgement be influenced more by sentiment than by sound reasoning, he was inclined to let them go.

Adams had remained inarticulately and fervently loyal to the memory of Mackenzie. Though Tozer was now preparing him for confirmation, neither Tozer nor Steere, with their cooler exteriors, had captured his allegiance. A burning ungrammatical *cri de coeur*, in an illiterate hand, went down the mountain to Waller. 'I cannot tell you my feelings and how I think of those who are gone, how dearly they loved all these boys and now for you and me to live to see them treated like this the Bishop is worse than a brute to treat them like this. It is like casting their souls into hell. Do have them up and give them a talking to and try to get them to stop with you till the ship takes them, and do your utmost to get the Doctor to take them all from here . . .'[1] Adams had been crying like a child at the news.

It was reluctantly admitted to be difficult to hold boys back if they wanted to go home. But it seemed, for example, to Alington as well as to Adams, that Tozer and Steere would not be displeased if they went. Each boy was asked whether he wished to go and told that he could have a piece of cloth to take with him. Alington compared the procedure to a schoolmaster walking into a room with a jam-pot and trying to persuade the boys to say that they would go to the moon.[2]

The matter was more complicated for the heads of the mission than Waller and Adams could see. Senhor Mesquita, the commandant of the fort at the Kongone, happened to be visiting Mount Morambala from 23 to 27 November. He told Tozer plainly that if he removed the African boys from the

[1] Waller MSS., vol. III, f. 180.
[2] W 4.12.63.

country he would be guilty of a crime against Portuguese law, the crime of smuggling stolen goods. He said that the soldiers at the mouth of the Zambezi would resist any such operation and would allow them to pass out to sea only if they possessed a permit from the governor of Quilimane. Waller, meeting Mesquita on his way down the mountain, was inclined to be belligerent. He told Mesquita that he and his little picket would be no match for the English. Mesquita admitted it. But he said with dignity, 'If you go, you must take me and my six men and put them down where you like. I will not have a stain on my character.' Unlike Waller, Bishop Tozer was not belligerent. He had been appointed with the special instruction to avoid violence and illegality. He was ill-fitted to engage in a smuggling operation.

Blair and Kallaway conducted the six boys in safety up the Shire to the Murchison cataracts. And for Waller the scene was transformed. Livingstone, hearing of the decision to leave the Zambezi and of the return of the six boys, was scandalized at the Bishop.

Livingstone had not shared Waller's pessimism about a mission upon Mount Morambala. Waller had repeatedly written to him that Morambala had no chance of success and that his heart could not remain in the enterprise. Livingstone admitted that the clouds which collected upon the mountain might be a hindrance; he saw (none more clearly) the arguments against being in Portuguese territory; he would have preferred Tozer to have inspected Mbami's before making his decision. But the Central African Mission was still his hope for the future of the African, even more since the government had recalled his expedition. On 5 November he was still writing to Sir Thomas Maclear of his hopes for Africa, how the mission might succeed where he had failed.[1] He was vexed when he heard of Waller's resignation on what he thought a minor issue. He had not clearly understood the argument, and had heard some 'trumpery story' that Waller had fallen into bad odour with Steere by banging his gun upon Mackenzie's crozier and breaking it.

It seemed to him—and for the rest of his life it would seem

[1] Livingstone to Maclear, 5.11.63, CAA.

to him, as he brooded over the retrospect in his solitariness—that Bishop Tozer was responsible for the final failure of the Zambezi expedition and of his plan for the destruction of the African slave-trade. He rose in wrath. He wrote one letter to Waller expressing his sense of outrage and declaring that he would bring down the river Wekotani and anyone else from Chibisa's who wished to come. He wrote another letter to the Bishop demanding from him the other boys.

Tozer, though distressed at Livingstone's fierce reaction, was not surprised. He had come to regard him as an unpredictable enthusiast who lived and acted more upon his feelings than his reason. Like Rowley and Stewart, but more austerely than either, he held Livingstone responsible for driving these bands of Englishmen into a wild goose chase, even a death-trap. And though he was displeased at the tone in which Livingstone demanded from him the care of the remaining boys upon Mount Morambala, he could not help feeling that the demand saved the mission much difficulty with the Portuguese authorities. He knew that he was responsible for all the boys who wished to stay with him and had no intention of leaving them behind. But he could foresee long complications and arguments about passports with the Portuguese authorities. Plainly the boys could not be abandoned but must be brought out of the country. And if Livingstone would relieve him of the awkward duty of getting them past Senhor Mesquita and his miserable contingent, whether with passports or without, so much the better. Perhaps Livingstone's claim that he had a 'right' to the boys had a measure of validity. He had liberated nearly all of them from the slave-traders, and had (in a sense) sent them to boarding-school with the mission; it might reasonably be argued that he was still *in loco parentis*. 'I daresay he can establish his claim to them far better than I can.'[1] 'I am singularly grateful to Dr Livingstone for stepping in at this crisis and taking the boys off my hands. The first is, that almost all of them are wild to go back to Chibisa's, and if I did not allow them to go, I should have to take them away against their consent; and secondly, I have reason to believe that the Portuguese authorities might at the last moment step in and prevent the boys

[1] Tozer to Woodcock, 6.1.64, UMCA.

accompanying us. With this latter difficulty, Dr Livingstone' (as H.M. Consul) 'can cope far better than a mere private individual like myself.'

Livingstone had accused Tozer of 'apparent cowardice'; and although he intended the qualifying epithet seriously, the imputation of cowardice pricked home. But he did not know his man if he supposed that Tozer could be diverted from his course by such an imputation. Tozer, whatever his faults, was aware that to evacuate the Zambezi against such opposition and such strength of sentiment was a deeper act of moral courage than the attempt to drift on until the mission collapsed in the inevitable calamity. He was unmoved by regard for his reputation, for sentiment, or for abuse.

* * * * *

There are authors of letters who suffer in later estimation because, by training or restraint or discipline or for whatever reason, they cannot put themselves into their writing. Letters alone are unreliable guides to character. But so far as the letters of Mackenzie and Tozer go, they afford a ground for comparison. You cannot read the papers of Mackenzie, published or unpublished, without warming towards the man who wrote them, without growing in affection—if it is legitimate to use the word affection of someone with whom no personal encounter is possible. You cannot read the papers of Tozer, published or unpublished, without admiring the reasoning and the system, without assenting to the logic; but your heart never loses its chill of neutrality. And there are some matters upon which men will only be persuaded if there is more to persuade them than sound argument.

* * * * *

On 10 to 12 January, the mission stores were being manhandled from the top of Morambala to the landing-stage, and thence to Sena where the inhabitants were agog to buy them. Additional stores had recently poured into the Kongone; but by the time that Steere had sold the goods, partly at Sena and partly at Quilimane, he had recovered for the mission more than £500. No one seems to know what happened to the harmonium.

Waller's Journal:

18 January 1864: (It was raining again.) 'Went down to the bank and to my very great surprise found the Bishop there. He had gone past my house without calling in to wish me good-bye and I had been waiting in a long time for him, never dreaming that I was to be denied even this courtesy though he has never during my more than four months' stay paid me a call.'

By 20 January everyone had gone except Alington. He had been left in charge of the boys, to join Waller and the girls until Livingstone arrived to take command. On 24 January Alington and Waller had service together. Waller found the common worship, the company, and the laughter and high spirits of the boys to be exhilarating. No longer would he stand daily on the high ground over the river, looking with longing towards the north. He ceased to sleep at nights—with nine boys sleeping in the hut, scratching and slapping mosquitoes, goats and rats scuffling or tumbling near by, fowls roosting in the goat house, women coughing, babies squalling, and the distant lion or hyena roaring.

On 2 February they saw in the distance the smoke of the *Pioneer*. Livingstone and Waller greeted each other with warm affection. On board Waller saw Wekotani, Chuma, and several others from Chibisa's. His own boys fairly rushed to jump aboard. In the pouring rain, Livingstone gave up his cabin at night as a dormitory for Waller's women. 'I have a boy,' he wrote to Bishop Gray, 'who was the favourite of Bishop Mackenzie and of Mr Scudamore, and a girl whom the Bishop carried on his back for six miles—an old woman decrepit—and a girl who would have been dead but for the unwearied attention of the missionaries.' Touched by the presence of the Africans, he found he was given new heart, amid his sense of failure, by carrying African boys and girls out of the country. He prepared to brook no interference from Mesquita, and gave orders to Lieutenant Young to 'pitch into the water' any Portuguese who tried to stop them.[1]

Knowing that Senhor Mesquita remained on his uncomfort-

[1] Livingstone to Gray, 30.3.64, UMCA; Livingstone to Maclear, 22.3.64, CAA.

able watch at the Kongone, Livingstone chose to sail to the Luabo mouth. There he found *H.M.S. Orestes* at anchor. The *Pioneer* took the boys out to sea and put them aboard the *Orestes*. Captain Gardner had always agreed with Bishop Tozer upon the ethics of smuggling human beings and was reluctant to receive the boys. He was persuaded with difficulty. Mesquita, when he heard the news, said that it was quite a weight off his mind.

The *Lady Nyassa* sailed round to the Kongone, where the women were kept below decks for fear of Mesquita. There they put out to sea and followed the *Orestes* to Mozambique. At Mozambique the women behaved freely, and were even seen in white company about the town. These proceedings caused mild irritation to the Portuguese. They said that the laws which existed to protect the black man and to prevent his forcible transportation from the country had been rudely violated by the very man who ought to be trying to maintain them. Tozer thought the illegal act 'indefensible'. But doubtless senior Portuguese officials shared the attitude of Senhor Mesquita. The emigration had been arranged with offence to no one's face. They viewed it with equanimity, perhaps with a measure of relief.

Captain Gardner, still convinced that it could not be the duty of a British naval officer to engage in illicit acts on the coasts of a friendly power, refused to take the women to the Cape and would not be moved by any persuasion. In the end they sailed with Waller in the *Pioneer*. Nor were the boys content at being separated from Waller and Livingstone. In Mozambique harbour, Chimwala was crying bitterly on the deck of the *Orestes*, imploring Waller to take him to the *Lady Nyassa*. As Waller's boat pulled away the boy became frantic, climbed out of a port along the barrel of a gun, and with a great sad wail jumped into the sea. Lieutenant Young managed to pick him up before the sharks winded him.[1]

Livingstone sailed away in the little *Lady Nyassa* across the ocean to Bombay, with a crew of nine and Chuma and Wekotani aboard, another perilous feat of physical courage. Waller, arrived at the Cape, diligently found homes and masters and

[1] W 9.3.64; Tozer to Gray, 1.4.64, Bishopscourt.

schools for his male and female children. One of them, Daoma, a girl whom Bishop Mackenzie had carried on his shoulders into camp during one of the Ajawa wars, became a serene and Christian adult and teacher. She corresponded with Waller every year and died as lately as 1937.

* * * * *

Everyone, except Livingstone, was agreed that the evacuation was necessary. Even Rowley and Waller, when they saw the rivers from London instead of from the bluff at Chibisa's, came to assent that the evacuation was necessary.

Yet something in the manner of it had bred distrust, a suspicion that Tozer was ill-fitted to be a missionary bishop. And this distrust inhibited Mackenzie's friends and followers, for a time, from assenting to the alternative plan which Tozer and Steere now proposed from the safety of Cape Town.

With their persistent, unemotional logic, Tozer and Steere argued thus. If the mission to the Shire highlands had shown anything, it had shown the necessity for secure communications with the stations inland, and therefore the necessity for a secure base at, or near, the coast. The history of the Shire venture had proved that to rush headlong into the interior, ill-found and ill-prepared and without adequate means for holding the goal attained at the first dash, was inviting disaster and retreat. They must first find a base to replace that base which they had tried so pessimistically to found on Mount Morambala. The base must conform to three conditions. It must be geographically suitable for access to the regions and the tribes of Lake Nyasa. Like Mount Morambala, it must be under a government so settled that there should be no need of Waller's muskets. It must be reasonably accessible to communication with England or the Cape now that the regular links between the Cape and Quilimane or the Kongone had been severed. As they surveyed the coasts of East and West Africa, they saw only one place which fulfilled the conditions—the island of Zanzibar. In Zanzibar was a settled Arab government, with a powerful English resident. There was regular sailing between Zanzibar and Bombay; and with the increasing importance of the overland route through Suez an easy connexion with England would soon be established. The island was the mart for the trade of East Africa. From it radiated the established routes for the caravans. Arab traders from Zanzibar penetrated as far as Tete on the Zambezi. In a manner, to start from Zanzibar was to revert to Livingstone's old policy of seeking a route to the north of Portuguese territory, the policy represented by the fruitless attempts upon the River Rovuma. The tide of African exploration seemed now to be flowing northward. Captain Gardner agreed that they were right in selecting Zanzibar. And accordingly they departed from the Cape for Zanzibar in the summer of 1864, without waiting for the approval of the committee at home.

The argument was unanswerable. The committee could not but accept the *fait accompli*. But its acceptance was not easily extorted. Before it heard that Tozer and Steere had already sailed for Zanzibar, it sanctioned (on 18.4.64), the transfer of the mission to Zululand. Geographical ignorance in England supposed that a chain of mission stations might be established from Zululand to the Lower Zambezi and the Shire, and so enable the mission to renew its endeavours upon the original parish.

Anne Mackenzie, who once had placed her highest hopes in Bishop Tozer, could not bring herself to recognize the new plan as the authentic inheritance of Mackenzie's tradition. She shared all the opinions of Waller upon the manner of the evacuation. For the remainder of her life she devoted herself, despite the committee and the continuity of its management, not to a Universities Mission which she could not accept as authentic, but to creating and backing a Mackenzie Memorial Mission in Zululand. Indomitable and almost unaided, she succeeded in raising for her new mission a capital sum equivalent to the original capital of the Universities Mission. Blair and Adams continued as members of the Zululand mission.

The manner of the evacuation was not the only ground for criticism. The objections of Waller to Mount Morambala applied *a fortiori* to Zanzibar. If Morambala was in slave-owning territory, Zanzibar was the greatest market for slaves in the whole of Africa. If Morambala was in an area where Christian instruction might be regarded as the duty of others,

Zanzibar had other Christians already working there or nearby —some French Roman Catholic Fathers, and the Church Missionary Society on the coast not far away. Livingstone thought that to transfer the mission to Zanzibar was to degrade the great venture to the rank of chaplaincy to an English consulate.

To move to Zanzibar was to abandon the first of the terms in the doublet 'commerce and Christianity'. You could not from Zanzibar teach the natives how to grow cotton and coffee, you could not instruct them how to survive without selling men and women. Tozer and Steere reiterated again and again that they regarded Zanzibar only as a base, the starting point which must be secured before operations could be extended outwards towards the Nyasa country. But the charge had substance in it. Tozer, though he had every faith in the evangelistic purposes of the mission, had no faith at all in its industrial purposes. From the summit of Mount Morambala he had come to regard Livingstone's plan for a colony of commerce and agriculture as a 'chimera of the wildest kind'. Shortly before his arrival at the Kongone the Portuguese had finally imposed duty on every article imported into the Zambezi; he had had to pay the duty on all the stores and equipment which he had brought. His experience of the union between missionary and artisan made him pessimistic about the plan. He thought the artisan could not be a dedicated person in the same way as the missionary, and the moment he was out of the Zambezi he disbanded all that side of the mission.

In a manner it was true. The 'industrial mission' was premature. But it was not impossible, as Stewart was to show with Blantyre and Lovedale. The Universities Mission itself would use 'artisans' again before many years had passed.

As with the argument over Mount Morambala, all these arguments were peripheral. If the critics had trusted Tozer's genuine intention to carry out Mackenzie's mission to Nyasaland, they would have backed his new venture. They could not bring themselves to trust him.

The failure to trust him helped to break Tozer. He had not been working there long when he suffered a severe breakdown in health, and thereafter was never much more than a passenger in the working of the mission. Not until Steere himself became bishop in 1874 did the mission again make its settlements in the interior near Lake Nyasa. But, even at its lowest ebb, the Universities Mission never forgot the grave at the Ruo mouth and the call towards Nyasaland.

Hardly anyone in this narrative, except Anne Mackenzie, failed to return, physically or in spirit. Rowley after two or three years, even Waller after seven or eight years, had turned in their English homes to back the Universities Mission, based upon Zanzibar, as the heirs of Mackenzie. Kirk began his great work as English consul in Zanzibar, and was to do more than any other individual to repress slavery at its headquarters.

Livingstone, though he could not forgive Tozer and died before he could see the return to Nyasaland under Steere, was always to remember the grave down the Shire. In 1866, like a Samson shaking himself free of the withers that had restricted him, the shoulder-chafing burden of consulate and ships and logistics, he disappeared again into the interior, a lone hand, to be found by no white man, except Stanley, until he died at Ilala in 1873. The two Africans who brought his body so remarkably to the coast were Chuma and Susi—Chuma who had been one of the boys released at Mbami's and nurtured by Bishop Mackenzie, Susi who had been first employed at Shupanga to fit the pieces of the *Lady Nyassa*.

Livingstone's death for the sake of the African recreated passion for his ideals. Round his funeral gathered Horace Waller, Captain Wilson, Young, and Stewart. It was Stewart, surprisingly, who took the initiative in founding a Livingstone Memorial mission in Nyasaland; the Mackenzie Memorial mission had moved to Zululand, the Zambezi-Shire route would again be used by a mission with the ideals of Livingstone for Central Africa. The Livingstonia and Blantyre Missions which sprang out of Stewart's initiative fascinate by their continuity with the early history of the Universities Mission—the problem of order and secular government and weapons, the calamitous casualties from fever, the applications from chiefs for armed assistance against other chiefs, the quest for a new and healthier site, even the mode of hoisting a harmonium up a mountain. The Blantyre mission had been intended to be sited at Magomero, and it was rather accident and fatigue than intention which sited it thirty miles nearer Chibisa's and the Shire. But these missions from the Churches of Scotland (Blantyre being from the Church of Scotland, Livingstonia being from the free Church), survived and in the end flourished—partly because the leader of Livingstonia, Dr Laws, was a leader of excellence and survived in continuous control until well into the twentieth century; partly because a shift in the sands at the Zambezi bar opened the Chinde mouth in the delta and enabled stores and passengers to avoid the overland haul from Quilimane; partly because the improvement of steamships rendered the passages to the Cape or to Zanzibar less uncertain; and partly because the opening of the Suez Canal in 1869 brought the eastern coast of Africa so many miles nearer to Europe.

Finally, it was the Makololo who precipitated that protectorate of Nyasaland by the British for which all the idealists of Mackenzie's mission or Livingstone's expedition had yearned. The reasons for that protectorate were complex and have recently been described in an admirable book.[1] The appearance of a less idealistic, and less ineffective, version of *commerce* in the person of Cecil Rhodes transformed the politics of the country. But it was the Makololo who set the chain of events in motion.

The departure of the British from the Shire and the Zambezi in 1864 left a vacuum of power which the Portuguese were then not able nor willing to fill. Kapene the Ajawa chief, whom Waller had imagined as the protector of the 'English' refugees at Chibisa's, held his ground in the highlands near Mount Soché and it was from him that the Blantyre missionaries were to buy their acres of ground. But his survival owed more to discretion than to valour; at the first sign of impending danger he would retire with his retinue of wives to the top of Mount Soché and leave his subjects to fend for themselves. He appears to have been transformed after his death into the god-spirit of Mount Soché. Meanwhile adventurers of the type of Mariano pushed northward up the Shire, never able to extend their influence far because they needed to face Portuguese control and restraint upon their southern side. From the north, from Lake Nyasa itself, Arab influence penetrated southward round Mount

[1] A. J. Hanna, *The Beginnings of Nyasaland and N.E. Rhodesia*, Oxford 1956.

Zomba, and in the absence of the whites, Islam spread as the religion of numerous villages of the Ajawa.

But in the centre—all up the Shire from the Ruo mouth to the cataracts—the Makololo held their ground and founded the little kingdom which Waller had so romantically conjured. Their methods of government were as rough and ready as ever. But they still maintained their affection for the English name, they still maintained the English abhorrence of slavery, they still said *Good Morning* as their tribal shibboleth, they cared tenderly for the graves of Dickinson and Scudamore on the bluff at Chibisa's, they sometimes looked for the return of the English up the river, they gave their children English names (one of Moloko's children was called Dickinson[1]), they thought of themselves as in some manner an English protectorate though they had no protectors. And when the Portuguese were at last pressing up the Shire, it was an appeal from the Makololo which was the immediate cause of the declaration (in 1889) of a protectorate in Nyasaland by the British government. It is no accident that the southernmost tip of modern Nyasaland is not far from Mackenzie's grave.

By 1894, the missions (the Universities Mission and the Scottish missions, the children of Livingstone, of Mackenzie, and of Stewart) were established in force through Nyasaland and the country between Lake Nyasa and Zanzibar. Commerce was beginning to flourish up and down the Lakes. Sugar, coffee, and cotton were being grown, slavery was vanishing. The ideal for which Livingstone had endured and which had seemed so visionary was turning itself into a reality. In 1863, Rowley had knelt in the long grass at the Ruo mouth and meditated upon the unsearchable workings of Providence; and without any evidence but the moral evidence of faith, had affirmed—not without effort, not without a consciousness that this was a cry of the soul because the soul could not but cry—that Mackenzie had not lived nor died in vain. Thirty years later it was plain that Rowley had been right.

Not long after her return to England, Anne Mackenzie settled in Hampshire, and paid a visit to Hursley to see old

[1] Dickinson had ministered to Moloko when he had been stabbed by the tusk of a wounded elephant.

John Keble. She showed that humble poet his own book, the little brown copy out of which Mackenzie had read verses to Burrup as they were waiting at Chibisa's to begin their fatal journey to the Ruo. The book was warped and stained by the waters of the Shire. Keble asked if he might keep it with him, quietly, for a while. When he gave it back to her, she found these words written inside the end page:

'Except a corn of wheat fall into the ground and die, it abideth alone; but if it die, it bringeth forth much fruit.'

Ad. Admiralty papers in the Public Record Office.

Awdry Awdry, F., *An Elder Sister.* 1878.

Bishopscourt Archives at Bishopscourt, Cape Town.

Blaikie Blaikie, W. G., *The Personal Life of David Livingstone.* London, 1880.

CAA The National Archives of Rhodesia and Nyasaland.

Coupland R. Coupland, *Kirk on the Zambezi.* Oxford, 1928.

Devereux W. Cope Devereux, *A Cruise in the Gorgon.* London, 1869.

FO Foreign Office papers in the Public Record Office.

G Harvey Goodwin, *Memoir of Bishop Mackenzie.* Cambridge, 1864.

K Kirk's Journal.

LJW ed. J. P. R. Wallis, *The Zambezi Expedition of David Livingstone.* 2 volumes. Oppenheimer Series 9. London, 1956.

Monk ed. Monk, W., *Dr Livingstone's Cambridge Lectures.* 2nd ed. Cambridge, 1860.

Narrative Livingstone, David and Charles, *Narrative of an Expedition to the Zambezi and its Tributaries.* London, 1865.

P Procter's Journal.

R H. Rowley, *The Story of the Universities Mission to Central Africa.* London, 1866.

RL Archives of the Rhodes-Livingstone Museum, Livingstone, Northern Rhodesia.

SJ Journal of James Stewart (parts unpublished) in CAA.

SJW ed. J. P. R. Wallis, *The Zambezi Journal of James Stewart.* Oppenheimer Series 6. London, 1952.

Steere R. M. Heanley, *A Memoir of Edward Steere.* London, 1890.

Tozer ed. Gertrude Ward, *Letters of Bishop Tozer and his Sister.* London, 1902.

UMCA Archives of the Universities Mission to Central Africa.

W H. Waller's Journal in Rhodes House, Oxford.

The Waller papers are of cardinal importance to the history of the venture. Waller kept the material for his journal in a number of small notebooks; he then wrote the material up, for transmission home, in a number of larger notebooks, every few days or weeks. Both the smaller series and the larger series are for the most part preserved for the whole period while he was on the Zambezi, the principal and important exception being the long notebook which he presumably wrote during his stay at Shupanga in the spring of 1862. These are at Rhodes House in boxes labelled Waller MSS., vol. IV and vol. V, MSS. Afr. 16.4.–5. Waller MSS., vol. I contains twenty-four important letters from Livingstone to Waller, and in the same volume ff. 92 following contain letters written in retrospect by Livingstone at Newstead, mainly while he was engaged on the composition of the *Narrative*. Waller MSS., vol. III, contains miscellaneous letters, from Kirk to Waller, from Mackenzie, Blair, Alington, Rowley, and others of the group.

Rhodes House also possesses the Thornton papers, but of these only two or three are relevant to the subject.

Procter's memoranda were partly destroyed in the fire at Chibisa's on 3 August 1862; his diary for October to December 1861 was lost in the fight at Manasomba's village. But he re-wrote the missing parts. Stewart brought a large part home and entrusted it safely to his family. About 1923 Procter's son-in-law Robert Lachlan gave it to UMCA.

Rowley in his will ordered all his papers to be destroyed. But the working up of his journal into the narrative published in 1866, as *The Story of the Universities Mission to Central Africa*, patently sticks very closely to the original (as would be clear from internal evidence even if Rowley did not assert it in the Preface), and is invaluable as a source.

The UMCA collection is composed of different sources. First, the letters which were sent by Mackenzie to the committee, usually to Strong: and since he intentionally sent all the letters via Bishop Gray of Cape Town, there is some overlapping with the material from the Gray collection in Bishopscourt at Cape Town. This includes three letters from Livingstone to the committee, and the remainder are bound in a letter book with the title *Letters and Journal of Bishop Mackenzie, 1861–2*. The Journal, however, is not the original and complete Journal. It consists of extracts—made quarterly, at least, in intention—from a fuller journal, for the benefit of the committee.

Similarly the letters of Bishop Tozer are bound in a letter book with the title, *The Letters of Bishop Tozer and Dr Steere*. Here again there is a measure of overlapping with the Bishopscourt collection, and for the same reason.

The second source of material came from Harvey Goodwin, Dean of Ely, and later Bishop of Carlisle, and his wife. Goodwin was a Fellow of Gonville and Caius College who had examined Mackenzie and been his colleague as a Fellow, and was the recipient of an intermittent correspondence. Goodwin, as an intimate friend, was asked by Mackenzie's family to undertake the publication of the Memoir of Mackenzie, and for the purpose was lent letters sent to the family. He published the *Memoir* in 1864. Goodwin did not keep the letters which he had been lent; but he remained in touch with the Universities Mission, gave it the profits of the second impression as well as the first, and had not the sense of breach with the mission which afflicted Anne Mackenzie herself after the withdrawal from the Zambezi. Thus the Goodwin letters, whether from Mackenzie or Miss Mackenzie, form an important second source of material in UMCA, and are bound in a letter book with a blue cover entitled *Mackenzie's Letters*: *Mrs Ware*. It is probable also that the Goodwins collected the two volumes of newspaper cuttings which are in the same collection.

In addition, UMCA possesses the minute books of the meetings of the UMCA committee of the time; a diary kept by Dr Steere while on Mount Morambala, though it is not labelled; the letters which Scudamore's family received from Scudamore or others; and a large collection of Steere's letters.

The National Archives of Rhodesia and Nyasaland at Salisbury possess a fine collection of Livingstone material, and in addition the papers of James Stewart. The Rhodes-Livingstone Museum at Livingstone possesses another important collection of Livingstone's papers. But David Livingstone's Journal or Journals for 1862, which would be of great interest for the history of UMCA, has not been found, though Blaikie had it under his eye in 1880, and though Wallis made every effort to find it (or them), when he was editing the Journals in the Oppenheimer Series.

* * * * *

Of printed materials those which are of principal importance as sources are mentioned under Abbreviations. In addition consult especially:

A. E. M. Anderson-Morshead. *The History of the UMCA 1859–1909*. 5th ed. London, 1909.

Buchanan, J. *The Shire Highlands*. Edinburgh, 1882.

Elmslie, W. A. *Among the Wild Ngoni*. London and Edinburgh, 1899.

Hanna, A. J. *The Beginnings of Nyasaland and North Eastern Rhodesia, 1859–95*. Oxford, 1956.

Hawkins, E. *Filio Desideratissimo*. Oxford, 1862.

Johnson, W. P. *My African Reminiscences*. Westminster, 1924.

Keable, R. *Darkness or Light*. London, 1912.

Livingstone, David. *Missionary Travels and Researches in South Africa*. London, 1857.

Livingstone, David. *The Last Journals*. Ed. H. Waller. 2 vols. London, 1874.

Livingstone, W. P. *Laws of Livingstonia*. London, 1921.

Macdonald, Duff. *Africana*. 2 vols. London, 1882.

Seaver, George. *David Livingstone*. London, 1957.

Tew, Mary. *Peoples of the Lake Nyasa Region*. (Ethnographic Survey of Africa: East Central Africa, Part I). London, 1950.

Wallis, J. P. R. (ed.). *The Matabeleland Mission*. Oppenheimer Series, No. 2. London, 1945.

Wilson, G. H. *The History of the UMCA*, London, 1928.

Young, E. D. *Nyassa*. London, 1877.

Young, E. D. *The search after Livingstone*. London, 1868.

INDEX

www.ingramcontent.com/pod-product-compliance
Lightning Source LLC
LaVergne TN
LVHW050618100826
845148LV00011B/1636

* 9 7 8 1 6 0 6 0 8 9 5 4 5 *